SWEDEN'S DARK SOUL

KAJSA NORMAN

Sweden's Dark Soul

The Unravelling of a Utopia

HURST & COMPANY, LONDON

First published in the United Kingdom in 2018 by
C. Hurst & Co. (Publishers) Ltd.,
41 Great Russell Street, London, WC1B 3PL
© Kajsa Norman, 2018
All rights reserved.
Printed in the United Kingdom by Bell and Bain Ltd.

The right of Kajsa Norman to be identified as the author of
this publication is asserted by her in accordance with the
Copyright, Designs and Patents Act, 1988.

A Cataloguing-in-Publication data record for this book
is available from the British Library.

ISBN: 9781787380097

This book is printed using paper from registered sustainable
and managed sources.

www.hurstpublishers.com

"I, as well as the government to which I belong, will, in every context, forcefully stigmatize [brännmärka] those who speak ill of Sweden abroad. We don't need those types of efforts now. Now, our success is in the balance. We need ambassadors for our cause."

Prime Minister Göran Persson in a parliamentary debate,
14 June 1995*

* Swedish Riksdag, Parliamentary Protocol 1994/95:120, 14 June 1995, p. 63.

CONTENTS

CONTENTS

PART THREE
THE DISSIDENT, THE IMMIGRANT,
AND THE FIGHT FOR THE UNIMIND

CONTENTS

PART FOUR
ON THE TRAIL OF THE CULPRIT

CONTENTS

PREFACE

In many ways, I am the Swedish norm. I look Swedish. I sound Swedish. And, for many years, I thought "Swedishly." I was born and raised in the north, in a series of near identical apartments built by the state to ensure that everyone had an equal standard of living.

My family has been working-class for generations. My mother worked in a cafeteria and my father in a sewage plant. Grandfather was in the lumber industry in Ådalen when the military opened fire on striking workers in 1931. The outrage fueled by the resulting deaths became the tipping point that launched the subsequent era of Social Democratic hegemony. It shaped him, it shaped my parents, and it shaped me.

I was 7 years old when our Prime Minister Olof Palme was murdered in 1986. The news of what had happened hit my father like a bullet in the chest, and when he sank to the floor crying, I did the same. We were socialists. Not active in the party, but part of the silent support base; part of the collective to which everyone we knew belonged. People like us thrived through the redistribution policies and welfare reforms that turned Sweden into one of the most egalitarian nations in the world. Unlike my grandparents and my parents, I never experienced poverty. Free education and healthcare ensured that I received the same opportunities as the children of the most affluent families in our town.

PREFACE

My Sweden was predictable and secure, but also boring. As a writer, I was always more interested in far-away places with greater passion and conflict. Consequently, I devoted my career to writing about dictatorships and political oppression in countries such as Cuba, Zimbabwe, and Venezuela. Then, one day, a disgruntled Afrikaner reached out to me. He had just read my book *Bridge Over Blood River*, about the post-apartheid landscape in South Africa, and was not happy with my portrayal. "Sweden's greatest export is unsolicited advice. Why don't you start by taking a look at your own country?" he suggested.

Meanwhile, Swedish crime literature had taken the world by storm, spurring a renewed interest in all things Nordic. By 2012, an estimated 50,000 to 100,000 news articles had been written about crime phenomenon Stieg Larsson and his *Millennium* trilogy. This translated to an advertising value of roughly $50 million, according to a government agency.[1] But what was being advertised? The agency concluded that the "Stieg Larsson Effect" had brought about an irreversible transformation of the Swedish brand:

> "The events [in the books] are in stark contrast to established stereotypes about Sweden: the safe country that many people imagine to be an egalitarian paradise turns out to contain extremism, racism, oppression of women, conspiracies, and a system that indirectly sanctions abuse of the weakest members of society ... Ill-will lurks even in the most idyllic of places and nature provides no refuge from evil ... The notion of Sweden as a conflict-free model nation is shattered."[2]

While obviously fictive and exaggerated, Larsson's books are filled with actual statistics that underpin the grim reality behind his stories of misogyny, cold-hearted bureaucracy, and Nazism. Beyond their pop-culture trendiness, there was something deeper about these stories of dystopic, systemic injustice that resonated with me. Perhaps the disgruntled Afrikaner was right;

perhaps I really ought to pursue the dark themes lurking beneath the polished surface of my homeland.

* * *

Then, one day, while living abroad, I learned of a real-life crime in Sweden so disturbing and strange that I was pulled into its web. I began the process of tracing the people involved and the events leading up to and following the crime, and soon picked up the trail of a series of invisible forces that seemed to have driven the behaviors of those involved. The more I learned, the more I understood that this crime was quintessentially Swedish, that my book about my country would be a non-fiction variant of Swedish noir.

While the protagonists of Scandinavian Noir tend to be troubled outcasts, the villains are often representatives of the state—personifications of a flawed system. The crime I was investigating had its cast of immediate victims and perpetrators, but, as in any good noir, the roots of the evil extended much deeper, as did its casualties. The more I dug, the more warnings I received: "Aren't you afraid?" "You realize you'll never be able to work in Sweden again." "They'll come after you hard." "If they can't discredit the message, they'll find a way to discredit you."

I was surprised, but also intrigued. As a journalist, as well as in my capacity as an army press and information officer, I have worked in many dangerous places. I have served the Swedish Armed Forces in Afghanistan and Mali, been chased by security police in Zimbabwe, and been threatened by Cuban intelligence officers in Havana. Yet, at no point have my Swedish family members, friends and interviewees expressed more concern regarding my personal and professional risk-taking than while I was working on this assignment. It seemed bizarre, but perhaps it was a sign; perhaps my country was not the exemplary democracy I had been raised to admire. In my research I was repeatedly reminded of a powerful quote by our former Prime Minister Göran Persson: "I, as well as the government to which I belong, will, in every context, forcefully *brännmärka* those who speak ill of Sweden abroad."

The Swedish verb *brännmärka* means to mark something with a burn. It is the process whereby a heated branding iron is pressed against flesh with the intention of leaving a mark. While mainly used with livestock, in the Middle Ages it was also used to mark heretics, who would be branded on the forehead with a B for blasphemy. Over time, *brännmärka* has become a colloquial expression, used as a harsher form of the verb "to stigmatize." When used about cattle, it conveys a combination of brutality and entitlement. But when used about humans, it betrays in its speaker a dangerous combination of contempt and fear. It's hard to know exactly what Prime Minister Persson had in mind when he made the statement. Did he think of the Swedish people as cattle? Or was it the medieval practice of branding heretics that prompted the association?

Fears of being personally victimized are as prevalent amongst segments of my own countrymen as amongst dissidents in the dictatorships I've scrutinized. Among my interviewees, psychologist Hans and police officer Lars asked to have their names changed, and "Hans" for the identity of his relatives to be protected, for fear of both professional and personal repercussions. However, my two main protagonists, dissident Chang Frick and Armenian immigrant Samvel Atabekyan, have both opted to keep their real names. One could argue they have less to lose; as you will soon learn, they are already outcasts, each in his own way.

* * *

This book is based on countless hours of interviews conducted between 2016 and 2018 with victims, witnesses, and experts; my protagonists; and some of the key people who have mattered in their lives—family members, childhood friends, mentors, and other important influencers. Based on these interviews, as well as recorded phone conversations between my protagonists and various third parties; police reports and official documents; and books and other written sources, I trace the forces that enabled a deeply disturbing crime, hoping to catch a glimpse of Sweden's soul in the process.

This book could not have been written without the support, trust, and courage of many people. Thank you, Chang Frick and Samvel Atabekyan, for traveling with me to your childhood neighborhoods, and for opening up your homes and your minds to me. On a journey that has taken me from Killeberg, Sweden to Yerevan, Armenia, you have introduced me to places, perspectives, and people I would never have found on my own. You've ducked no question and fenced off no area of your lives. You constitute the perfect proof that two mutually contradictory truths can co-exist in parallel.

The epigraphs opening the chapters "Go Back to Poland, Chang!" and "Agents of the Unimind," taken respectively from Thom Lundberg's *För vad Sorg och Smärta* (Stockholm: Albert Bonniers Förlag, 2016) and Roland Huntford's *The New Totalitarians* (London: Allen Lane, paperback edition, 1975), are reproduced by kind permission of their respective authors. The epigraphs opening "The Murder of the Prophet," taken from Andrew Brown's *Fishing in Utopia* (London: Granta, 2008), and "The Fight for Control of the Unimind Begins," taken from Tomislav Sunić's *Against Democracy and Equality* (London: Arktos Media, 2011, 3rd edition), are reproduced by kind permission of the respective publishers. Every effort has been made to trace the copyright-holder of the 1916 poem *Ångest* by Pär Lagerkvist (d. 1974), an extract of which forms the epigraph to "Samvel and Swedish Angst" in my own translation. The author and the publishers would be grateful for any information which might help to trace the identity or address of the copyright-holder(s).

PREFACE

Thanks to Professor Benjamin Teitelbaum for sharing his expertise in Nordic studies, advising on sources, and giving my text the benefit of his academic scrutiny. Thanks to my publishers at Hurst: Michael Dwyer, my editor Lara Weisweiller-Wu, and everyone else who has played a part in the production of this book. I'd also like to thank my late mentor, Henning Mankell, who pioneered the art of crime fiction as a vehicle for social criticism. I know he would argue passionately against many of the points in this book, while fighting just as passionately for it to be published. Henning once told me that if you're going to write about a strike, portray it from the perspective of the strikebreaker. In that spirit, I've chosen to depict the Swedish system through its outcasts.

Lastly, I'd like to thank Noelle and Hannah for their loving support, and my husband Matthew who is the first to call me out whenever I return to Sweden and once again become blind to its peculiarities. "You only have a few days of clear vision before you begin to change," he once told me, "before you immerse back into Swedishness and begin to tell me all the things that I cannot say or think and all the ways in which Sweden is best."

Here it is, then, my attempt at balancing the distance and proximity needed to deconstruct the system that created me.

PART ONE

THE CRIME

WEDNESDAY 12 AUGUST 2015

"We are very aware that there are those who suffer distress at the festival and we are also aware that this is a prevailing emotion in society at large," says the voice carrying over the ether. It belongs to Lisa Nilsson, head of communications at the We Are Sthlm festival.

Radio Sweden reporter Filip Hannu cuts in to provide a summary:

> On Tuesday We Are Sthlm kicked off in Kungsträdgården with Zara Larsson as headliner. It's a festival for young people between the ages of thirteen and nineteen that usually attracts some 200,000 visitors. The festival is fed-up with the groping taking place in the audience and the disrespectful comments. All people working with the festival have received training in spotting violations and visitors will be taught to set boundaries.

Nilsson continues, "It is of course tied to the fact that we have acknowledged that this is a problem area that we need to address in a very active way."

Hannu: "Only a couple of police reports dealing with sexual assault have been filed in the last couple of festival years, but unfortunately Lisa Nilsson believes the problem is much more common. That's why, this year, extra resources are being spent on stopping the violations and convincing more girls to file charges."

Nilsson: "People's safety and wellbeing are naturally our top priority, combined with having a great experience, but those three parts are connected when one arranges a festival. That's why this is one of the most important issues we work with. Naturally."

It is 5 a.m. when Radio Sweden airs this broadcast of 1 minute and 23 seconds.[1] All of Sweden must be sleeping.

SATURDAY 15 AUGUST 2015

Kungsträdgården Park in downtown Stockholm is packed with thousands of people out enjoying one of the last nights of summer at the teen music festival We Are Sthlm. Alleys of lush, green linden trees frame the outer edges of the park. Dominating the background are the pale-green copper patina roofs of St James' Church.

It's still warm and pleasant out when Hans, a middle-aged psychologist, arrives with his two teenage relatives. His discerning gaze takes in the scene as the trio approaches from the cobblestoned Lantmäteribacken, delivering them to the heart of the festivities. The area is buzzing with activity. Along the perimeter of the park, different organizations have set up tents offering children and teens the opportunity to engage in sports and crafts. There's football, a skateboard park, and an obstacle course, but the canopy-covered stage to their right is the main draw, featuring hip hop artists like OIAM, Kaliffa, and Panetoz.

Popular Swedish singer Zara Larsson is the evening's main attraction. Hans doesn't much care for her music. To him, Swedish pop all sounds the same. Much like the nation's furniture, it is built from familiar blocks and styled to the height of blandness, or bland to the height of style—it's impossible to know which. But his young relatives are excited. They talk, smile, and point towards the stage as preparations for the next act get underway. Meanwhile Hans looks around for a place to buy a hot dog, but there isn't much in the way of food—and no beer tents, since it's a teen event.

Summer is finally peaking. June and July were cold, offering little in the way of solace for the sun-starved Swede, but in the last week or so, the heat has done its magic, melting bad tempers like warm honey. Pink patches of exposed skin testify to the Swedes' desperate efforts to soak up as much of the brief summer as possible. Like Vladimir and Estragon waiting for Godot, Swedes frequently wait eight months for a summer that never arrives. When this happens, the collective mood stays decidedly darker for the remainder of the year.

The best part of Swedish summer is the enduring light. Even in Stockholm, which doesn't get the midnight sun of northern Sweden, days can seem infinite. By mid-August, however, summer is already giving way to fall. By 9 p.m. the park is bathed in twilight. The lightest days are behind us, Hans reflects. Next week school will start again and most people will be back at work.

As evening comes, the families with young children and strollers leave the park to be replaced by more teenagers. The collective excitement builds as Zara Larsson's performance draws nearer.

Hans hasn't been a part of Stockholm's nightlife scene for many years now. When he sees the first set of girls roaming about on their own, he is reminded of just how long it's been. This is meant to be a festival for teenagers, but they look so very young. Cherub-faced, with the honey-hued, pre-pubescent complexion that has not yet turned oily, Hans doubts most of them have even turned 13. Lanky and gangly, they are dressed in hot pants and tight, short tops, not unlike the stage outfit of their idol Zara Larsson. Exposing their frail shoulders, undeveloped chests, bare indrawn stomachs, and boyish hips, Hans wonders how their parents can let them out half-naked like that. Then he catches himself. It sounds like something his father would say, not an opinion he thought he would ever share.

Hans is just starting to regret having agreed to accompany his relatives when he notices a few familiar faces among the police officers on duty. One of them is Lars, who is standing talking to some colleagues. Hans has previously worked with Lars and several of the other officers in his capacity as psychologist. He sends his wards off to roam about on their own for a bit, then makes his way over to catch up with Lars and the others.

"Long time, no see. How've you been?"

"Working as always," Lars replies in his usual grudging tone, but then he smiles, obviously pleased to see Hans.

* * *

Vera is only 15, but when she arrives in Kungsträdgården with her friends, she feels old. Around the edges of the festival different organizations and even political parties have set up tents to offer activities and information. Several of them serve free candy and *saft*, Swedish squash, to the children. Vera and her friends do a loop to sample the treats and put some in their pockets for later. This is supposed to be a festival for teenagers, but most of the girls look like they're pre-teens, running around with push-up bras in an effort to hide their flat chests. Vera is wearing jeans and a top with her long, blonde hair down. She is pleased to note that her arms, normally very pale, have finally caught a bit of a tan. She and her friends opted to put their miniskirts back in the closet after being told by others who had attended in the past to expect hands in their panties if they dressed "provocatively." Better safe than sorry, she figured, but now she feels ridiculous for having worried. While the donuts with soft-serve ice cream are tempting, she can't escape the disappointing feeling of being at some younger sibling's birthday party. She much prefers to feel like the youngest at an event for young adults, than the oldest at an event for kids.

She brushes the feeling off. After all it's free, and it's the music they have come for. Vera loves to dance. She grabs her friend Angela by the hand and they start to make their way towards the stage.

* * *

As darkness descends, Hans detects a shift in mood. Groups of teenage boys and young men move about in packs, eyeing the young girls in hot pants. In the last few months, thousands of unaccompanied minors have arrived in Sweden, and, like most Swedes, Hans has learned to recognize the features and high cheekbones common among the Afghan Hazara minority. "Mainly from the suburbs," comments one of the police officers, following Hans' gaze.

What a culture clash, Hans reflects. It makes him uneasy. Many of the men look much too old to be here. Hans notices a stubbled face, peeking out from deep inside a raised hoodie; eyes glazed over with lust, like some contemporary Humbert Humbert gawking at his adolescent Lolita. His spine tingles. If he had a daughter, this is the point where he would take her home—no matter what she was wearing.

It isn't long before his concerns begin to materialize. Less than an hour after arriving, two girls come running up to the police officers next to Hans. They look 15; not the youngest girls Hans has seen, nor the most scantily dressed. Their faces are oily with sweat and acne. "They're groping us," exclaims the tallest girl agitatedly, pointing towards the sea of people. One of the police officers shrugs: "There's not much we can do," he responds.

Hans is baffled.

"Come on," he objects. He looks at Lars, eyebrows raised. "Aren't you even going to try?" Lars appears resigned, but shoots his colleagues a quick glance, then turns to the girls: "Show us who it was."

The officers pave their way towards the stage with the girls cautiously following behind. At the very back is Hans. He watches as the girls lean in to the officer's ears and point at four or five young men.

"I didn't do anything," gestures the first boy they approach. The officers motion for him and a couple of others to come along. The boys laugh and talk amongst each other in a language Hans can't understand. He is amazed at how unfazed they appear to be by the presence of the police. A few of their friends follow behind of their own volition. The officers escort the apprehended boys backstage, where large, white tents have been set up. Hans follows a few meters behind the officers and watches as they struggle to communicate with the young men, who don't appear to speak any Swedish. He waits outside the tent. Although he can't see all the way in, he can see that many more have been rounded up. Some are lying face-down with their hands zip-tied behind their backs.

After a few minutes, Lars and his colleagues emerge from the tent. The girls are long gone. Lars looks defeated. "They'll be released in an hour or so," he says. "They laugh straight in our faces and there's nothing we can do."

* * *

A DJ is playing in anticipation of the evening's main act: Zara Larsson. The hits of 2015 succeed one another, like an anthem to the highlights of summer. It's a beautiful evening. One of Sweden's rare, balmy nights where one doesn't need a jacket. Surrounded by a sea of people, Vera would even go so far as to describe it as warm. In a few days, school begins again and Vera will start ninth grade. Best to enjoy the moment.

She closes her eyes and focuses on the beat when she feels a hand take a firm grip around one of her butt cheeks. When she spins around another hand grabs her breasts. Then a hand starts touching her crotch. Some seven guys have surrounded her and Angela, rubbing up against them and assaulting them with their hands. As soon as Vera turns to fight one off, she feels new hands coming from other directions. As though in perfect sync, they attack from whichever way she isn't facing, then retreat back to box her in. She feels the panic rising. She looks over at Angela and sees her own fear mirrored in her friend's face. Vera begins to scream, but her assailants don't even flinch. While their hands violate her body, they seem to stare right through her as though no sound is coming from her mouth, or as though she isn't even there. She screams louder, hoping people further away will hear her and intervene, but any glance she manages to catch is marked by indifference. The music drowns her screams and no one reacts.

* * *

Hans and the police officers stand talking when the noise of a car engine interrupts the conversation. They follow the sound to the edge of the park. A young man is flaunting his old American ride, revving repeatedly. A couple of the officers head over to talk to the driver, while Hans and Lars remain chatting.

"It's systematic," Lars explains: teenage boys and men group together to surround and sexually assault young girls. Using the cover of the crowd, the men surround the girls. They shove their hands up the girls' skirts, down their blouses, or into their pants. Some girls have even been forced down onto the ground and sexually molested while lying down. One girl had her pants pulled down and fingers inserted into her vagina. "But most girls don't want to file a police report. It's very hard to prove who did what in the crowd," Lars says. "Sometimes they won't even tell us themselves, but other girls will come and say what they've seen done to someone else."

Hans is frustrated. As a psychologist he is well aware of the mechanism of shame. He is certain many of the young girls won't even dare to tell their parents what they've been subjected to, embarrassed, no doubt, even to use the vocabulary needed to describe it. They will blame themselves; think that somehow it was all their own fault. Maybe they flirted, maybe they danced, maybe they even enjoyed the attention for a brief moment until things suddenly went horribly wrong.

Hans stands on the sidelines, straining his eyes in an effort to make out what is going on out there, but it's dark and the crowd is a sea with a thousand bobbing heads. Along the perimeters he watches as girl after girl staggers out from the crowd to appeal to the festival's security guards. Their young faces are marked by shock, tears, or anger as they reach out for anyone to ensure their safety. Every few minutes, the guards elbow their way into the crowd only to reappear shortly thereafter, sometimes with a few guys in tow, other times with nothing but a look of resignation. Hans keeps a rough count. He estimates that during the course of the evening police and security guards round up some ninety boys and men who are evicted or taken to the tents in the back. But the sheer number of perpetrators, combined with the victims' vague descriptions and sometimes unwillingness to participate, make arrests difficult. Police focus on removing perpetrators from the area to prevent further attacks.

"It's sick when you think about it. This has been going on every evening since the festival started last Tuesday. My daughter will never attend an event like this, I can tell you that much," says Lars.

No parent in their right mind would send their teenager, let alone pre-teenage daughter here, if they knew what was going on, Hans reflects. He sometimes feels that Swedish media take their feminist agenda too far, but tonight they have his full support. The angular bodies of little girls shivering with trauma will haunt him for a long time. For them, what was meant to be the last night of summer will now be remembered as the last night of childhood.

SUNDAY 16 AUGUST 2015

Hans is an early riser. Even on a Sunday morning after a late night, he struggles to sleep in, and this Sunday is no different. The late summer light seeps in through his blinds, making it even harder. He closes his eyes again and tries to fall back to sleep, but the images from last night keep coming: the young girls in their tiny outfits, the insidiousness of the men stalking them, the uncanny sensation of watching packs of predators hunt helpless prey.

Finally, he gives up and rises to brew his morning coffee. He returns to bed and grabs his laptop to read the news. The top headline of Sweden's leading daily *Dagens Nyheter* (DN) declares that Swedes are turning away from their once robust habit of joining associations. The Scouts and the Swedish Outdoor Association are losing members. To make matters worse, fewer parents are choosing to place their children in childcare co-ops. The journalist gives the example of a co-op that will soon close down. "The pre-school is ... picturesque and cozy with beautiful nature. The house neighbors a coltsfoot-covered meadow where horses graze peacefully. On the other side it smells of barbeque and newly cut grass." The journalist portrays the co-op and its closing with a sentimentality that borders propaganda:

> Parents take down shelves and curtains. Everything must go. Books, board games, and toy dinosaurs are thoughtfully packed away in

boxes. In the hallway, virtually all that remains is a pair of boots, some plastic bags, and a lone photograph. The portrait belongs to 6-year-old Loke Westberg ... With a resolute gaze he reaches on tip-toes for his photo. If the pre-school were a creature this would be the moment when its heart stops. In just a few months the pre-school building will become a private home.[1]

Hans flips through all *Dagens Nyheter*'s stories, looking for news about the festival and the sexual assaults. Then he turns to the competing daily, *Svenska Dagbladet*. Nothing there either. He tries the tabloids. *Aftonbladet. Expressen.* No luck. He stares across the room for a moment at a blank spot on his bedroom wall.

He returns to *Dagens Nyheter*, the most influential of Swedish media outlets and the flagship of the powerful Bonnier group. He reads the editorial by Editor-in-Chief Peter Wolodarski, titled "Listen to the police who warn of an atmosphere of lynching." It concerns whether or not it is right to publish the origin of suspects or perpetrators. A few days ago, on 10 August, a Swedish woman and her son were stabbed to death at IKEA in Västerås. The perpetrator was an asylum seeker from Eritrea who had just been denied refugee status. Established media, including *Dagens Nyheter*, eventually published the nationality of the perpetrator, but only after this information had long been available on social media. "If wild speculation and acrimony continues to increase on the Internet, we can be certain that lawmakers will respond by curtailing freedom of speech," writes Wolodarski.

MONDAY 17 AUGUST 2015

Again, Hans starts his morning by scanning all the newspapers for reports from the festival. Still, there is nothing.

Wondering now if they simply don't know what happened, Hans decides to reach out to *Dagens Nyheter*. He knows the story will be considered sensitive, but Hans is a well-respected professional, and he can provide them with contact information for several police officers who were there and can corroborate his story.

That evening Hans sits down to craft his message.

Hello,

I have a tip for a truly important article about the vulnerability of young girls and how they are systematically subjected to sexual abuse at We Are Sthlm in Stockholm.

I have the contact information of police officers who can provide you with background information.

Call me and I'll tell you more.

Best regards,

Hans does not mention that he perceived the perpetrators to be mainly young refugees from Afghanistan. He signs with his name and title, then hesitates. He wants to use his professional credibility to ensure he is heard, but he knows how sensitive these matters can be. He knows if word gets out that he was the one to point the finger at unaccompanied refugee minors, he will be branded a racist. Instinctively, he knows that sympathy for the refugees trumps sympathy for the girls. Lord knows, these young boys have been through enough, people would say. He adds: "p.s. Because of my profession as a psychologist, I wish to remain anonymous." At 9:32 p.m., he hits send.

* * *

Swedish cowardice bothers Hans. When deciding whether to publish a story, he knows that journalists are affected not only by the real consequences of their actions, but also by the imagined consequences. Well, apparently so is he, and he is ashamed to acknowledge it. In Sweden, everyone knows so well what the accepted position on any given issue is; what others are thinking and how they will judge you if you deviate from that. Hans has never before reflected on where that comes from—why it is that he is able simply to tap into a pool of knowledge that will offer a near-foolproof prediction of how any comment or action will be received. Is this also the case in other cultures? Somehow, he doubts it.

And when it comes to victims and perpetrators, the prevailing mythology dictates that a victim is also morally superior and good. Among his profession, this notion is particularly common, as protecting the victim is considered crucial to any psychologist. Logically, a victim can also be a perpetrator. In fact, it is not uncommon to be a victim of some kind before becoming a perpetrator. Hans knows this. But he also knows that it doesn't change anything. To direct accusations at unaccompanied refugee minors would ruin his career. People might not tell him to his face—they might even think he did the right thing—but few would admit to this publicly, and when the time came to award an assignment or a promotion, it would be easier to pick someone else; someone with an impeccable reputation.

* * *

Hans is visiting with family when the journalist calls. He steps out onto the balcony for privacy. It's still fairly warm out. In the distance he sees the rooftops of Stockholm spread out like a colorful quilt beneath him.

He tells the journalist what he has witnessed and is pleased to note that she seems very interested. But when he mentions that many of the perpetrators, the vast majority in fact, appeared to be Afghans, the tone changes.

Or is he imagining it? It's not anything she says, but he is used to interpreting cues. After all, it's what he does for a living. The conversation continues, but the journalist is noticeably colder. She thinks he is out to blame the refugees. But it's not about blame, and Hans is not the only witness. There were thousands of people in the park; she doesn't have to trust him. He has plenty of contacts among the police officers who were present. He can put her in touch with any one of them. Not only can they corroborate his story, but they can likely give more details than he can, as they have worked throughout the festival, not just the one August night Hans visited.

He gives her the number of Lars, the police officer he spent the most time with that night. Lars had worked other nights at the festival and was right there next to Hans for much of the Saturday. He too had been upset, albeit more disillusioned, by what they witnessed. The journalist says she will call him.

* * *

Over the next few days, Hans opens his web browser every morning, hoping to find the story. He no longer bothers to brew his coffee first, but reaches for his MacBook on the floor as soon as his alarm sounds. And every morning he is met by the same disappointment: the story isn't there. Instead he is overwhelmed by endless trivia. In the tabloids he reads about the number of pills famous criminologist Leif G.W. Persson consumes, and about what one can do to lower one's interest rates. Even the weather forecast makes the front page, as another heat wave is expected. The more serious dailies inform him that there have been fewer applications to open charter schools, that narcotics are being sold with increasing openness, and that a 24-year-old woman has died in a fire. If the images from the festival weren't eating at him, Hans would think that nothing ever happened in Sweden. It scares him to realize that this steady stream of non-news would probably leave him feeling content and reassured to live in such a boring and peaceful place, had he not known that there was another, untold, dimension—one that apparently could not be discussed.

Hans emails two other news outlets to tell them about the incident. There is no reply. After a few weeks, he finally gives up and stops reading the news altogether. His original suspicion was right; this type of blame cannot be cast.

Hundreds of young girls have been sexually molested, abused, and humiliated. In a public place, at a tax-financed event, under the supposed supervision of responsible adults. In a country that claims to be one of the most feminist places on earth. And for some, unspoken reason, there will be no action. No justice. No story.

PART TWO

OUTCASTS AND THE RISE OF THE UNIMIND

IN THE BEGINNING THERE WAS DARKNESS

Scandinavia was long unchronicled and unknown. The first written account of its inhabitants stems from Caesar and the Romans, who described the people of the north as savages; cruel, uncultivated, and uncivilized; a cautionary tale for Roman people. Later, they would be portrayed as barbarians of the north: primitive, warlike, and destructive, yet simple, with a pure, untainted way of life, in sharp contrast to the people of the hedonistic Roman Empire.[1]

The Viking Age in the eighth century CE marked the Swedes' first real entry into the history books. While the Vikings of Denmark and Norway headed west, those from Sweden advanced to the east. These inland Vikings were known as the Rus and are often credited with having established the medieval state of Kiev, out of which modern Russia grew.

With the exception of the Viking escapades, these northerners lived largely in isolation, excluded from the most important experiences and intellectual currents of Western Europe. Never occupied by the Romans, the early Swedes were also spared the upheaval brought about by the fall of Rome. Christianity wasn't firmly established in Sweden until the twelfth century, five centuries after Britain. This geographical and cultural isolation ensured the region was populated by an unusually homogenous people.

In 1397, the Scandinavian kingdoms of Norway, Sweden, and Denmark formed the Kalmar Union, aiming to join forces under a single monarch in order to block German expansion to the north. While the arrangement served its purpose, over the next hundred years Swedish nobility became increasingly open about their dissatisfaction with Danish dominance over their affairs.

On 4 November 1520, King Christian II of Denmark celebrated his coronation in Sweden. After three days of festivities, the king—known in Sweden ever after as "Christian the Tyrant"—locked the palace, effectively capturing his guests. In the following days, he marched nearly 100 Swedish noblemen, one after another, out to the great square in front of the palace to be publicly executed. The event became known as the Stockholm Bloodbath.

Gustav Eriksson, of the Vasa noble family, had declined his invitation to the coronation party, but his father and two of his uncles were among those slaughtered. Realizing his life was also in danger, Gustav fled to the province of Dalarna, where he managed to spark a rebellion against King Christian. Other rebellions followed around the country. Enlisting support from the affluent German free city of Lübeck, whose merchants felt threatened by King Christian's aggressive economic policies, Gustav drove out the Danish army, securing Swedish independence in 1523.

On 6 June that year, Gustav Vasa became the last elected king of Sweden and Finland. In portraits, his appearance varies, but according to a written description by his nephew, Per Brahe, Vasa was a large man, with a round head, yellow hair, a beautiful, large, long beard, sharp eyes, a small, straight nose, red lips, and rosy cheeks, with "not a spot on his entire body large enough to place a needle upon, beautiful proportionate hands, fairly strong arms, ample body and thin legs, delicate, beautiful feet; somewhat hairy." His nature was said to be that of a hot-tempered, sanguine man.

More importantly to the history of Sweden, Vasa was a gifted strategist and a master of propaganda. In the mid-1500s, he commissioned his very own historian, Bishop Peder Svart, to chronicle his life and destiny. The resulting book is filled with legendary, death-defying adventures that supposedly took place while Vasa was struggling to liberate Sweden from the Danes. The mythology soon took on a life of its own and secured Vasa's positive image as the founding father of modern Sweden. In 1606, the city of Vaasa in what is now Finland was named after the House of Vasa. To this day, he remains popular, despite the fact that we now know he was a harsh ruler; a suspicious, vindictive, and cruel tyrant who would place the heads of those who disobeyed him on spikes outside his castle. Even in modern times, people continue to honor him. A massive statue of Vasa is the first sight that greets visitors to Stockholm's Nordic Museum, and every year some 15,000 people participate in Vasaloppet, the largest cross-country ski event in the world, retracing Gustav Vasa's flight from Christian II's soldiers in Dalarna province.

But more than just propaganda, Vasa laid key parts of the foundations upon which modern Sweden would be built. He strengthened the position of the state by imposing heavy taxes on virtually everything. He introduced the Reformation to Sweden and, in the process, confiscated the assets of the Roman Catholic Church, thereby solidifying the power of the state. He also laid the groundwork for the modern Swedish bureaucracy, even turning the Lutheran Church into an arm of the state and the clergy into bureaucrats. Using land formerly owned by the Catholic Church to bribe the nobility, Vasa convinced the Diet to abolish Sweden's elective monarchy, introducing instead a hereditary monarchy that would ensure continued power for House Vasa and its successors, stretching all the way to the current Bernadotte royals.

Like no other monarch of his time, Vasa understood the political implications of Martin Luther's doctrine: better, deeper control of his subjects and their lives. Luther opposed the vast influence of the Catholic Church on worldly matters, dismissing it as corrupt. Salvation was the free gift of God granted to those who believed in Jesus Christ, and could neither be earned through good deeds, nor purchased. Luther wanted to replace the authority of the Catholic Church with God's words as outlined in the Bible.[2] This suited King Gustav perfectly; he commissioned the first Swedish translation of the Bible. Vasa was said to be indifferent when it came to religion but welcomed the opportunity to diminish the influence of any power players, including the Church.

Vasa's approach to state-controlled Lutheranism shaped Swedish life for hundreds of years. His insistence that everyone read the Bible and learn to correctly interpret the texts for themselves significantly sped up literacy and education. By the early 1800s, the majority of the adult population knew how to read, despite Sweden's extreme poverty.

While Catholics regarded celibacy as righteous, Luther considered sexuality one of God's gifts to humanity. What should one do when plagued by the Devil and despair? According to Luther, one should eat, drink, and escape to other thoughts, to dance, or to beautiful girls. A good Christian was no longer a chaste monk or nun. Instead, in Protestantism, the good home was given a near sacred position.[3]

Vasa nationalized the Church and stripped the clergy of their immunity from civil courts, essentially turning Sweden into a Protestant society without priests. The king strove for the politics of the new movement without its religion. For the awakening of the religious spirit, Swedes would have to wait until the late nineteenth century, when revivalism and the rise of Social Democracy took on evangelical proportions. Gustav Vasa, like the Social Democrats centuries later, used the Church to foster the concept of Swedish nationality. Not until the year 2000 was the Church finally separated from the state after almost 500 years of allegiance.[4]

While Vasa laid the foundation for Sweden's professional army and founded the Swedish navy, he maintained a policy of isolation. His sons, however, had more ambitious objectives. Periodically for the next 250 years, Sweden fought Russia and Poland for control of the Baltic. But it was during the reign of Gustav II Adolf that Sweden became a great military power. In an era marked by constant war, he led his armies as king from the age of 16 in 1611 until the Battle of Lützen in 1632, where he was killed leading a charge.

Like all educated Swedes, Gustav II Adolf had read the chronicles of Johannes and Olaus Magnus, who portrayed the Swedes as the heroic heirs of the Goths. The king regarded himself as a direct descendant of King Berig, the legendary Goth king who supposedly left Sweden to conquer vast European territories. Known variably as "The Golden King," "The Lion of the North," and "The Father of Modern Warfare," Gustav II Adolf felt it was his duty to follow in the steps of his heroic ancestors.[5]

Paintings of Gustav II Adolf suggest he had the receding hairline that would plague future generations of Swedish men, but he compensated for it with a rather impressive ginger-blond beard. The king also had talents that extended beyond the battlefield. A remarkable combination of soldier and civil servant, he was as passionate about keeping things organized as he was about fighting. He was assisted by one of the great bureaucrats of history, Count Axel Oxenstierna, the Lord High Chancellor of Sweden, who also acted as regent after his death.

Together, they reformed the structure of administration, shaped the modern Swedish government, and began parish registration of the population so that the central government could more efficiently tax and conscript the people. This gave the king the resources he needed to fight his wars and a method of rapid mobilization, which ensured access to a strong and agile army. Under Gustav II Adolf, Sweden rose from the status of a mere regional power to one of the great powers of Europe and a model of early modern government. Within only a few years of his accession, the Lion of the North had conquered vast territories, making Sweden the largest nation in Europe after Russia and Spain.

Neutral in the Thirty Years' War when it broke out in 1618, Sweden eventually came to the aid of the struggling German Lutherans. The armies of King Gustav II Adolf drove the Catholic forces back, regaining much of the lost Protestant territory and preventing the further expansion of the Holy Roman Empire.

By the time the Thirty Years' War ended in 1648, Sweden had become an empire, and the continental leader of Protestantism.

GO BACK TO POLAND, CHANG!

"How it hurts when the child realizes it will never be accepted, never included among the many … Among the Romani there are stories about the hateful actions of the ordinary people … They wear the overcoat of the gracious school magistrate, the garment of the well-meaning priest. They take the shape of the neighboring family's protective father, the meek visitors of a Sunday mass, the easily thrown gazes of the villagers on market day, the comrade who remains your friend until your origin is revealed."

Thom Lundberg, *För vad Sorg och Smärta*[1]

It's 5:30 a.m. Eleven-year-old Chang Frick wakes up feeling cold. In the winter the wood furnace doesn't quite manage to keep the house heated until morning. He rubs the sleep from his eyes and remains still for a few moments, listening to the faint sounds of the house. There's the odd, stifled creak from boards and beams, as though the house is trying to stay quiet so as to avoid attention.

No one else appears to be awake. Chang slides out of bed. His bare foot nudges the radio-controlled car he's left sitting on the floor. Good thing he didn't step on it. That could have woken Mother. He picks up yesterday's tracksuit bottoms and hoodie from a pile of clothes on the floor. He puts them on and tiptoes downstairs to start a new fire in the furnace. That way it will be warm for his brother. Then, he stops by the fridge. The seemingly bottomless bowl of beetroot soup from which they've scooped their dinner for four days straight is still the only edible item on the shelves.

"Shit."

He knows Arnold has a school trip today. He'll show up empty-handed and get in trouble for forgetting to bring a packed lunch. It won't be the first time. Neither he nor his younger brother would ever admit to the teacher that they have no food. And if they did, they would probably be accused of making excuses. It's not for lack of money. Their mother works on and off, and the government benefits keep coming. She and her new man Lennart just don't prioritize things like grocery shopping. They'll spend all their money on a new stereo and go hungry for a week. Or they'll simply forget to buy food.

If he can't eat, there's no point brushing his teeth. And he doesn't care about brushing his hair. It wouldn't make a difference. The son of a Polish Jew and a Roma Traveler, Chang is the school's *svartskalle*, or "black skull," a derogatory Swedish term for people with dark hair and brown eyes. His very un-Swedish name, Chang, doesn't exactly help to soften his foreign image. He has his dad, Georg, to thank for that. Georg is from a branch of the Roma people known in Swedish as *resandefolk* (Travelers) or, more commonly, by the derogatory term *tattare* (originally from a misconception that these people were Tatars).

Historically, most Swedes made little distinction between *tattare* and gypsies. Both groups had long been marginalized in Swedish society. They spoke a similar Romani language and led a similar nomadic existence, but while the gypsies started arriving in the late nineteenth century, the Travelers have resided in Sweden for over 500 years. Unbeknown to most Swedes, many Romani words have even made their way into modern Swedish. *Tjej*, the most common word for girl or girlfriend, is really a

Romani word, as are the words *puffra* (Swedish slang for gun), *bak* (joint or establishment) and *vischan* (countryside). Travelers would earn their keep taking seasonal jobs on local farms, with traveling fun fairs, or working as craftsmen, such as wire makers or copper kettle makers. Their nomadic lifestyles did not fit the Swedish model of reliability and stability. They were generally disliked and often accused of thievery and violence. Hundreds of years later, much of the prejudice lives on.

Chang heads straight for the front door. He grabs his coat, steps into his brown winter boots, and leaves the house. His light blue bike rests against the white brick wall of the house, waiting for him like an expectant friend. It's cold, but there's no snow or ice on the ground. Chang rides south along Sven Månsagatan.

In the yellow, wooden house next door lives a family with two kids; a chubby girl in first grade and her big brother Emil, who looks just like the mischievous little blonde protagonist in the famous Swedish fairytale of the same name. Next door to them sits a white brick house on the corner of Björnstigen Street. This is home to a lady that Chang refers to simply as The Socialist, because everyone knows she is a big supporter of the party. She has the juiciest prunes on the street and Chang sneaks over to steal some whenever they're in season.

He breezes past the playground and the remaining row of colorful, idyllic houses on Sven Månsagatan. Here, people don't have to lock their front doors or their bikes. In these gardens, neighbors find any excuse to get together. The yearly highlight is the neighborhood crayfish party in late summer, but there are many other events tied to the local football club, Treby IF. Chang has smelled the barbeques and heard the laughter on many occasions, but his family has never been invited. He suspects it has to do with Mother.

When Chang reaches Hallarydsvägen, he turns right. Halfway towards the local car repair shop he turns onto a small bike path that cuts to Länkvägen, letting him out behind Rune's farm. Back here he can bike in parallel with the main road. The landscape is open and pastoral. About 600 people live here in Killeberg, on the border between the southern provinces of Skåne and Småland. Frequently depicted in the stories of children's author Astrid Lindgren, it is the quintessential fairytale land of safe, rural Sweden. A place where carefree, blond children roam.

Biking past the turn-off to the sewage and wastewater plant, Chang holds his breath. On a hazy day like today, the stench can be terrible. A few minutes later he arrives at school: a single-story, wooden building in bleached yellow.

* * *

"Roger," shouts one of the team captains. A blond, freckled boy runs over to join him. "Johan A," exclaims the other captain. A tall boy with a swimmer's physique rushes forth.

At gym, the PE teacher likes to assign one student as the captain of each team and asks them to take turns picking team members from the class. Today they're playing *brännboll*— Swedish baseball.

"Niklas!" continues the first captain. A short, sturdy boy with a ruddy tuft, steps up. Soon, all the boys except for Chang have been picked. "Cornelia," says the first team captain, less enthusiastically. A girl with long, blonde hair and a pointy nose runs up. "Alexandra," the other replies.

And so it continues, until all the girls have also been picked. Left standing is Chang. Always. Regardless of the sport, he is always the last to be chosen.

Some of the more savvy kids even have the system down to a science, immediately figuring out whether there is an odd or even number of kids on a given day, and so whether it makes more sense to start picking first, or to offer this privilege graciously to the other, perhaps less cunning, student.

* * *

It takes a few seconds before Chang registers the sudden silence in the changing room. He has just undressed after PE and is about to head to the shower when he notices the wide-eyed stares from the other boys:

"What the hell have you done?" "Why the fuck do you look like that?" They've stopped whatever they were doing and stand in a semi-circle gawking.

"Nothing. What do you mean?" Chang counters. He doesn't understand what they are talking about.

"You're all purple!" "You look like you've been hit by a car."

Chang's stomach sinks. He's forgotten to shield himself.

"I've heard you get beat up at home," Johan comments and begins to laugh. A few of the other boys join in. Chang doesn't say anything.

"I got a lot of bruises from skiing once," another Johan interjects. "It doesn't have to be because he's been beaten up."

Chang still doesn't say anything. He knows Johan is trying to help, but it's too late. His back, bum, and thighs are tender from last night's punishment, when Mother chased him into a corner and beat him from behind with a wooden brush. He doesn't even remember what brought it on. As usual, he crouched down to protect his head, and as a result his back ended up taking the brunt of the impact until her arms grew tired. He doesn't even remember how long it lasted.

Until now, he's been pretty good at hiding his marks, either rushing to shower first or lingering until the others are done before taking his clothes off. But today, for whatever reason, he forgot. Perhaps because it no longer hurts as much as it used to. He has learned to take his mind somewhere else. He can't see what his back looks like this time, but judging by his classmates' reactions, it must be bad.

A wooden bench traces the walls of the small locker room. Chang grabs his towel from one of the hooks above it and walks to the set of four showers. There's nothing he can do about it now. There are no shower curtains. No place to hide. He steps into the closest shower, turns his back on them, and presses the button. The jet stream of lukewarm water washes over him. His face burns with shame. He keeps his eyes fixed on the light-blue, plastic floor and waits. Like Mother's arm, their comments and snickers will eventually tire.

* * *

"Where did you buy those? At Ica Maxi?" Cornelia comments, pointing at Chang's brown winter boots. Her pretty face is framed by a straight-cut bang, while the rest of her long blonde hair is tied back with a bow. She wrinkles her small, pointy nose as though she has just smelled something unpleasant. Alexandra and Julia giggle.

"Can't you afford proper shoes?" Alexandra joins in. She too has blonde bangs and wears her hair tied back with a similar bow. The two friends wear almost identical, striped sweaters. They never miss an opportunity to let Chang know what is wrong with him, whether it's his hairstyle, his clothes, or, most frequently, his parents. Each day the trio seems to search for new ways of letting Chang know he doesn't belong, and Mother makes it easy for them. She decks him out in worn, washed-out donations she has found at second-hand stores or thrift shops.

Chang feels his cheeks burning with shame again. How do they know Mother got his winter boots at the local grocery store? He is standing by the wooden fence that divides the schoolyard from the football pitch. It's solid and square, ideal for bouncing tennis balls. Chang wishes he could sink through the tarmac and resurface somewhere far away.

Finally, the moment passes and the girls continue their stroll across the schoolyard. Chang watches as they walk away. Then Cornelia turns around and delivers her favorite jibe: "Go back to

GO BACK TO POLAND, CHANG!

Poland, Chang! You know we don't want you here." But Chang has never even been to Poland and his mother has never spoken Polish to him. Sweden is all he knows.

THE FALL OF THE SWEDISH EMPIRE

Sweden's extensive warfare earned the country many enemies and more territory than there was money or manpower to defend. Shortly after the passing of King Carl XI in 1697, several of the country's foes decided the time was right to retake what they had lost.

Carl XII, who became king at the young age of 15, was only 17 years old when Denmark-Norway, Poland, and Russia agreed to attack Sweden, launching the Great Northern War (1700–21). But they had underestimated the young king. Carl XII was a competent commander, quickly forcing Denmark to capitulate and abandon its alliance with Sweden's enemies. Then, in November 1700, he humiliated Russia at the Battle of Narva, crushing an army more than three times the size of his and killing some 10,000 men. Lastly, the king set out to remove the Polish King August II and conquer the Polish crown, rejecting both Polish and Russian peace proposals.

Carl XII believed in leading by example and liked to ride at the head of his troops. He shared the hardship of his soldiers, living and eating as they did and exposing himself to the same dangers. Paintings of him were radical for the time as they lacked the symbols typical of traditional royalty. Instead, Carl insisted on his portrait being completely realistic. A precursor to the strict egalitarian style of future Swedish leaders, he wore a simple, blue soldier's uniform and no wig (unlike most royals of the era), and his short, disheveled blond hair looked as though it hadn't even been combed. He insisted that even his scars and tan be portrayed, and refused to allow any decorative background. He wanted to look like one of his soldiers, who were frequently farmers or of simple background.

He also distributed the financial hardships more evenly. Everyone had to help pay for the costly wars according to their ability to do so. Under him, the nobility became less privileged, and promotions were increasingly based on merit rather than family ties.

While Carl XII was busy fighting in Poland, Russian Tsar Peter the Great reorganized his army. In 1703, he was able to conquer the fortress Nyenschantz in the town of Nyen, capital of Swedish Ingria, and begin building the Peter and Paul Fortress; the embryo of present-day St Petersburg, on what was then still Swedish territory.

In 1707 Carl XII decided to march on Moscow. But the Russians employed their classic "scorched earth" defense, burning the farms in the Swedes' path, thereby starving the Swedish army. Unable to acquire enough food for his troops, Carl eventually opted to change direction and head south to recuperate. However, the following winter was unusually harsh and many soldiers froze to death. By the spring of 1709, Carl had lost more than two thirds of his troops. He decided to put the fortress city of Poltava under siege, hoping to force a large, decisive battle. By the time the Swedes finally faced the newly modernized Russian army, they were worn down and badly outnumbered. To make matters worse, Carl had been shot and injured in the foot some ten days previously and was unable to command his troops. The Russians forced the Swedes to retreat, leaving behind 7,000 dead Swedish privates and officers. "Like a Swede at Poltava" remains a Russian expression for "utterly helpless." Many of the Swedish soldiers who became prisoners of war after the subsequent capitulation at Perevolochna were put to work constructing the future St Petersburg.

Carl XII escaped to the Ottoman Empire, hoping to enlist its support against Peter the Great. In his absence, Russia raided Sweden's coasts unchecked and conquered the Baltic territories, including Riga and Tallinn, from the Swedish realm. In 1715, Carl finally returned to Sweden with what was left of his army. After spending a year trying to get the strained Swedish war economy back on its feet, he attempted to conquer Norway from Denmark, as compensation for his Russian failure. For the king, preserving Sweden's position as a leading warrior nation was paramount. However, in 1718, he was killed by enemy fire while inspecting the trenches outside Fredriksten Fortress in Norway.[1] His death put an end to Sweden's era as a great empire. The Swedes retreated and, by the time the Great Northern War was over in 1721, Sweden had lost almost all of her foreign territories. Russia was now the leading power of Northern Europe.

SAMVEL ATABEKYAN

"On your left, Dane," shouts one of the young boys, preparing Samvel Atabekyan for the fact that the ball is about to appear from underneath the car beside him. It's dusk and the scorching Armenian summer sun has finally relented, taking the oppressive heat with it. Because of his albinism, early mornings or evenings are the only times Samvel can be out playing. The other kids call him "the Dane" because they think he resembles Manchester United's ultra-blond Danish goalkeeper, Peter Schmeichel.

Samvel has always known he is different. The way people stare at him, it's impossible not to. In Armenia, a country with one of the world's most ethnically homogenous populations (over 98 per cent Armenian), he's the misfit. Fair-skinned with light blond hair and blue eyes, he stands out from the predominately dark-haired people around him.

Born in 1986, Samvel's life began as the Soviet Union was coming to an end. He lives with his parents, grandparents, uncle, and baby brother on the fourth floor of a typical Soviet apartment block, in the suburb of Raykom some 15 minutes away from downtown Yerevan. To the outsider, the buildings all look very similar—but the residents, who know them intimately, are well aware of the differences. Samvel's family live in one of the better buildings: made of stone, not concrete. The structure right next door is even fancier, because it contains two-story flats. This is where the neighborhood doctor lives, and Samvel can't understand why his family didn't pick an apartment like that when they had the chance. Then again, anything is better than the concrete block on the opposite side of the small square. Its walls are paper-thin and everyone knows the wind blows straight through them.

The kids play soccer outside the building on an asymmetrical, concrete pitch, squeezed in between the parked cars, benches, and other random objects. Games are often more reminiscent of an obstacle course than a match, but it's what they're used to. They've drawn the goal in black chalk on the wall. Save for the one spruce planted firmly in the center of the small square, there are no green spaces around. Yerevan is a city of concrete. A creation of the Soviet Union: uniform, characterless, it could have been located in any of the Soviet republics. Armenia's beauty and uniqueness is in the mountains, in nature—but Samvel and his family are city-dwellers.

Samvel's grandparents Garik and Svetlana (named after Stalin's daughter) work in a light bulb factory. It's a delightful place that Samvel loves to visit. The weird machines and odd sounds make him feel as though he is inside the brain of some sci-fi giant. Sometimes his brother Hayk will also come along. They have a daycare center they can go to, but much prefer the excitement of the factory, where they can wander around and watch production. Samvel goes there almost every day. He's not sure if it's allowed. There are never any other children, but no one objects. The atmosphere in the factory is quite laidback and nobody expects his grandparents to strain themselves too hard.

"They pretend to pay us and we pretend to work," the workers often joke. Many people are undoubtedly driven by a sense of duty, but there is no incentive to put in much extra effort. There are those who cheat the system; Samvel has heard his grandparents talk about that. People who claim salary at a job where they do next to nothing, only to spend their time on prohibited side gigs, such as smuggling foreign merchandise to resell at hefty markups. It's hard to blame them; the factory hasn't been able to pay out any salaries for a very long time. Instead, the workers receive odd items, and an infinite supply of light bulbs.

In Samvel's neighborhood, Raykom, no one sees the end coming. Even though Gorbachev introduced glasnost and perestroika, people are convinced change will be slow. But then everything rapidly falls apart. People with an education flee abroad, but in Raykom, most inhabitants have only a basic education, as propaganda long ago replaced critical thinking on the curriculum. Higher education is not for the masses. It requires contacts, and in Raykom people aren't particularly well-connected.

There are small signs that Western-style capitalism has arrived. An American University opens in Yerevan. Someone puts up a KFC advert on the elevator in their building. People can be seen kissing on television, which was unthinkable under Soviet censorship. But when it comes to the fundamentals, at first, much trends in the wrong direction.

Under capitalism, Armenia has little with which to compete. The many Soviet-era industries and factories are dated and inefficient. Before long, the light bulb factory where Samvel's grandparents work shuts down. Possessing no other marketable skills, his grandparents, now in their 50s, are left unemployed. As they haven't received a salary in years, they are allowed to keep the corporate white RAF-977K van used to transport light bulbs as compensation. Samvel's grandfather Garik loves it. He repaints it gray and spends the bulk of his days maintaining it, but to the rest of the family it's of little comfort. In the pantry, light bulbs take the place of food.

Families like Samvel's are allowed to buy the apartment they were allocated during communist times at a reduced cost, but there are no jobs and the economy is in ruins. A brewing conflict with Azerbaijan, which began in 1988, escalates into a full-blown war in 1992. As a result, both Azerbaijan and Turkey close their borders and impose a blockade, severely affecting the economy of the fledgling republic. Armenia, landlocked and surrounded by hostile neighbors, struggles to import food. The situation quickly deteriorates. Overnight, chaos and desperation replace the predictable patterns of their previous existence.

While there was a lack of products during Soviet times, it mainly manifested itself as a lack of choice. Samvel's family, neighbors and friends have never gone hungry before. Many felt they led a decent life. They felt safe and didn't have to work too hard. Now people don't know what to do. They have no experience with a liberal market system and no real chance of succeeding in it. Samvel spends hours with his mother in queues to buy bread. The family has ration books, but there is nothing to buy. They survive on potatoes.

* * *

Samvel is 7 years old and has just started school, but he hasn't attended in months. It's the winter of 1993 and Yerevan is buckling under the effects of the post-Soviet crisis. Unable to heat the classrooms, the schools have closed. They announce that they will open as soon as possible, but week after week passes while the harsh winter refuses to release its grip on Yerevan. Electricity is rationed; each home gets served for an hour or two per day. During that short interval of light and heat, families have to do everything for which they need power—rushing to cook, do laundry, shower, and heat a small area of their home where they try to trap the warmth for the rest of the day.

People burn anything they can get their hands on to stay warm, constructing special tubes to channel the smoke out of their apartments. Some even invent their own heating solutions.

In Samvel's home, the strategy is to keep one room above freezing. The whole family crowds in together, wearing winter coats and using every blanket and cushion they can muster as a shield against the cold. Huddled in the dark around their small black-and-white television, powered by a car battery, Samvel's family watches Yeltsin praise the market economy.

Eventually, they get hold of a gas heater. On these long winter days with no school, Samvel and his younger brother Hayk don't stray far from it. They spend hours curled up there, soaking up its heat and looking out the window at the passing cars. Samvel pretends he owns all the cars approaching from the left, while his brother pretends to own all the cars coming from the right. They compare and compete over who has the nicer collection. They watch the Soviet VAZ or Lada cars putter past. Before independence in 1991, there was only one Armenian car manufacturer, JerAZ—known for their RAF-977K vans, but they are so ugly only Grandpa Garik can love them. The boys pretend not to see them so they don't have to include them in their collections. A foreign make, on the other hand, is the grand prize. Whoever catches sight of a Mercedes, Ford, or—even better—a BMW, wins. It doesn't matter how old or how rough, in the boys' world, foreign trumps Soviet every time.

There is no lack of toys in the former Soviet republics, and Samvel and his brother have many. But this winter they rarely play with them. Toys provide neither warmth nor nourishment. What they yearn for is escape.

SWEDISH COLONIALISM

From the sixteenth century, many European nations began to conquer vast territories in Africa, Asia, and the Americas where precious metals, plantations, and mines generated great wealth for their masters. Focused on expanding and defending its territory around the Baltic Sea, Sweden had largely neglected entering the colonial race and had thereby been excluded from the lucrative slave trade.

In the mid-1600s, Sweden had made a couple of attempts at establishing overseas colonies. New Sweden by the Delaware River in America lasted a mere seventeen years, and Cabo Corso in modern-day Ghana fell even faster.[1] But in the late 1700s, when the rest of the European nations were working to end slavery, Sweden saw its chance to move in. Under King Gustav III, Sweden would intensify its efforts at acquiring overseas territories and becoming a colonial player. Having lost its position as a great empire, a colony would lend the country much-needed prestige, especially important given that Sweden's main rival, Denmark, already possessed three islands in the West Indies: St Thomas, St John, and St Croix.[2]

In 1784, Sweden finally acquired the Caribbean island of Saint-Barthélemy (St Barts) from France in return for trading rights in Gothenburg.[3] The Swedish West Indian Company was then formed to transport enslaved Africans to the Caribbean, with the king himself as the largest shareholder.[4] The acquisition did not stir much excitement in Stockholm. St Barts was isolated, with poor soil, and lacked its own drinking water. The French Abbé Guillaume Raynal described its inhabitants as so poor that even the pirates felt sorry for them and paid honestly for whatever the islanders could offer.[5] The island's one redeeming factor was the excellent, deep harbor, Le Carénage.

It was decided that the best way to make the colony financially lucrative was to turn it into a free port where the import and trade of black slaves, so-called "new negroes from Africa," would be tax-free for all nationalities. A fee was charged for each slave leaving the island. Swedish nationals only had to pay half the fee, thereby giving Swedish ships an advantage in the transportation of slaves to the island and then on to other islands or to the American mainland.[6]

In 1788, the British Society for the Abolition of the Slave Trade sent the Swedish anti-slavery activist Anders Sparrman to convince King Gustav III to ban slavery. The king replied with a direct denial: nobody in his country had participated in the slave trade and he would ensure it stayed that way.[7] Meanwhile, the number of slaves on St Barts had tripled from 281 to more than 1,000 in the three years that had passed since Sweden took possession of the island.[8]

A total of 5,334 slaves were transported from Africa to St Barts under the Swedish flag. The peak years were 1801 to 1805, when Swedish ships brought some 1,870 slaves to Gustavia—as Le Carénage, the capital and main port, had been renamed in the king's honor.[9] From the seventeenth through the nineteenth centuries, Swedes organized some fifty shipments of slaves; in all, 34,941 slave ships crossed the Atlantic.[10] Thus, Sweden was obviously a small player, but for lack of opportunity—not lack of will. Under Swedish rule, Gustavia was home to the largest slave auctions in the Caribbean. When the United States and Great Britain went to war in 1812, many of the slaves from the neighboring island colonies fled to St Barts; the Swedish crown later made great profits from the sale of these war refugees.[11]

In 1815 the leadership of Europe met in Vienna, where it was agreed to abolish slavery. Sweden signed the treaty and promised that all slave trade on St Barts would cease within five years. However, no measures to that effect were taken. In Gustavia the slave trade would continue until 1847, long after France, the United Kingdom and the northern United States had all banned it.[12]

Unable to make the island lucrative by other means, Sweden returned it to France in 1878 for the modest sum of 320,000 francs.[13] This remains one of the great historical regrets of the sun-starved, modern Swede—at least if one is to believe the countless pages of nostalgic scribbling in the guestbook of Le Select bar, the contemporary meeting place for Swedish visitors to Gustavia.

PROFESSED VALUES

Chang sits alone at the back of the fifth-grade classroom, staring down at his light blue desk. At the front his teacher Sven, a cautious, gaunt man from Stockholm, is explaining the assignment. He is wearing his usual jeans and shirt, with a checkered, blue V-neck sweater on top.

"Not everyone is as fortunate as us. There are schools that have problems with both bullying and racism and it is important to be prepared so that one knows what to do should it happen to us. That's why, today, I want you to work on developing an action plan for what you would do if you saw someone being bullied."

Sven is a nice guy, but very timid. Chang bets he has never in his life dealt with a conflict.

It's supposed to be a collaborative assignment, but when Chang walks around trying to find a group everyone tells him they are full. He returns to his desk and begins to take notes. "Action plan against bullying. Regardless of background, everybody has the right to be treated the same..." Chang is well aware of his school's professed values. He begins to list them: Inclusiveness. Standing up against bullying. Zero tolerance of racism. If someone is having a rough time, it's important to be a good friend and offer support.

He pauses and looks around the classroom. Next to him a group of girls have pulled their desks together. They look focused and sincere as they work away at the assignment. For a moment, Chang dares to hope. Perhaps, by being forced to reflect, some of the kids will realize that they are mistreating and bullying him for being different. But then he overhears a comment: "Let's start off by saying how proud we are about the fact that no bullying takes place at our school."

This very same girl has called him *svartskalle, tattare*, and told him to go back to Poland on several occasions. Chang feels an odd, anger-like feeling rising inside him. While the young Chang is not yet able to fully understand or articulate the source of his frustration, this seemingly innate ability of Swedes simultaneously to emphatically maintain a moral position while actively participating in its violation will become a recurring thorn in Chang's side. Apparently, you are judged on what you say, not on what you do.

Sven interrupts his thought process. "Chang, I see you've opted to work by yourself," he comments. "That's totally fine too."

VIKING REVIVAL

"The wind and the waves are changing their strain,
But the Viking's memory shall ever remain
And the brave will never forget it."

Erik Gustaf Geijer, *Vikingen* (The Viking), 1811[1]

In the wars against Russia in 1808–9, Sweden lost 20,000 soldiers and had to concede Finland and the Åland archipelago. Finland had been a part of Sweden since the early Middle Ages. It made up more than a third of the Swedish territory and a quarter of the population.[2] Its loss was a heavy blow, prompting a surge in nationalism. Authors and intellectuals of the time set out to infuse new pride in the broken Swede and inspire him to fight for the recovery of the lost eastern territory.

Many of these nineteenth-century Swedish poets and authors found their inspiration in Norse mythology, where gods such as the hammer-wielding Thor aroused a fighting spirit. And, if one should fall, paradise awaited. Valkyries—female warrior-spirits or shield-maidens—would soar over the battlefields choosing who lived and who died, before escorting half of the slain to Valhalla, where the one-eyed god Odin presided. At Valhalla, the slain heroes would spend their days fighting, but come evening all their wounds would be healed, and they'd be served an amazing meal of meat from the boar Saehrimnir (who is resurrected each time he is butchered) and an endless supply of mead served by the beautiful Valkyries. Those not chosen for Valhalla would go to Freyja's heavenly field of warriors, Fólkvangr. Of this place, less is known, but as Freyja is the goddess of love and sex, what awaited was probably not entirely unpleasant.

Real-life Norse heroes also acted as inspiration, such as Erik the Red, who founded the first Norse settlement in Greenland, and his son Leif Erikson, believed to be the first European to have discovered continental North America (before Christopher Columbus), establishing a Norse settlement on Newfoundland. Norse heroes had kin, and came from societies with strong traditions and rules, but their destiny was entirely their own. They had to submit to their personal fate, but to no human or god. This resonated deeply with the zeitgeist of the early nineteenth century: the individual was alone.[3]

In 1811, Erik Gustaf Geijer, Esaias Tegnér, and Pehr Henrik Ling founded the Gothic League, a patriotic club aiming to revive the Viking spirit. Geijer romanticized the Viking and the land-owning Swedish farmer (*Odalbonden*), who, with his ties to the land, was more Swedish than any nobility could ever be.[4] The Gothic League portrayed the Swedish people as the core of the nation. The free farmers were the proud descendants of Odin. They had successfully resisted all destructive foreign influences and southern vanities. Steeped in a spirit of endurance and self-reliance, they had worked the land with their own hands, untempted by superficial pleasures. Geijer's poetry was filled with male virtue, bravery, endurance, and independence.[5]

While the members of the Gothic League would have loved to see Sweden take up arms and fight to reclaim Finland, the royal family did not share their nostalgia. In 1810, one of Napoleon's former marshals, Jean-Baptiste Bernadotte, was elected the heir-presumptive to the childless King Carl XIII of Sweden. He ascended the throne in 1818 as Carl John XIV. All subsequent monarchs descended from him and the present royal house of Sweden still bears the name Bernadotte. Carl John was reluctant to spur a new cycle of conflicts with Russia by attempting to retake Finland. He decided that it would be smarter to expand to the west, thereby creating a compact peninsula stretching all the way to the North Sea. Foreseeing the collapse of France, in 1813 he allied Sweden with Napoleon's enemies, including Great Britain, Russia, and Prussia. In 1814, he received his reward as the Treaty of Kiel forced Denmark to cede Norway to Sweden. The Norwegians objected to Swedish control and declared independence, but after a short military intervention—Sweden's last war to date—they were forced to submit.

The Norwegians never really accepted Swedish rule, and in 1905 the unhappy union was finally dissolved by the Norwegian Parliament. In the subsequent Norwegian referendum, 368,208 voted in favor of the dissolution, while only 184 Norwegians wished to remain united with Sweden. While initially outraged, Sweden decided against military action and the terms of separation were agreed peacefully. "However important the union may be for the safety of the Scandinavian people," said King Oscar II, "it is not worth the sacrifices that forceful measures would command."[6]

SOVIET NOSTALGIA

Gayane looks down from her glassed balcony onto the small square where the old men sit playing chess as though nothing has changed. Beside them, watching attentively, is her son Samvel. His little head, with its tuft of thin, blond hair, is the beacon her eyes find in any crowd. She feels a pang of tenderness in her chest. His entire life, she has worried about his health and wellbeing, constantly trying to protect him from the sun, the heat, and most importantly, the evil remarks of strangers. People often comment, point fingers, or otherwise mock the different-looking child. Gayane has to be on constant alert, always ready to protect and defend him. It's emotionally exhausting. They tend to stay close to home. Here, in their local square, everybody knows Samvel, and to know him is to love him; of this she is certain. His dazzling intellect is already the talk of the block: the brilliant, little boy who taught himself English by locking himself in his room reading.

She looks around for Hayk, but he is nowhere to be seen. He's probably off somewhere with his friends, she figures. She doesn't worry about Hayk. He is a happy child, not a brooder like Samvel. Popular, handsome, and caring, Hayk dreams of becoming an actor. He is as extroverted as Samvel is introverted. The two boys couldn't be more different. She loves them both equally but in different ways. The tenderness she feels for Samvel is so intense it can sometimes feel like a raw, exposed wound.

Gayane scans the square, the center-stage for much of her life, for other familiar faces. Not many people are out today— just the old, devoted chess players. The world could collapse and they would still be there. In many ways, one could argue the world has collapsed, although things mostly look the same; just more deteriorated. She looks at the building on the opposite side of the small square. It's covered with patches; its doors and windows a mismatch of different types and sizes. Some windows are missing entirely, gaping empty like a lost tooth in the mouths of the old men on the square. Some windowless holes are covered with plastic or tarpaulin; some are boarded shut. Each family has to care for their own unit, resulting in a patch-work of solutions. In Soviet times, such lack of standardization would never have been tolerated.

Since the fall of the Soviet Union, everything is different, for better and for worse.

Gayane is glad to be rid of the constant trepidation that came with never knowing how free one could be in words or deeds. There was always the risk that a neighbor would call the KGB and make up a story that could land you in big trouble. But at the same time, she misses the warmth she felt characterized human relationships during Soviet times. There was a greater sense of community. As long as one accepted one's lot and didn't overstep, life was simple. And she's never been one to be tormented by subversive thoughts. She doesn't need much to feel content and this, she has learned, is a blessing. There weren't enormous pos-sibilities, not at all—but one was part of something bigger; a link in a chain, a community of closed-knit human relationships.

Back then, neighbors and friends would often gather to do things together. Gayane looks down at the wooden tables and benches in the square, remembering where they used to all congregate at the end of a hot summer's day. Sometimes they would head in to town to attend a concert. Most cultural events were state-sponsored, so everybody could afford to participate. Besides, everybody had more or less the same amount of money to spend, which made social relationships less complicated. While life in the Soviet era is often described as gray, Gayane likes to think of it as colorful. She doesn't remember any shortage of anything she needed. Society was more secure and she knew what her salary would be at the end of each month. While it wasn't much, it was reliable, predictable.

Now, one has to be very careful with money. Gayane feels it takes a toll on relationships with friends and neighbors, as well as within the immediate family. It's the reason she is standing here alone now. The fall of the Union has caused the family to split. Unable to find work and provide for the family in Armenia, her husband Garnik has had to leave for Łódź, Poland. There he works and sends money home. She doesn't know when she will see him again; when he'll be able to afford to visit. Bringing the family along was never an option. It took years just to sort out the paperwork for his own permits, and he didn't want Samvel and his brother to have to go to a Polish-speaking school. After all, it's only supposed to be a temporary solution. Whenever they speak, Gayane and Garnik both pretend they still believe this— but the years go by, and in her heart Gayane knows that Garnik isn't coming home any time soon.

Overcome by a sudden weariness, she takes a seat on the balcony's soft, green sofa. Her mother has replaced and patched the worn fabric so many times that Gayane no longer remembers what its original color used to be. This is where the whole family used to sit. When the summer heat got too oppressive inside the apartment, they would carry out extra chairs and have their evening meals around the foldable camping table. Immediately to her left, next to the balcony, is the small, cool pantry where, after the fall, the family attempted to conserve enough food to last them through the winter.

"Do you remember my mother's chicken tabaka?" Garnik will often ask her over the phone. He likes to reminisce about the "good old days" of Soviet rule. While Gayane is more conflicted, she'll usually indulge him just to hear the enthusiasm in his voice. They both miss the Soviet youth camps. While some criticized the camps as merely another vehicle of ideological indoctrination, Garnik and Gayane both remember them as wonderful teenage adventures far away from home.

Garnik yearns for the past even more than she does. During his childhood, Garnik's parents operated their own restaurant, which meant access to plenty of food. He likes to tell mouthwatering stories about coming home from school to delicious treats like the cheese-filled bread Khachapuri and Kharcho soup served by his Georgian mother. As a child, Garnik even received an allowance, which was very unusual at the time. "And I'd spend it all on Pedro," he would giggle to Gayane. Pedro was a rare brand of imported Czech chewing gum; an exclusive treat. It was a reality far removed from the hunger experienced during the crises after the fall, and makes for a depressing comparison with the meager supply now stacked away in the family pantry.

INFLATABLE BARBARA

"Wonderful, inflatable, Barbara," the radio blasts. Barbara Frick sighs loudly. In a fake foreign accent, renowned Swedish singer Robert Broberg sings about a plastic, inflatable sex doll named Barbara who, unlike normal women, never nags. "If you are lonely just say YES to wonderful, inflatable Barbara," the song continues. "She spends all day in bed, nice and quiet. She is the most wonderful woman you've ever kissed."

Chang chokes back a giggle as he watches his mother rush over to the radio in an effort to turn it off before Broberg reaches the part she detests most: "Her butt! You can pump it up. Aaaaaahhhhh!" Soon she'll start her usual rant about how she can't believe that this is considered a perfectly acceptable song, popular with adults and children alike. The song is so popular, in fact, that all sex dolls are now marketed as "inflatable Barbara." But Chang won't tell his mother that small piece of trivia, of which the kids at school have been sure to inform him; that would be suicide. He carefully watches her face to see how worked up she is this time. She turns to meet his eyes. He lowers his gaze, grabs his jacket off the chair, and begins to head for the door. He does not want to be around if she blows a fuse.

"Where are you going?" she demands.

"Out biking," he says quickly, as his brother Arnold enters the room, oblivious to the bomb about to go off.

"I don't want you spending time with worldly kids," she admonishes them.

Barbara has become increasingly conservative; turning to religion, perhaps in response to an environment whose value system she does not share and where she does not feel welcomed. While she preserves her non-religious Jewish traditions and symbolic possessions such as the menorah, she is now a devoted Jehovah's Witness. Chang and his brother are repeatedly told they can only have friends who are also Jehovah's Witnesses.

"Be home by five," she warns. Chang knows the consequences of disobedience. The beatings are frequent. Arnold bears the grunt of it. He always seems to provoke a greater fury in their mother than Chang ever managed. Unlike Chang, Arnold openly disobeys, and talks back to Mother. She, in turn, begins to channel most of her rage onto him.

The boys mumble agreements as they push out the door to safety.

* * *

Chang hears his younger brother's screams from the bathroom. Ten-year-old Arnold has arrived home an hour late after spending time with his friend Ola. Mother is beside herself. Peeking in through a crack in the door, Chang sees how she has him by the hair, banging his head into the wall. She is a sturdy woman, no longer the delicate lady Chang has seen in pictures from her younger days. Her blouse is slightly too small and when she raises her arms rolls of fat hang out around her waist. It reminds Chang of fermenting sourdough. A wisp of black hair has escaped from her ponytail and sticks to her sweaty forehead as she bangs Arnold's head into the wall again. He screams even louder. Then she leans over and bangs it with all her might on the edge of the bathtub. With a thump, the screaming stops.

This time she has killed him. Chang is sure of it. He can't see his brother's head, just his limp body. She adjusts her grip on the small boy's frame. Chang runs silently for his room. Bang. Bang. Bang. The echoes of his brother's head repeatedly hitting the porcelain enameled steel of the tub chase him down the hall. They enter his room with him. He covers his ears, and then uncovers them again repeatedly. If she kills him, the police will come. He won't tell; if they interrogate him, he won't say a thing.

Finally, the banging stops and Chang hears his mother walking out.

When it sounds like she's far enough away, Chang sneaks into the bathroom. Arnold's limp body lays flaccid on the floor. There is blood on the wall, blood on the tile, blood in the bathtub; even blood on that weird porcelain bowl that Chang has learned is called a bidet. And Arnold is covered in blood. He lays completely motionless. Chang feels the panic rising. Then he sees the blood bubbling in Arnold's nose. Little bubbles of blood bursting. That means he must be breathing. He must be alive! Chang rolls him over on his side and sneaks back to his room. He's too scared to even imagine what his mother will do if she catches him in the bathroom.

THE CRADLE OF COLLECTIVE MENTALITY

The old agricultural system required absolute submission to the demands of the collective. Until well into the nineteenth century, Sweden—with some exceptions in the north—had a system of strip farming. Holdings were not continuous but made up of disconnected patches so narrow that they could not be cultivated separately. The land of each village had to be worked collectively as one large farm. That way, all would share burdens and favors equally. Financially, each village was regarded as a unit, and sales were handled communally.

The early industrial settlements were also characterized by a powerful sense of community. Starting in the 1600s, hundreds of isolated and self-contained outposts, known as *bruk*, developed around local industries across the country. The *bruk* master owned not only the community's industry, but its houses and all its facilities as well. Housing was tied to the job and the owner had a responsibility to take care of his workers, providing them with healthcare, schooling, and old age pensions. Most workers were very loyal to their masters and the *bruk* are often regarded as the cradle of both the Swedish industrial revolution and the Swedish welfare state.[1]

Conformity and strong social control characterized life in the *bruk* as well as in the collective farms, where the village council supervised church attendance, morality, and everyday behavior. The individual was strongly pressured to behave as the community demanded, with no personal deviation permitted. This produced a collective mentality in which personal identity was determined by membership in a group.[2]

As suffocating as this collective lifestyle must have been, its eradication proved even more traumatic. In 1827, strip farming was abolished to pave the way for more effective and efficient means of crop production. The land was redistributed to form the consolidated holdings of modern agriculture. Farmers were meant to mind their own land, instead of sowing and harvesting together. They were given six years to remove their old homes in the village and move out to their estates.[3] This broke up ancient communities and disrupted the traditional way of life. Walls and fences were built to separate properties. Used to living together in villages at the center of their fields, people were now spread out in isolated farmhouses.[4]

However, though physically separated, the collective mentality persisted. In order to preserve the social connections they had known before, farmers began to form associations, which grew rapidly into national popular movements. "Temperance societies," whose members were teetotalers advocating sobriety, were the first to appear and quickly became very popular. The urge to belong to a collective was so strong that it wasn't uncommon for people to take the pledge required to join while secretly continuing to drink.[5]

THE BURDEN OF FREEDOM

Samvel, his brother, and their mother share a bedroom in their grandparents' apartment. The room is big, with large windows and beautiful, light green curtains that dance in the draft whenever they open the panes to air the room. There are three single beds, a couple of wooden armchairs with worn fabric, a TV, and a VCR. Each year, the Armenian government extends the hours that electricity is available and, from the mid-90s, quality of life slowly improves.

Samvel has grown into a gangly young man, whose thick glasses magnify his perceptive blue eyes. Like the bulk of his generation, he has little sympathy for his parents' nostalgia for the past. As soon as he is old enough to reason, he debates with his parents, trying to show how they have been limited in ways they don't even realize.

As far as Samvel can tell, Soviet citizens were not very demanding of life. As long as there was food on the table and they received a low but stable salary, people were content. He is convinced a great deal of the discontent and nostalgia among older people stems from their inability to be successful under the new system. They can't use the freedom they have gained, so they end up on the sidelines. After the fall, people's strongest memory of the Soviet period seems to be the yearly, subsidized vacation to the Black Sea. Once a year they would leave their anonymous city of concrete, and travel to a government-sponsored coastal resort. When the system collapsed, that yearly glimpse of the ocean was forever lost. Many can never again afford to return.

Overnight, people like Samvel's grandparents had been rendered worthless—all because they were trapped in a system and now they don't know how to function outside of it. "It was Gorbachev who ruined the Soviet Union," Grandpa Garik always says. He and many others seem to believe that going back to the old order would fix things. When Samvel wants to understand that generation, he tries to put himself in their shoes. It can't be easy to have the life you have always known suddenly vanish overnight. All rules upended, all that predictability suddenly replaced by unpredictability. It's hard to imagine how he would have felt had he been older when the change came. But Samvel isn't old; he is young, and for him what matters most is freedom, even if it takes generations. He realizes, however, that freedom is very demanding in many ways. It seems most people can't handle it; don't even want or need it. A person who is free is accountable for their decisions and actions, but when someone else defines your existence and sets the boundaries, the weight of personal responsibility is lifted.

SHAPING THE *VOLKSGEIST*

Between 1860 and 1880, the population of Sweden grew from 3.9 million to 4.7 million. But the new generation was in for a very different reality from the idealized life of the free farmer portrayed in Geijer's poetry. Agricultural reforms made life tougher for those who lacked land of their own. Young men and women had to take up employment as maids, farmhands, crofters, or so-called *statare*, agricultural contract-workers who, contrary to other farmhands, were paid in kind with food.[1]

People abandoned the rural areas for the cities. However, there was a surplus of labor and many could not find work. The lower classes lacking political rights continued to grow. This spurred a wave of emigration to the United States during the late nineteenth century. In this period, Sweden produced the third most European emigrants relative to its population size. Between 1851 and 1910, about 1 million people undertook the arduous journey across the Atlantic to America. This worried the elite, and in 1907 the Swedish Parliament launched an extensive investigation into the causes of this great emigration.[2] As an appendix to the investigation, Professor Gustav Sundbärg published *Det svenska folklynnet* (The Swedish Disposition), which claimed to describe the national temperament. He argued that the most prominent characteristic of the Swede was his great love of nature; a longing for vast, depopulated forests filled with spruce trees and isolated streams. This love of nature was coupled with indifference towards other people. He portrayed the Swede as stiff, alienated, borderline autistic, and hopelessly unpatriotic; constantly dissatisfied with all that made him and his country different, but quick to praise the national aspirations of others. The hearts of Swedes were empty; they didn't much care for each other and experienced no natural solidarity. This, according to Sundbärg, had created the discontent that was leading many to emigrate.[3]

Letters from Swedish immigrants in America stoked anti-national sentiment amongst the population. The letters told of religious tolerance, political freedom, and plenty of opportunities to improve one's lot in life. This contrasted with the dominance of the Swedish state Church, the arrogance of the country's ruling elite, and the social injustices of the time.[4] Up until this point, foreign influences had been the concern of the upper classes alone, while the masses had been immersed in a national tradition. Now, repatriates and letters from abroad were teaching the lower classes of Sweden about America, while their rulers remained under German influence.

* * *

For a few decades at the end of the nineteenth century, Scandinavia peaked as an intellectual hub. A common theme among authors and artists at the time was the conflict between individual and society. Solitude was glorified as a means to free oneself from the masses, society, and the different forms of community. Henrik Ibsen, August Strindberg, and Georg Brandes became renowned not only in Scandinavia, but abroad.[5]

Strindberg built on the ideals portrayed by Geijer: individualism, independence, and the role of poverty in shaping the Swede. The poor but noble Swede was idealized.[6] Civilization was false and corrupted. Only in the solitude of nature could man truly be free. Towards the end of his life, Strindberg became the people's poet; the voice of a people who "paid tribute to the collective but desired the individual."[7]

Geijer had claimed that to develop the *Volksgeist*—the unique spirit and character of the nation—people had to know their history; their roots. It was important to preserve the old Nordic ways. Consequently, enthusiasts set out to collect traditional objects and document the old songs, legends, and beliefs of the rural folk. There, they argued, lingered the true soul of the Swedish people. The cultural history embedded in the objects uncovered by archeologists, or in the lifestyle of traditional farmers in the countryside, constituted the core of Swedishness.[8]

This idealization of the free farmer helped bridge some of the social and class-based divides of the time. The *folk* (the people) belonged together because they were alike. The Swedish people were portrayed as an extended family of sorts, whose members each carried the common people's soul (*folksjäl*) within. It wasn't long until these ideas began to affect politics. Based on this natural sense of kinship, shouldn't the nation be built on the will of the people? Then the country would stand on firmer ground than if royal dynasties had all the say. The people should rule themselves, or at the very least have more influence. Slowly, society was becoming more liberal and democratic.[9] Rich or poor, every Swede was first and foremost Swedish and ought to feel a shared responsibility and deep loyalty towards his land. Beyond paying their taxes, the upper classes were also expected to have their children educated in public schools, and, if need be, take up arms for the nation. In 1872, a system of military conscription was introduced, and it was no longer possible for the wealthy to buy their way out or pay someone to serve in their place. The fact that the cultural elite now portrayed the Swedish people as belonging to one big family helped to encourage acceptance of these radical changes.[10]

Education was a part of the national project of modernization. The people had to be molded to fit the new nation. They had to learn to read and write, but also to cherish their country. School textbooks underwent massive reforms. In 1868, *Läsebok för folkskolan* (Reading Book for Elementary School) was published. It was to be the standard schoolbook of Swedish literature, printed and distributed in a way that had previously only been achieved by the Bible, the Book of Psalms, and the Catechism.[11]

Artur Hazelius, a young teacher and linguist, was asked to choose texts for the first edition of the book. Although largely unknown, Hazelius was patriotic and had many ideas on how best to influence the next generation. Hazelius had written his PhD thesis on *Hávamál*, an old Norse poem from the Viking age. The idea of the Swedish people sharing an ancient Nordic soul resonated with him and was reflected in his selection. He picked romantic poems about Vikings and peasants, tales from Norse mythology, fairytales, songs, and historical anecdotes by poets like Geijer, Tegnér, Atterbom, and Stagnelius. The *Läsebok* would become a classical canon for the new, official nationalism. The texts that Hazelius was unable to include he published himself, under the title of "Patriotic Reading for Children and Youth."[12]

Clas Theodor Odhner, a university history lecturer, was tasked with reviewing the Swedish history textbooks. Odhner had been a part of the same circle of Uppsala students as Hazelius and shared the same influences—Geijer and Scandinavianism.[13] His history book for Swedish students, first printed in 1870, would dominate the teaching of Swedish history for generations. It was reprinted until the mid-twentieth century.[14]

One important topic of Odhner's book was the national character. Children were taught that their ancestors had a war-like, independent, and defiant disposition; that they had wanted to rule themselves and not be dependent on anyone else. Every spring, the men had set out on their dragon boats and were not seen again until the fall. "To be one's own lord and not depend on anyone else was the aspiration of every free man. Strength, valor, and courage were the traits most highly regarded by our ancestors and they entitled a man to honor in life and fame after death," Odhner wrote. The farmers made up the core of the people, he argued, but they were not a passive mass; they embodied the common will.[15]

CHANG'S SILENT VICTORY

It's the dead of winter in Killeberg. Eleven-year-old Chang forces his bike through the mud, slush, and snow. School is out for winter break and he is headed to a kids' table tennis tournament, taking place in the neighboring village of Hökön. It's only 9 kilometers away, but on icy paths it feels much longer. Chang hopes he can at least avoid running a flat. His old, light-blue Monark seems to be a magnet for anything that can pierce its tires.

The tournament takes place in Hökön's old school; a beautiful, old building painted traditionally red with white corners. It's the natural center of the village. With its mere 150 inhabitants, there's not much here save for the old sawmill, a small car repair shop, and a few houses.

Chang enters, takes off his shoes and hangs his jacket by the front door. The venue smells of coffee and wet socks. A woman is busy pulling muddy winter boots off someone's little brother. She glares at Chang.

"So, you're here to play some ping-pong?" A worn, older man approaches. He looks a little out of his element, like someone who has spent his whole life in the forest but who has finally been forced indoors, by some circumstance beyond his control. He motions for Chang to continue up the wooden staircase to the second floor, where two ping-pong tables have been set up. Only four children, including Chang, have turned up.

His first opponent is tall and looks a couple of years older than Chang. He is a good player, so Chang is pleased that he still manages to put up a decent fight. Sliding around in his socks, he returns a few tricky serves that he is certain will miss the table. By the time he is finally defeated, the sweat covers his forehead and he can feel it trickling down his spine.

The second game is an easy win. By now Chang is warmed up and unstoppable.

Because of the low number of participants, the tournament doesn't last long. When it's over, the children all head downstairs where three medals lie waiting in a neat row on the table. Engraved pieces of metal have been glued to wood painted gold, silver, and bronze. Everybody congregates by the front door. Chang stands to the side. He looks around. All the other kids have their parents there.

The elderly organizer announces the winner. Everyone applauds as the big kid who beat Chang walks up to receive his gold medal. Then the runner-up is called. Again, everyone applauds; even louder this time, as though they feel sorry for him for having to settle for second place. But he doesn't look disappointed. Chang suspects that, just like himself, the boy probably didn't expect a medal at all. "And in third place," the organizer continues, "Chang Frick."

The announcement is met with complete silence. In his slippery socks, Chang slides over to the organizer who hands him his medal. No one applauds. No one speaks. The room is so quiet Chang can hear his belly rumbling. The moment doesn't last long before the organizer quickly moves on to the third runner-up. The last boy steps up to receive a participation certificate. The applause from the adults resumes.

Biking home through the slush and snow, Chang ponders the feeling in his stomach. It's not sadness. He feels strangely excited. He showed them all. Instead of staying home, out of sight, like he knows they'd prefer, he claimed his space and won the medal that the fourth-place boy would otherwise have received.

And because the tournament went so quickly, he has time to stop by at his friend's house on his way home without Mother finding out.

* * *

Kim's dad Håkan sits at his big, kitchen table looking out through the window.

The red paint is peeling from the walls and some buildings look like a gust of wind might knock them over. New roof tiles have been stacked against one of the ramshackle buildings for years now, but Håkan can't find the time to replace the crumbling metal roof. Lord knows there is enough work to go around on the farm anyway.

Over by the stove, his wife Rosy is making meatballs. She is a sturdy lady and an excellent cook. The tempting smell already fills the kitchen, but Håkan knows dinner is still a little ways off. He has time for one more snuff. Håkan has just pulled out his snuff container from his back pocket and popped its lid, when Chang Frick walks in.

"So, it's you, boy," he comments. As always, Chang looks a little disheveled—like a farmer's boy, but without the smell of manure. "What brings you by?"

"I just played in the Hökön table tennis tournament. I thought I'd pop in on my way home," Chang explains. He falls quiet for a few seconds, but judging by his secretive, defiant smile, Håkan suspects there is more coming. Before long, Chang has told him all about his experience at the tournament and the silence that reigned when he won the bronze.

"The fuckers!" Håkan exclaims and spits his snuff out on the table. "The envious, petty, narrow-minded, little fuckers!" he continues. "Don't let them get to you, boy."

Håkan is a white-haired, fairly small, and slender-limbed man, with delicate features. But there is nothing delicate about his personality or temper. An avid hunter, every inch of wall space in his home is filled with antlers and other hunting trophies. Agitated now, he cracks open another beer. It helps numb his chronic pain. He seems always to be nursing some injury he has sustained on the farm or working in the forest. Once he put a chainsaw to his leg; another time he took down a tree and had part of the stump spring back up and hit him straight in the face, knocking his cheekbone loose. For the longest time, he was able to scare the kids by moving it around.

"They're fucking socialists all of them," Håkan continues, "so concerned about being the same." He motions for Chang to take a seat. He has warned the boy about the socialists before, but it can never be said enough times. In particular, it is worth repeating the Law of Jante—the Nordic social code of egalitarian conformity, as laid out by the twentieth-century Dano-Norwegian author Aksel Sandemose. The boy has to understand this list of social commandments, by which all Swedes are pressured to abide:

1. You shall not believe that you are someone.
2. You shall not believe that you are as good as we are.
3. You shall not believe that you are any wiser than we are.
4. You shall never indulge in the conceit of imagining that you are better than we are.
5. You shall not believe that you know more than we do.
6. You shall not believe that you are more important than we are.
7. You shall not believe that you are going to amount to anything.
8. You shall not laugh at us.
9. You shall not believe that anyone cares about you.
10. You shall not believe that you can teach us anything.[1]

"That's exactly what they said when I got the top mark on my test," Chang comments. "Those exact words: 'Don't believe that you are someone.'"

"That's right, boy. And don't you listen to them. They're just envious at anyone who works hard and achieves something, so they try their best to bring them down."

The Law of Jante can be traced all the way back to the early democratization process. In England and the USA, the goal had been to raise the people to the level of the aristocracy; liberties traditionally reserved for the few were to be given to the many. In Sweden, the opposite development took place. Democratization was about bringing the aristocracy down to the level of the people, by abolishing any special rights or privileges the elite had previously held.[2]

Håkan knows the other kids are hard on Chang. Hell, the whole village is. But if he can at least help him understand why people act the way they do, it might make it a little easier to bear. "No one is allowed to be good at anything; no one can stick out or they'll be shunned and trash-talked. Don't ever get mixed up with them socialists, Chang. Don't ever become one of them."

Having heard the commotion, Kim enters the kitchen. "That goes for you too, son!" Håkan says, acknowledging the short, blond boy in the doorway. "Don't let anything they say get to you." Håkan stands up, jabs his right arm forward at jaw height, and says: "Just hit them right in the nose if you have to, boys."

Kim and Chang laugh and head off to play Nintendo. Håkan sits back down and returns to his snuff. Kids can be mean anywhere, but he knows the kind of issues that Chang struggles with are in a league of their own. He knows, because he heard of the kid long before he ever met him. Back when the boys first started preschool, parents were telling their kids to stay clear of the *tattare* kid. Håkan could never understand what made the boy so threatening. One day, he'll tell him how people used to talk about him and his family. But not today; it will have to wait a few years. Chang is still much too young.

THE BIRTH OF THE PEOPLE'S HOME

The social democratic ideology that dominated Sweden for much of the twentieth century was disseminated not only by the Party, but also by its various supporting branches, such as the workers' movement, the unions, the co-operatives, and various popular movements (*folkrörelser*). From their humble beginnings in the 1850s, when voluntary organizations were mainly about temperance and religious revival, popular movements grew to encompass causes such as women's rights and workers' rights.[1] By 1920, these movements had about 1 million members: a quarter of the population over the age of 15. They began to exert great influence on social and political discourse.

While they each addressed different issues, they all helped to school their members in collective individualism—a combination of individual independence and collective action. People were encouraged to work, take responsibility, and show solidarity, while cautioned not to give in to urges.[2] The goal was to uplift the entire collective and create independent individuals, free from alcohol addiction and from humiliating submission to employers, charity, priests, or other representatives of the class society.[3] Many of the young people who joined the workers' movement hoped for more than higher wages, better working conditions, or political influence. They wanted to assert their individuality and be respected as thinking, feeling beings.

One of them was Per Albin Hansson, who would go on to become one of the founding fathers of Swedish socialism. In the social democratic youth association that he joined as a young man, there was an individualistic, heroic rhetoric that was more reminiscent of Nietzsche than of Marx. The goal of socialism was the creation of a new, superior human. Through the brave struggle of the working class, the proletariat would be elevated to new, better men. From the filth would rise a modern *Übermensch*.[4]

At the same time, collective behavior and the punishment of deviations were necessary components of these movements if they were to maintain their strength. They instilled an ideal of *skötsamhet* among their members. To be *skötsam* means to conduct oneself in a proper and orderly manner, and to be free from vices. People were supposed to keep in line, avoid conflicts, strive for compromise, and put the collective above and before the individual.[5]

In 1920, Hjalmar Branting became Sweden's first Social Democrat prime minister. The party was then the single largest in Parliament, but lacked sufficient support to achieve a majority. The decade was characterized by a series of weak, short-lived Social Democrat governments, until the Conservatives regained power in 1928.

The Social Democrats realized that, in order to achieve a broader appeal, they would have to tone down the radical rhetoric about class struggle. Instead, they began to emphasize peaceful, gradual reform. This, they hoped, would help realize their ambitious plan of becoming the one party for all Swedes.[6]

In 1928, Per Albin Hansson, now leader of the Social Democratic Party, gave a famous speech to Parliament in which he described the party's vision of creating a *Folkhem* (people's home). The term was borrowed from right-wing politician Rudolf Kjellén, but Hansson repurposed it and transformed it into a metaphor for the nation as a safe place where all social classes could come together and feel at home, as though part of a single family:

> The good home knows no privileged or deprived [individuals], no special favorites or stepchildren. No one looks down upon anyone else, no one tries to gain advantage at another's expense, and the strong do not suppress and plunder the weak. In the good home there is equality, consideration, co-operation, and helpfulness. Applied to the great people's and citizens' home this would mean the breaking down of all the social and economic barriers that now separate citizens into the privileged and the deprived, into the rulers and the dependents, into the plunderers and the plundered. Swedish society is not yet the good home for its citizens. There is formal equality, equality of political rights, but from a social perspective, the class society remains, and from an economic perspective the dictatorship of the few prevails.[7]

Universal suffrage, achieved in 1921, had been an important milestone, but now it was time for the next step: an economic leveling that made citizens not only politically, but also socially equal. Encapsulating greater individual autonomy and a stronger sense of national communion,[8] the metaphor of the *Folkhem* would become the Swedish social ideal and the key to the future hegemony of the Social Democrats.

In the 1930s, the Social Democrats expropriated much of the national mythology and symbolism of the nineteenth century. The party's leaders portrayed themselves as descendants of Geijer's brazen, free farmers. But instead of patriotic farmers taking a stand against an arrogant aristocracy, it was now about the workers standing up to the capitalists. In other European countries, nationalistic sentiment and symbolism often ended up in the hands of rightwing radicals or fascists. Indeed, Per Albin Hansson came to power with his vision of a *Folkhem* (people's home) in 1932, just as Hitler was rising to power in Germany with a not-dissimilar vision of *Volksgemeinschaft* (people's community), aiming to unite people across the class divides to achieve a national purpose.[9]

The Social Democrats fused socialism with nationalism. Freedom was about the independence of the nation and the right of all Swedes to be equal as citizens.[10] No one was subordinate to anyone else; or rather, no ethnic Swede was subordinate to any other.

CHANG'S SAFE HAVEN

"What about that one?" Chang points to a Volvo 245 in the yellow shade of cigarettes, resting amidst the other cars and rubble.

"She runs," replies Lasse, the owner of the car repair and paint shop in Killeberg. "But she needs some work." Slim and sinewy, Lasse is an expert at bringing old cars back to life and rejuvenating them with a fresh coat of paint. His yard is always filled to the brim with the carcasses of old vehicles and their amputated parts. Today, young Chang has come by to tell him he wants to buy a car. The Volvo he has his eyes on is in rough shape.

"I bought her from The Gulp," Lasse continues. The Gulp is a local alcoholic who earned his nickname by allegedly asking the police officers for one last gulp after being arrested for DUI. To any other customer, Lasse would never volunteer that The Gulp was the former owner.

"That should bring the price down," Chang immediately counters.

"It's 2,000 SEK," Lasse continues.

"I'll give you 1,500," Chang replies with feigned disinterest. He wears the stone-faced expression he has learned to perfect at school, where any sign of emotion is interpreted as weakness.

Lasse watches the young boy's face. There's a lot of his father in him, he reflects. Only 14 years old and already negotiating his first car deal like a seasoned businessman. He can't help but soften. "Alright," Lasse agrees. "And you can do chores in return for the parts that you need." He hands Chang a checklist with all the things he has to fix or verify in order to have the car pass the motor vehicle inspection. "Use any tool you need, and holler if you need help," he says.

Lasse is friends with Chang's dad Georg. They are in the same line of business—used vehicles, machines, and their parts—and both live surrounded by their merchandise. Lasse knows Georg as a heavy drinker who fits the stereotypical perception of the Traveler well. While Killeberg is his hub, he travels anywhere there is a deal to be done, particularly in Eastern Europe. He has an affinity for all things Eastern, especially Poland. That's where he met Chang's mom Barbara—or Sara, as she recently renamed herself, tired of being associated with an inflatable sex doll.

Born in 1929, Georg is 34 years older than Barbara. And Lasse knows there were many women before her. Georg believed in spreading his seed and had fathered children with many different women across the country, and quite possibly the continent. According to population extracts from the Swedish tax authorities, he has acknowledged fathering ten different children with various mothers across Sweden. It's probably best there's no equivalent data source covering all of Europe, Lasse muses, smiling as he watches Chang excitedly propping up the hood of his new car.

In 1983, about two months before the birth of Chang, Georg, then 54 years old, brought 20-year-old Barbara to Sweden. A year later, their second son was born. Georg named his boys Chang and Arnold after two scrap dealers in Karlskrona. The marriage didn't last long, and ever since the divorce Lasse hasn't seen much of Georg. No one has. The split exacerbated his drinking problem and Georg was pulled further and further down into his bottles.

Lasse feels for the boys and does his best to make sure they know they are always welcome at his house. In an effort to avoid their mother, the two brothers hide here as often as they can. Lasse wishes Georg would stop by to see them some time, but for some reason he never does.

* * *

Lasse watches from the shop as Chang gets straight to work. He meticulously searches through the droves of spare parts until he finds the tailgate of another Volvo 245 that he can use to replace the existing one. It, too, is quite rusty, but reparable. The boy has a good eye for this stuff, Lasse reflects. The speedometer is also broken, but Chang figures out that it's the cable attached to the gearbox that is flawed. He dives back in to find the spare he needs to replace it.

Lasse shows him how to remove the rusty metal with a bolt cutter. Then he helps him bend a piece of sheet metal and weld it on to replace the missing piece.

While they are working on the car, they hear the revving of an engine outside.

Lasse steps out just in time to see Arnold come rushing past on a motorcross. He slides back and forth in the mud; his eyes lit up. It's the only time Lasse has seen the boy come close to anything resembling happiness. While Arnold plays in the mud, Chang begins the tedious task of filling, grinding, sanding, and polishing his new car. Lasse is impressed by the boy's drive and dedication.

"You'll have to paint the new tailgate to match the rest of the car," he says. Chang nods.

"But I suppose that can wait," Lasse adds. Unless of course he decides to follow in his father's footsteps and flip it, he thinks to himself. Aloud, he says, "You're still four years away from being able to drive legally on a proper road."

"As long as I stick to the quarries, no one will notice," Chang smiles.

They are interrupted by a shout from across the yard. "Where are the boys?" Lasse looks up and sees Sara marching towards them.

"Relax, Sara," he shouts back. Instinctively, he walks towards her, putting himself between Chang and her anger. He knows she doesn't like them coming here. It's as though she hates to see them enjoy themselves. Now they'll get an earful.

If he just stands there for a while and lets her scream at him, perhaps there will be a little less energy left over for the boys. He worries about them, Arnold more so than Chang. Chang is resilient, he doesn't let their mother's abuse get to him; but Arnold takes it to heart. When Sara tells him he is worthless and will never amount to anything, Arnold believes her.

SAMVEL DISCOVERS BERGMAN

Mikael isn't picking up the phone. That usually means he is depressed, hiding under his covers. Mikael lives with his near-deaf grandmother, which enables him to monopolize the phone and play loud black metal. It's Friday night. Teenage Samvel feels like going out, but apparently Mikael can't be bothered.

Samvel has few friends and is used to being alone. When he was younger, he would sometimes repress parts of his personality in a desperate attempt to fit in, but as a teenager, he has stopped trying. There is nothing he can do about his foreign appearance, and his albinism prevents him from going swimming or taking part in most outdoor activities under the hot Armenian sun. But his difference goes beyond looks. Samvel doesn't feel particularly Armenian. He has learned to enjoy solitude, values his personal space, and cannot relate to the passionate disposition common among his countrymen. He doesn't even like his relatives—the ultimate sin in a country where family is everything. He prefers to spend his time in the company of the great philosophers, especially Nietzsche, who confirms his conviction that man is alone in the world.

But tonight is different. His small room feels suffocating; he needs to get out. He tries Mikael one more time. Samvel doesn't expect enthusiasm—any expression of *joie de vivre* would run contrary to their image—but perhaps he'll at least pick up the phone. Samvel likes Mikael. He can relate to him. They met at school and shortly thereafter Mikael played Samvel "Dead Human Collection" by Cannibal Corpse, which describes a life of pain and graphic suffering before the singer experiences sweet relief at joining the dead human collection. Samvel suspects Mikael was trying to shock him, but instead the growling words resonated with him, opening the door to new depths of darkness.

The phone rings, but still no answer. When this happens, Samvel usually gives up and settles down with a book, but tonight he decides to head out on his own. He runs a comb through his long, blond hair, puts on a black t-shirt, a pair of skinny jeans (a rarity, as most Armenian men consider the cut too feminine), and a long, dark green coat. He avoids the ancient elevator and takes the stairs down. On the street outside his building, renamed Azatutyan poghota or Liberty Avenue after the fall of the Soviet Union, he waves down a white Russian GAZelle minibus. The buses are meant to have fixed stops, but the drivers are so hungry for a fare that there is no point making one's way to a designated stop. They pull over to pick up any pedestrian who even glances their way.

Samvel pulls out 100 dram and squeezes onto the crowded bus. His neighborhood, Raykom, sits at the top of a hill. The road to town is a long, curved slope with some of the best views of Yerevan.

Around 15 minutes later, he disembarks at the Kaskad, a giant limestone stairway linking the downtown Kentron area with the Monument neighborhood. Trendy teenagers hang out near the Yerevan Opera House, which resembles a giant unglazed, clay-colored ceramic; Samvel prefers Yerevan's only alternative pub, Jeansnos (literally "the place where one wears jeans"). But he won't go there by himself. When he is alone, he likes to climb the 572 steps to the top of the Kaskad. From here he can see central Yerevan and even Mount Ararat where, according to the Bible, Noah's Ark washed ashore following the great flood.

SAMVEL DISCOVERS BERGMAN

To most people, that is a big deal. Armenia was the first country in the world to officially adopt Christianity, and growing up here means growing up in a religious society where all aspects of life are based on divine interpretation. While the Soviet state preached secularism, Christians in Armenia were largely left alone to practice their faith. Unlike in Russia, where the Bolsheviks had tried to eradicate any trace of religion, the many Armenian churches and monasteries had not been touched.

While raised a Christian, Samvel was never particularly religious, and as a teenager any last remnants of faith vanished when he developed an interest in black metal music. After his first exposure to Cannibal Corpse, Samvel discovered much of the genre had Nordic origins, with bands like Dimmu Borgir, Immortal, and Emperor from Norway; Marduk, Dark Funeral, In Flames, and Therion from Sweden, and Nightwish from Finland.

Samvel remains at the top of the Kaskad for a long time, looking out at the lights of the city. In his childhood, the city was completely dark. During the post-Soviet crisis, streetlights were hardly a priority since there was not even enough electricity for basic necessities; but now, in the new millennium, Yerevan is finally lit up and starting to feel like a proper city.

Samvel decides to walk all the way home. He loves to roam the streets at night. On his way, he stops at his favorite video rental store, with its discreet basement location. An old-fashioned bell sounds as he opens the heavy door and follows the steps down. He usually comes here with Mikael, who showed him the special shelf at the back, housing European alternative movies by directors like Pasolini and Fellini. They've watched some odd and disturbing films together, like the horror art production *Salò, or the 120 Days of Sodom*. But tonight Samvel really takes his time, digging through all the obscure piles they haven't yet explored. At the very back, Samvel discovers the Swedish director Ingmar Bergman. There is something oddly appealing about the old, yellowed covers with their silhouettes or close-ups of tormented, frightened, and defiant faces. Samvel settles on one featuring a blond man playing chess with the grim reaper: *The Seventh Seal*.

It turns out to be the start of a love affair. Through Bergman's classics such as *Persona*, *Cries and Whispers*, and *Shame*, Samvel develops his understanding of Sweden. In the desolate Swedish forests, on the rocky shores of Stockholm's archipelago, or amidst the awe-inspiring, towering *raukar* of Gotland,[1] Bergman takes on existential themes such as loneliness, isolation, and angst. The son of a priest, many of Bergman's movies deal with religious faith, or lack thereof. God is present mainly through His absence. If He exists, He is silent, and as humans we are all alone.

WEEDING OUT THE DREGS

ENGINEERING BIOLOGICAL HOMOGENEITY

"The goal is a healthier race ... let all of us become A-people;" "Let's build a healthy Sweden!" "We can't afford to have any B-people in this house!"

Advertisement by the Milk Propaganda association from
the late 1930s.[1]

Geographical isolation was believed to have protected the original purity of the Nordic people and their Aryan origins. By this logic, Swedes had all the prerequisites to stay pure and healthy if they only took care to maintain the "quality of the national material" and weed out the anomalies.

In 1921, the year that Adolf Hitler became leader of the Nazi Party in Germany, Sweden founded the world's first Institute of Racial Biology in Uppsala, thereby granting racial hygiene the status of recognized science.[2] The institute was run by Herman Lundborg, who, that very same year, published *The Swedish Nation in Word and Picture*, promoting identification and segregation of "superior" Nordic races and "inferior" non-Nordic ones. Some of his findings were presented at the Svea Rike exhibition in 1930. Here, he attempted to link Sweden's glorious political and cultural history to the supposed racial superiority of the Nordic types.[3]

The mid-thirties saw a shift from biology to sociology as the key to improving the quality of the population.[4] Two of the most influential social engineers, who would be instrumental in drafting the social policies needed to mold the new Sweden, were Alva and Gunnar Myrdal. They were regarded as the patron saints of Swedish social democracy. Gunnar was a respected economist who would receive some thirty honorary doctorates from universities across the world and a Nobel Prize in Economics in 1974. Alva was primarily a sociologist and social reformer who would go on to head up the UN Department of Social Welfare, and later the Department of Social Sciences at UNESCO. She would also receive numerous awards and honorary doctorates, including the Nobel Peace Prize in 1982 for her efforts advocating disarmament.[5]

Together, the Myrdals sought to carve a path to modernity for Sweden. They considered themselves role models for the "little lives" of ordinary Swedes and used their own marriage to provide a living example of a rational union of equality and companionship, in which their three children were raised in a "sensible" manner.[6]

The Myrdals rose to prominence in 1934 when they published the book *Crisis in Population*, addressing the widespread fear across Europe that the population was degenerating. Falling birth rates could lead to depopulation, and to make matters worse, it was the least desirable segments of the population who were reproducing. Industrialization seemed to be overriding the process of natural selection, as even the most basic forms of social assistance were allowing "inferior people" to survive and multiply. As a result, their psychological and social defects were supposedly passed on to the next generation.[7]

The book was extremely influential, and within months the political sphere expressed its willingness to introduce sociopolitical reforms. In 1935, the government appointed a Population Commission with Gunnar Myrdal among its commissioners. His and Alva's ideas, even entire sections from their book, were incorporated into the Commission's seventeen reports. Within a couple of years, most of their proposed reforms were carried out, including maternity grants, children's allowances, free school meals, after-school childcare centers, birth control through abortions and contraception, sex education, and tax reform.[8]

In 1934, Sweden also introduced racial hygiene laws that enabled sterilizations.[9] In order to improve the quality of the national "material," not all individuals could be allowed to reproduce. Best, then, to exterminate all physical and psychological inferiority within the population: idiocy, illness, and undesirable character traits. However, research in this area called for caution, as it seemed that society was partly to blame for some of these flaws. Unlike many eugenicists of the time, the Myrdals rejected the notion that differences between the social classes were determined by heredity. If members of the lower classes were given the opportunity to develop their talents, most of them could be transformed into "valuable" members of society. However, there were some people who should be strictly forbidden from reproducing: people who were too well-functioning to be institutionalized, but who suffered from hereditary mental illnesses and physical defects. The Myrdals called them the "dregs of society," "whose propagation is undesirable in terms of racial hygiene."[10] These "individuals who are quite unfit for life" must be "thoroughly weeded out."[11]

In 1941, Parliament unanimously extended the legislation to include "anti-social individuals." Such individuals could not take care of their children, and more of their kind should be prevented from coming into the world to reduce social pressure. Alva Myrdal argued that child benefit payments must go hand-in-hand with systematic campaigns of sterilization in order to restrict the fertility of those who would make poor parents in genetic or social terms.[12]

It was up to three doctors—and, post-1947, two politicians—to determine who was "asocial." Their decision was final and could not be appealed. For the following thirty-five years, sterilizations were carried out completely out of reach of the judiciary.[13]

While other European nations instituted power-sharing principles and, eventually, individual citizens' rights, Sweden kept a form of government that had its roots in the 1600s, with a very strong central power and only rudimentary separation of powers. The constitution that was in place until 1976, contained very little in the way of individual rights.[14]

Even today, Sweden is unique in that its constitution does not guarantee the independency of the judiciary vis-à-vis government and Parliament. Until Sweden joined the EU in 1995, it wasn't legally possible to argue that the sterilization laws had violated the foundations of democracy. Prior to this a parliamentary majority had complete power to decide what was democratic and what was not.[15]

Swedish doctors urged people to enter only into "genetically sensible marriages." Abortions and sterilizations, forced if necessary, were meant to prevent the births of "abnormal" and "backward" children.[16] Those targeted were not living up to the expectations of independence and self-reliance that had become ingrained in the national self-image. Common causes for sterilization were illness, or being anti-social, or feeble-minded.

However, feeble-mindedness was not necessarily synonymous with intellectual disability or even "idiocy." It was, just as much, a social, moralizing diagnosis that could be applied to anything that deviated from the ideal of conformity.[17] "Inferiority" or "feeble-mindedness" could express itself in extravagant or unkempt clothing, disinterest or exaggerated interest in one's children, shyness, being too talkative, restlessness, unemployment, apathy, stubbornness, hubris, promiscuity, wastefulness, cheekiness, laziness, painted fingernails, obstinacy, dyslexia, black hair, cleft palates, and so on. By listing the characteristics, behaviors, and even dress codes that were deemed so undesirable that they constituted cause for sterilization, the medical records from this era provide a kind of blueprint of the ideal citizen of the People's Home. While no one was sterilized because of painted nails or black hair alone, these constituted ingredients that could, in aggregated form, paint a picture of deviance. The doctors were rarely able to make precise judgments, but there was something about these citizens—the presence of some inconclusive, yet easily sensed vice—that led physicians to conclude that their future offspring would be a burden on society.[18]

Most victims were women. A man could be promiscuous without running the risk of being characterized as feeble-minded, whereas it could be enough for a poor, unmarried girl to go out dancing too often for the local authorities to file a report recommending sterilization.[19] There were even cases of 16-year-old virgins being forcefully sterilized because they lived too close to army barracks.[20] A common sign of feeble-mindedness in any woman was bringing a child into the world whom she would be unable to support. Such lack of responsibility was an indication of low intelligence, even if the woman scored well on the intelligence tests that were often conducted.[21]

Women who applied to have an abortion were often coerced into sterilization.[22] If the doctor deemed it likely that a woman would not consent or show up for the sterilization appointment, she could be unknowingly sterilized at the time of her abortion. This, in spite of the fact that having the two operations performed at the same time quadrupled the risk of fatality. Between 1935 and 1951, over 100 women died having abortions. Half died of complications because they were sterilized during the procedure. Upset by this practice, a group of doctors wrote to the Medicines Agency, arguing that it was unreasonable to make sterilization a condition for abortion when the risk to the woman undergoing dual surgery was so great. The Agency opted not to change its policy, and immediate sterilization continued to be a condition for some types of abortion until 1975.[23]

Author Maciej Zaremba has gone through hundreds of records and letters from Swedes who were sterilized between 1939 and 1965. He concludes that even "voluntary" sterilizations were rarely completely voluntary, but frequently a condition for something else. What the victims had in common was rather their poverty, helplessness, and dependency on the care of the welfare state.[24]

Sterilization, thus, was not just about preventing further genetic undesirables, but also about managing the socio-economic implications of infant mortality among the undesirable segments of society. Hence, as the welfare state grew, so did the number of sterilizations. Most of them took place after 1945.[25]

After the war, the Scandinavian countries were the only ones in Europe to apply laws that aimed to categorize people as "adequate" or "inferior," in order to deprive the latter, with varying degrees of compulsion, of their ability to reproduce.[26]

In 1946, Alva Myrdal argued for mass sterilizations of welfare recipients.[27] The increased social obligations of the majority created financial incentives to weed out unproductive members of society who constituted a burden on the rest. Before welfare reforms had been implemented there were few financial incentives to sterilize the "feeble-minded" or single mothers.[28]

In the Sweden of the 1930s, few people saw anything wrong with doctors and authorities taking control over certain citizens' ability to reproduce. The personal integrity of groups considered to be on the margins of society—the feeble-minded, alcoholics, anti-socials, and *tattare*—were far from top priority. The burden on society of countless poor children, without proper providers, was a much bigger concern.[29] With *tattare*, the media would even occasionally use the term "exterminate."[30]

Travelers had been part of the Swedish population for centuries, but when the government concluded that their way of life had become too divergent from the norm of industrialized society, they were deemed a biological threat. In 1937, the National Board of Health and Welfare concluded that further assimilation of the Travelers would be counterproductive because of the risk that their "fundamental, foreign disposition" would live on in future generations who might look like Swedes on the surface, but whose hidden influence would "give rise to a divergent way of life."[31]

In 1942, Minister of Social Affairs Gustav Möller, known as the father of the Swedish welfare state, ordered an inventory of all *tattare* and gypsies present in the nation. The Institute for Racial Biology measured many skulls, but concluded that it was not possible to distinguish *tattare* from proper Swedes solely based on their skull size. Instead, reasons such as "vagrancy," "unmistakable *tattare* features," or an "asocial way of life" became more common on sterilization records. "Thievery" and "pleasure-seeking" were other behaviors that could effectively be combined with the categorizations "inferior" or "of *tattare* blood." The implicit message was that these were people who were both different and a societal burden.[32]

It was deemed illogical or even "undemocratic" for those subjected to sterilizations to be granted any legal ways to object to these violations. As Zaremba summarizes the creed of the time: "Why should the sick cells have any rights at the expense of the healthy body?"[33] Between 1935 and 1975, more than 60,000 individuals were sterilized in Sweden, with varying degrees of coercion—at least 20,000 of them entirely against their will.

In 1975 the sterilization laws were quietly revoked.[34]

CHANG VISITS HIS FATHER

Every so often, growing up, Chang catches a glimpse of his father. He sees him drive past, or turn a corner somewhere in the village, but he never stops. Sometimes Chang bikes past his house. He can describe every white brick of the ground floor with his eyes closed. The second floor is yellow and made of wood, as though it was added at a later stage. The yard is full of trucks, the odd excavator, and lots of old-school American cars parked on the grass. Most vehicles stay around for a week or two before being sold. By keeping track of the inventory parked outside the house, Chang has a pretty good idea of the state of business.

One day, Chang decides to stop and ring the doorbell. He has been told he is the spitting image of his father, but the man who opens the door is old and white-haired. There is an air of virility and authority about him that Chang did not expect. If Georg is surprised to see him, his face does not betray it. He simply steps aside, allowing Chang in, as though visits from his son are normal and expected.

A Chinese lantern with red tassels is the first thing that catches Chang's eye. Underneath it, on the left side of the hallway, sits an old piano. To the right is Georg's office. It has a large window overlooking the road so that he can see anyone approaching.

"Do you want anything to drink?" Georg leads the way to the kitchen. It's cluttered with dirty dishes and dried stains on every surface. On the floor, old mail and newspapers lie scattered. There is a green, moldy lump floating in the orange juice, so Georg pulls out the vodka instead. "Let's sit upstairs," he smiles, revealing a few missing teeth.

A wooden staircase bends up to the second floor. It's obvious that this is where Georg spends the bulk of his time. To the left is his small bedroom and to the right a living room of sorts, with a worn sectional sofa, a few cabinets, and a very old gramophone. Chang can picture him here with his drinking buddies, bragging and telling tales.

Georg puts the bottle down and throws a bag of sweet peach candy onto the table. The varnished, slightly sloping, wooden floor creaks as he walks over to the cabinets and takes out two shot glasses. He pulls out a vinyl record from a large stack. The title is in Russian, so Chang has no idea what he is about to hear until the patriotic tunes of Soviet marching music begin to play. Flipping through his father's collection, it seems to be all he listens to. The sounds of communism, Chang reflects. Soviet music and American cars; his father's two passions.

"Let's see who's the strongest," Georg suggests and grabs hold of Chang's arm. He begins to pull. He is strong and fit, with the body of a much younger man. Chang makes the bulk of his allowance performing physical labor. He cleaves and stacks wood, and helps out at the nearby farms, so he is by no means weak, but his old man easily beats him. Georg laughs and pours them a shot of vodka each. They take a seat in the worn sectional. Georg downs his shot and immediately pours another one. "So, how is school?" he asks.

"Well, there's this girl that I like," Chang replies. "She's called..."

"Just go ahead and fuck her, son," Georg interrupts.

Chang is stunned.

"I'm only fourteen," he eventually replies.

"Shit, I hope you're not a bloody virgin at fourteen. When I was twelve I was already at it and oh my God did I fuck," Georg replies. "You better get the hell started so that you become a proper man."

"How many have you slept with?" Chang asks sheepishly.

"Oh, I don't know." Georg looks up at the ceiling and performs a rough estimate. "Thousands."

"Did you know I used to own a Ferrari?" Georg continues. He launches into a long story about all the expensive cars that have once been in his possession. As Chang listens to his father talk, a memory that he didn't know existed returns to him. He sees himself sitting in the back of his father's old-school American car. His mother is in the passenger seat and his brother, just a toddler, in a car seat beside him. They park their big, ostentatious car across three parking spots outside the grocery store. "This will drive them mad," Georg laughs. They pick up the few items they need, and when it's their turn to pay, Georg pulls out a 10,000 SEK bill.[1] The cashier doesn't know what to do.

"I've never seen one of those. I'm not sure I'm allowed to cash it," she comments.

While she phones her manager to check, Georg pulls out a thick bundle of identical bills. Flashing them before the queue that has formed behind them, he says: "Well, I sure hope it turns out to be genuine, because I have quite a few of them."

What an un-Swedish thing to do. Remembering it now, Chang is not surprised all the villagers hate them. But as he looks around the room, at all that is different and unique about his father's place, he feels strangely proud. The furniture may be worn, but it is not from IKEA. His father may be an old drunk, but he is not a loser. He is the American car, blasting Russian marching music, speeding ecstatically past a road full of Volvos all tuned in to pop radio, flashing their lights disapprovingly.

Chang may not know him as well as he would like, but he knows his father will never bow down to the Law of Jante.

Chang tunes back in. His father is still talking. "And I still have a lot of money stashed away in Luxembourg." Judging by Georg's stories, he has done everything in life worth doing. And he is distantly related to anyone that matters. It can't all be true, of course—but some of it must be. Lasse and his friends have told Chang that his dad wears leather bags full of cash under his clothes; that he straps them with a rope behind his neck so that they rest tightly against his chest underneath his shirt. He doesn't trust anyone, least of all banks, and he never pays tax, they say. For a moment, Chang is tempted to ask Georg to take off his shirt so he can see if it's true, but he suppresses the impulse.

Georg keeps pouring the vodka, but Chang is careful only to sip. If he comes home drunk his mother will kill him. She has no idea he is here, and Chang knows he can never tell her. But he'll come back. Next time he'll bring a video camera to film his father, so he won't forget what he looks like again; the way he gestures when he tells his stories. For now, mental pictures will have to do. Chang focuses on registering everything. The slightly offset floor. The way his father smells of onion and vodka. The feeling of his hand when he grabs him to show how strong he is. The beat of the marching music.

ENGINEERING SOCIAL HOMOGENEITY

By the 1900s, the *bruk* (autonomous, industry-centered local communities) and the popular movements had paved the way for the social homogenization of the Swede. The Social Democratic leadership continued the paternalistic traditions of the *bruk*-owner, providing for the population and making sure their material needs were met. Starting in the 1930s, the political and academic elites also began to consciously deploy social engineering techniques to shape the individual, in order to effect desired societal change. Like children, the collective had to be taught how to behave and express itself.

The large families of the past were no longer the norm. Still, many women remained at home to take care of fewer and fewer children. "That a grown person, most often the mother, should devote her day to the home in order to shepherd one or two children, is quite unreasonable," social engineers like the Myrdals argued. "This is not only inefficient, but will result in the mother becoming lethargic, fat, selfish, and under-stimulated."[1] The Myrdals envisioned a new society that favored social solidarity, one in which the entire nation took a shared responsibility for the children who would form the next generation.[2]

But it wasn't just mothers who had to be liberated from their offspring. The children too had to be freed from discontented, overstressed, and inadequate parents whose ignorance kept the children from developing properly. Instead, they ought to be brought up collectively in crèches and schools where they could be taught socially appropriate behavior and the essentials of a rational lifestyle.[3]

A co-ordinated system of community care was needed to provide children with a pedagogically grounded education and socially enhanced level of care. The notion that mothers knew best what was good for their children was deemed outdated. Rather, this notion was believed to be the cause of discontent, psychological malaise, bad habits, a lack of adaptability, ineffectiveness, resentment, criminality, and the death of thousands of infants each year.[4]

Even an upbringing in a healthy family was contaminated by emotional factors and personal relationships that rendered both parents and children vulnerable. The collective crèche, on the other hand, would provide a "democratic" education, characterized by neither coercion nor uninhibited freedom, but order, brought about by universal, impersonal rules. "The trick is to get the child to accept, of his own accord, the universal rules that govern our action," wrote Alva Myrdal.[5] If there was a need for punishment then this should be imposed through isolation or through "social disapproval."[6]

Teachers and trained professionals must supervise the children in order to note and, if necessary, correct any deviation in their mental, social, or physical condition. At the end of each day, these normalized children would return to their families and do their bit to help mold their parents, in so far as this was still possible. In this way, the state would, without coercion, forge individuals, families, and society into a harmonious, healthy unity. Over just a few generations, this process would result in a new, superior type of citizen.[7]

Statistics determined what needed to be fixed, blurring the boundary between "private" and "public." If the experts were working for the common good, then so must the ordinary person. People must allow themselves to be investigated and educated in how best to modify their behavior. This would enable them to fit into a community which "itself generates the principles of utility to which individuals must then adapt."[8]

The state had a duty to help its citizens in times of hardship and improve their living conditions, but an equally important task was to regulate their lifestyle. Traditions were "obsolete" and stood in the way of progress. A whole range of measures and potential interventions were designed to bring people into line and force them to lead an "orderly" lifestyle. Socially maladjusted individuals were ostracized.[9]

In 1936, the Authority for Health and Safety launched a department for home inspections. The Authority determined a set of minimum requirements with regards to things like square footage per resident, heating, light, and ventilation.[10] Housing inspectors then enforced these requirements. An inspector could even request to spend the night if he suspected that a home would not be able to maintain the minimum temperature overnight.[11] Once residents had learned the rules, those who wished could contact inspectors themselves to draw attention to substandard living in an effort to improve their lot.

However, this did not mean that residents could duck responsibility. Gunnar Myrdal and architect Uno Åhrén, among others, argued that poor living was frequently the result of laziness, avarice, and ignorance. Many didn't know how to live well, nor did they care.[12] This was a problem, as ignorant parents and inferior social environments clearly undermined the potential of the next generation. People had to be educated on how to "dwell" properly.[13] Hence, home inspections became a way to inspect not just the home itself, but also how people lived. Overcrowding was considered morally detrimental. It was believed to cause illness, crime, and even prostitution.[14]

The Myrdals argued that the interests of children must supersede "the prevailing liberal ideology" that everyone should be able to spend his money as he sees fit. When "asocial" parents made "socially defective consumption choices," for example investing in entertainment and clothes rather than their homes, the psychological and physical health of their children suffered. As a result, "the family must be compelled to change consumption choices," and create more positive habits.[15] "People have to get used to brushing their teeth and eating tomatoes, before they will come to appreciate this type of consumption, and the same goes for sensibly arranged homes," they insisted.[16] "Bad habits must be turned right. The unwise enlightened. The irresponsible awoken."[17]

The Myrdals considered the respect for privacy a remnant of the 1800s:

> in the future it will not seem socially indifferent how people spend their money: what living standards they keep, what kind of food and clothes they buy, and above all, to what extent the consumption of their children is met. The tendency will be towards a social political organization and control, not just of the distribution of income in society, but also of the direction of consumption within families.[18]

The desired morals of society had to be turned into norms, according to Alva Myrdal. These norms could then be used to wage influence over and correct the individual reason.[19]

In 1946, it was established that there should be no more than two people to a room and that nobody should sleep in the kitchen.[20] Only a certain number of occupants were allowed in each home and if necessary children could be removed from crowded accommodation and placed in appropriate homes.[21]

Municipal institutions like the child welfare authorities and the authority for temperance conducted home inspections and investigations. Child welfare officials had the power to order the police to force an entry and remove children without recourse to the judiciary. An administrative order issued by a petty official was sufficient to take a child away from their parents and have them brought up by any person or institution deemed fit.[22]

At first, education on how to "dwell" was voluntary and disseminated through courses, lectures, leaflets, and home visits, but over time inspections became mandatory. According to the 1936 guidelines, the inspection should "foster inhabitants and supervise the nature and upkeep of homes."[23] Swedes were instructed to air their homes several times a day, at least 15 minutes every morning and every evening. In the kitchen and bathrooms, chokes were always to be left open, a daily fire would keep moisture out and stonewalls should not be covered with paintings or furniture. The inspectors could also criticize home décor, furniture, and color choices. It was not uncommon to demand that residents repaint dark walls in lighter colors, and any wallpaper had to be light. Tables meant for work had to be well lit and no plants were allowed to block the light.[24] Swedes were taught that modern people did their laundry in the designated laundry space, did not play their radio too loudly, and did *not* wear shoes indoors.[25]

In the early 1900s, the average Swedish worker had spent about 20 per cent of his wage on alcohol,[26] and despite temperance movements, alcoholism had remained a problem. But it was believed that, with better homes, women would become better mothers, and men would spend less time on the town drinking.[27] The first residents of the new, modern apartments in the late 1930s and the 1940s had to prove that they were not plagued by vices like drinking. Not everyone was deemed capable of modern living and it was important, especially for families with many children, to prove themselves worthy and show that they could live up to the ideal of *skötsamhet* (proper behavior). Those who were approved as residents of the first modern homes were provided with courses on how to "dwell" like a proper, modern Swede. Some buildings even had hostesses who helped new residents get settled in the right way.[28]

No detail was too small. Everything could and ought to be changed and improved: how and what to eat, how to dress, how to make one's bed, how to express oneself, how to structure relationships. The goal was to find the single best approach for the minutiae of "the little life." Narrowly setting norms for what constituted "the right way" to live would cement the feeling of "us."

It also created "the other."[29]

BROTHER ARNOLD

Chang stands outside his house waiting, his stomach in knots. It's a few weeks after the midsummer celebrations. It's nice and balmy out, but Chang still shivers. The family has just received a phone call. Someone has spotted Arnold roaming about drunk and called his mother to pick him up. Chang knows this will be bad.

Finally, he sees his mother's gray Opel Omega approach. She pulls in to the driveway and leaps out of the car. Her face is contorted with rage. Chang can't see Arnold, but when their mother yanks open the backseat door, his head falls out. Arnold has apparently passed out. Then she slams the car door on his head. Chang shrinks back as she does it again. And again. The old familiar dread returns. This time she will actually do it; this time she will actually kill him.

"You're not my son," Mother spits.

That night Chang watches over his brother. He really should be taken to a hospital, but Chang is too scared to call an ambulance. He can't even remain by his brother's side for fear that Mother will catch him. Contradicting her is enough to be beaten senseless, so to take Arnold's side in a situation like this is inconceivable. Instead, Chang lies in his bed, pretending to sleep; but every 15 minutes or so, he sneaks over to his brother's room. Arnold is still unconscious but has been dumped in his bed, where he lies in a pool of vomit and blood. Chang can't clean it up because Mother would notice, but he makes sure Arnold's airways are unobstructed so he doesn't choke. Then he tiptoes back to his own room, slips in between the sheets, and lies completely still, listening. As soon as he hears Arnold vomit, he sneaks back over to check on him again.

CONSTRUCTING UTOPIA

THE SWEDISH MODEL

There had been no master plan, it was more a vision of the end result; power sharing rather than class war—reform, not revolution. The Social Democrats aimed to provide a form of basic material security available to every citizen, granted on the basis of standardized, uniform criteria that would be financed through tax. Beyond the rhetoric of the leadership stood plenty of sensible and sober economists who believed that reforms without resources would yield financial disaster. The first task, therefore, had been the creation of prosperity. Social benefits would come at a speed justified by the rate of economic growth. But the vision depended on a labor force that was willing to internalize the ideal of productivity and embrace rational thinking. Workers had to regard themselves as part of a whole, as cogs of a machine aiming to liberate them from competitive struggle and poverty.[1]

In the 1920s, Sweden had more industrial disputes than any other country in Europe.[2] Relative to its size, it had the highest number of strike and lockout days in the world.[3] But by the late 1930s the environment had been entirely transformed. The workers' unions accepted the importance of growth to drive the economy. They agreed not to seek conflict but to support rationalization within companies, since a more lucrative industry would be able to pay them higher wages and provide their unemployed friends with jobs. Rather than prevent progress, the unions embraced modernization. In return, the employers rid themselves of strikebreakers, accepted the right of the unions to make deals and tolerated the state's efforts to construct a welfare system. And the state agreed not to meddle by imposing laws. Capitalism would be allowed to flourish if industry provided the state with growth and resources to redistribute through the public welfare system.[4]

This "peaceful coexistence" would become known as the "Swedish Model."

As early as 1935, Prime Minister Per Albin Hansson proclaimed the democratic Nordics as a model for people in other countries. The following year American journalist Marquis Childs published *Sweden: The Middle Way*, a highly idealized portrayal of Sweden as a utopia perfectly balanced between the extreme capitalism of America and the oppressive communism of the Soviet Union. Childs' book would become influential, particularly among Swedes, as it provided "an outsider's unbiased confirmation that Sweden—our Sweden—was better than many other countries."[5] Strengthened by this positive reinforcement, the political leadership proceeded to mold their citizens to become the "people of the future."

In 1938, industrial peace was formalized with the signing of the Saltsjöbaden agreement, under which the Swedish Trade Union Confederation and the Employers' Confederation agreed on a centralized, collective bargaining system whereby they could negotiate for the whole country, abolishing the confusion of individual unions or employers negotiating separately from one another. Workers and capital had agreed on a set of rules for handling labor market disputes that allowed them to avoid state influence. The signatories committed themselves to the peaceful settlement of industrial disputes. The right to strike was not abolished but outlawed for as long as the agreement was in force.[6] In order to strike one had to reject the agreement, which required at least two weeks' notice, preventing action taken in the heat of the moment. Trade union membership soon covered the vast majority of the working population.[7]

The industrial power of Sweden was mobilized in a way usually only seen in dictatorships or countries at war. Meanwhile the state took responsibility for spreading the wealth of this progress. What the capitalists produced, the state distributed. It was a way of reaping the benefits of capitalism while avoiding its inequalities. Nationalization, which would have been a simpler way of controlling the industry, was avoided for reasons of inefficiency.[8]

Modernity was hailed as the force that would lift the country out of its poor past while at the same time welding it together as a nation. The bodies of all Swedes constituted the nation's wealth. It was the patriotic duty of each citizen to take great care of their health and fitness, as failing to do so was the equivalent of squandering society's resources.[9]

During this time, Sweden was transformed from a poor agrarian society into one of the wealthiest nations in the world. Generations of Swedes saw their lives improve in remarkable ways. However, the powerful combinations of isolated geography, biological similarity, social engineering, collapsed class structures, vilification of conflict, and shared nationalist pride had intensified and deepened the homogeneity of the citizenry, creating an internalized herd mentality that shunned difference and sought consensus at all cost.

Over the ensuing decades, the depth and breadth of homogenous experience developed into a collective consciousness amongst the population—a "Unimind" of sorts. Containing all the unspoken rules and values of Swedish culture, it enabled Swedes to know instinctively what was expected of them. What was right; what was wrong. What to say. What to think. What to do. Swedes relied on this collective intuition as their moral compass; using it both to judge and to predict the judgments, thoughts or actions of others.

* * *

In Social Democrat Sweden, the majority lived in very similar, functional, flats, shopped at the local co-op, had a bank account at the Sparbanken co-op, filled up on gas at oil co-op OK, insured their homes with co-op Folksam, and were buried by burial co-op Fonus.

The idea behind the co-operatives had been to break the power that normal shopkeepers had over their clients, and to forbid credit, which trapped many poor workers in severe debt. However, over time the Co-operative Federation, KF, took on a life of its own. It became a core institution intimately tied to socialist Sweden, and the main provider of the accouterments of the modern Social Democratic lifestyle. Fittingly, the symbol of KF was a blue infinity loop on a white background. It became the trademark of the Federation's very own product series, which was meant to be brandless and subject to no marketing, thereby making it cheaper than other products. White letters against a blue background simply announced what kind of product it was: "toothpaste," "cornflakes," or "deodorant," for example. Ironically, these "brandless" blue-white products became the most widely recognized product brand of the 1970s.[10]

The various co-operatives, unions, and Social Democrat institutions cross-fertilized one another, and it wasn't long until they had spun a web across all areas of Swedish life. From the 1930s to the 1970s, the KF accompanied people from the cradle to the grave. During the time of Social Democratic hegemony, one could live a whole life without coming into contact with anything but Social Democrat-approved institutions, products, and services. The pressure to conform had mutated and, by now, it came from within as much as from without.

THE END OF FEAR

Arnold stands for a long time staring at his own reflection. He is a scrawny boy, lighter than Chang; blond and blue-eyed, but with the same hated *tattare* blood. He scrutinizes all his scars; not just the fresh, sore cuts and bruises, but the pattern of the whole. A lifetime of abuse. A childhood of fear. He has just showered and washed away all the dried-up vomit and blood. Sure, he shouldn't have drunk so much, but it didn't give her the right to nearly kill him. Over the years, he has received more beatings than food from Mother. He doesn't understand how anyone can treat their children the way she treats them.

It ends now.

Soon, he will be a teenager. He can already see his body changing. It responds differently to physical exertion. Some days it's like he can feel his muscles growing; swelling inside, even when he is still. They say his father is a strong man. He too can become a strong man. He flexes his biceps and envisions a much bigger man. He can get there; he just has to help his body along a little bit. He is done with fear.

Sure enough, by the time he is fourteen, Arnold's body, and attitude, explode. Nobody dares to call him a fucking *tattare*. Anyone who attempts to lay a finger on him pays dearly. Shortly thereafter, Social Services place him in a foster home. Arnold is relieved. Receiving three meals a day helps grow the body even more.

And now he doesn't have to kill his mother.

GARBO FEVER

"Why should anyone study Spanish?" Samvel exclaims. He looks around at the indifferent faces of his fellow students in Spanish class. The newly renovated classroom feels almost Scandinavian, with its minimalistic and bright design; white walls, white benches, white chairs, and a whiteboard on the wall to top it off. It's small, suited for ten to fifteen people, and could have been perfect had it not been for the language of instruction. "It's so positive, happy, and irritating. I want to study the Scandinavian languages instead. That would be much cooler."

"Well, that's not possible," counters the lecturer, Tigranuhi. "Besides, nobody cares about Norwegian," she adds in her usual, monotonous voice, as though answering a question like any other. Tigranuhi is short and fairly young, a recently graduated lecturer. She has spent time in Europe, Samvel can tell as much from the way she dresses. It only takes a quick glance to determine that the types of jeans and t-shirts she wears have not been purchased in Armenia. Her youth and inexperience make Samvel's obstinacy easier, but he'd like to believe that he would have said the same thing had the lecturer been an older, male professor, dressed in one of their typical dark suits.

Samvel has had enough of Spanish. As a freshman at the Russian-Armenian University in Yerevan he made an effort, but now he's a sophomore and no longer cares about arriving in class prepared. As part of his International Relations studies, Samvel is expected to study a European language. He signed up for Spanish, but regretted his choice almost immediately. The language is easy enough to learn, but Samvel struggles with the cultural aspect of the studies. It's so far removed from his personality. Besides, everybody speaks Spanish. What's the point of learning that? Why doesn't anyone care about the Scandinavian languages?

That early childhood nickname—"The Dane"—seems to have stuck with Samvel on some subconscious level, for his longing for all things Scandinavian has only deepened with time. The cold and the dark appeal to him. In Armenia he is different, in Armenia he is strange, but perhaps in Scandinavia he would fit in; perhaps there he could be happy.

On his walk home to Raykom, Samvel stops at the video rental store again and picks up another Bergman movie: *Wild Strawberries*. While the rest of his family members are still out, he can occupy the living room and immerse himself in Swedish film. Then, once they come home, he'll switch to reading. Strindberg's *The Red Room* sits on his bedside table, but as Strindberg was such a prolific writer, there is much more to explore. With some thirty books and over sixty plays, his canon will keep Samvel busy for a long time. Come midnight, Samvel will go online. The family has a special Internet plan that allows them cost-effective surfing between midnight and 8 a.m. It suits Samvel perfectly. While the rest of the family is sleeping, he'll research Swedish culture and learn more facts with which to inundate his unsuspecting peers.

While the kids in his class talk about Jennifer Aniston as their favorite actress, Samvel admires Greta Garbo. He finds her beauty overrated, but there is something about her personal history that enthralls him. She suffered from lifelong melancholy, and the depressive, lonely aspect of her story captivates Samvel. Garbo never married or had children, and when her beauty began to fade, she locked herself away and lived out the rest of her life in reclusion.

While living the Californian dream, she talked of how she missed being enfolded in the "marvelous melancholy" of the Swedish rain. Samvel is fascinated. In interviews, Garbo expressed that she had an innate need for solitude: "as early as I can remember, I have wanted to be alone. I detest crowds, don't like many people," she explained. Samvel can relate. And it doesn't hurt that in Armenia, no one knows who she is.

Swedish actresses such as Garbo, Britt Ekland, and Anita Ekberg, immortalized in Fellini's *La Dolce Vita*, fueled the notion of Swedish sin, along with the avant-garde creations of directors such as Vilgot Sjöman and Ingmar Bergman. In the '50s and '60s, a skinny-dipping scene was enough to cause a scandal; but the association with nudity and sex undoubtedly helped promote Bergman's films to international audiences. In the United States, some of his films were even given titles that were directly misleading. *Summer Interlude* was marketed as *Illicit Interlude*, and *Summer with Monica* became *Monika—The Story of a Bad Girl*. "Men wilt under the touch of her lips," read the poster. "So daring we recommend a babysitter."

Bergman played along, stating that skinny-dipping should be compulsory in all Swedish films. Even when reviewing *Persona*, one of Bergman's most complex films, the critics got hung up on sex: "Ingmar Bergman has followed the Swedish freedom into the exploration of sex," wrote the *New York Post*. "Bergman at his most powerful! A sexual frankness that blazes a new trail," concluded a reviewer of *The Silence*. These quotes were also exploited in the films' American trailers.[1]

In Germany and France, the expressions *Schwedenfilm* and *films suédois* became synonymous with pornographic films.[2]

Initially, the political leadership of Sweden protested against the perception that its people should be particularly promiscuous or immoral. However, it wasn't long until the notion of Swedish sin came to be regarded with a defiant sort of pride. There was nothing wrong with Sweden; it was the rest of the Western world, especially the United States, which was "retarded." Swedes argued that they simply had a more natural relationship to sex. It was "rational, democratic, and utopic."[3]

There were those who took it one step further, arguing that the liberal, Swedish attitude towards sex was the result of clever manipulation by the political leadership. According to the British journalist Roland Huntford, in Sweden, freedom existed only in sexual matters.[4] "Because he is sexually emancipated, the Swede believes that he is a free man, and he judges liberty entirely in sexual terms." Huntford referred to Aldous Huxley, who argued that sexual freedom tended to increase as political and economic freedom diminished. Any dictator was wise to encourage that freedom, he argued, as "it will help to reconcile his subjects to the servitude which is their fate."[5]

* * *

Samvel pulls his thin, white legs up underneath him on the gray family sofa. As far as he is concerned, servitude with sexual liberty is better, at any rate, than servitude without it. In *Wild Strawberries* Professor Borg has just been forced by the Inquisitor to relive an old memory where he watches his wife having sex with another man in the forest. "You are guilty of guilt," the Inquisitor informs him.

"What will the punishment be?" Borg asks.

"Oh, the usual," says the Inquisitor darkly. "Loneliness."

SWEDISH NEUTRALITY

Since 1814, Sweden had successfully avoided armed conflicts. It stayed out of the First World War, and at the outset of the Second in 1939 it declared itself neutral once again. The political leadership was intent on keeping the country out of the conflict.[1] However, after the occupation of Denmark and Norway in April 1940, this became increasingly difficult. Pressured by Nazi Germany, Sweden began to allow the transit of unarmed German troops between Norway and Germany.[2] In the name of neutrality, Stockholm had refused similar requests to allow the transit of British and French troops.[3] After the invasion of the Soviet Union in the summer of 1941, Nazi Germany requested more far-reaching logistical support, including the transit of the fully armed 15,000 strong 163rd Infantry Division from Norway to Finland. Agreeing to this demand would be a serious breach of neutrality, but Sweden acceded.[4]

One hundred and five Swedish trains were set aside for the purpose, and 15,000 Swedish soldiers were called in to supervise the transports and protect the German soldiers. This turned out to be unnecessary as there were no visible protests. Instead, members of the public showed up at the different stations along the route with chocolates, fruits and flowers for the Nazi troops.[5] Swedish trains also transported large amounts of German war materiel, in addition to thousands of injured German soldiers.

Unarmed military aircrafts were permitted to fly across Sweden, and German ships not only were allowed to enter Swedish territorial waters, but even received escort by the Swedish navy, a privilege denied to all other foreign warships. The Wehrmacht also enjoyed access to equipment from the Swedish army's mobilization stocks, including 4,000 large tents with stoves, providing shelter for the German soldiers fighting the Soviet army in the dead of winter.[6]

By the time the transit traffic ceased in 1943, 2,140,000 German soldiers had passed through Sweden.[7] In addition, 75,000 railway wagons of German war materiel had crossed Swedish territory.[8]

Most upsetting to the Allies, however, was Sweden's support of the Nazi war economy. By exporting large amounts of high-quality iron ore, Sweden essentially kept Germany's war machine running. As far back as November 1934, Hitler had acknowledged the significance of Scandinavian ore by arguing that its absence would make it impossible for Germany to go to war. In September 1939, British MP Ralph Glyn claimed that Sweden had the power to end the war in six months, if it refused to export iron ore to the Germans. But Sweden's dependency on Germany for the import of vital products like coal and coke, as well as various kinds of chemicals and fertilizers, gave the Reich great leverage.[9] Stockholm ignored the pressure from the Allies, finding ways to circumvent the trade agreements signed with Britain in 1939 to freeze levels of iron ore exports to Germany.[10] By April 1940, all bets were off, and Sweden gradually increased its exports to Nazi Germany. By 1941, 45,000 tons of iron ore were being shipped to Nazi Germany every day. Soon, 90 per cent of Sweden's foreign trade was with the Germans.[11]

In November 1942, US Secretary of State Cordell Hull emphasized that "the traffic of iron-ore is the most important single contribution, in terms of raw material, made to Germany by any nation outside its pre-war borders."[12]

Churchill would later accuse Sweden of "calculated selfishness,"[13] while Peter Tennant, the man in charge of the British Special Operations Executive in Sweden, argued that Stockholm's economic concessions to Germany's war economy were of such significance that they virtually amounted to "a direct act of war against Britain."[14]

Between 1933 and 1939 some 300,000 Jews fled from Germany. Sweden took in approximately 3,000 of them, but the growing number of Jewish refugees caused the country to review its policies. After 1937, Jews were no longer considered political refugees. Then, in September 1938, Swedish consulates and border control agents were instructed to introduce special border procedures for so-called "Aryan" Germans. To make it easier to separate and reject the Jewish Germans, a special request from the Swedish and Swiss authorities caused Nazi Germany to mark Jewish passports with a red "J." This made life harder for all Jews trying to leave Germany, regardless of their destination. As far as the Roma population went, Swedish restrictions were even harsher, with a total ban on immigration until 1954.[15]

In September 1939, all non-Nordic foreigners were required to have a visa to enter Sweden. The Swedish public was against allowing in too many Jewish refugees, as many feared that integration would prove difficult. Not until Nazi Germany was losing the war did the policy change, and Sweden start accepting Norwegian and Danish Jews. At the end of the European conflict, Sweden took in hundreds of thousands of refugees.[16]

In 1943 the British government estimated that 80 per cent of the Swedish population favored the Allies.[17] Still, the country continued to profit from its trade with Nazi Germany. Pressured by the Allies, Sweden finally curtailed the transit traffic and cut the export of iron ore and ball bearings. However, while exports of ball bearings decreased in 1944, supplies of ball-bearing steel and ball-bearing production machinery increased, ensuring that

Nazi Germany's ball-bearing sector as a whole continued to receive a satisfactory supply.[18]

Swedish press and radio were ordered to play down the troop transits and, with few exceptions, journalists obliged. Half a century after the end of the war, there was still no mention of them, or of Sweden's neutrality breaches more generally, in Swedish history textbooks; few members of the public were even aware of their existence.[19] The first post-war attempts at scrutinizing Sweden's actions during the war amounted to nothing. The commission appointed in 1946 to investigate Swedish Nazis drew a blank. A few members of the cultural elite who had admired Hitler were stigmatized in the media, but public figures who were less well-known could calmly cover their tracks and go on with their lives as though nothing had happened.[20] In some cases, many years would go by until old sins were dragged out into the open.

In 1994, it was revealed that Ingvar Kamprad, the founder of IKEA, had been an active Nazi.[21] Kamprad was of German origin and his ties to Germany remained strong after Hitler came to power and throughout the war. Between 1942 and 1950, even after the full horrors of the war had been revealed to the world, Kamprad was actively involved in pro-Nazi organizations. He sympathized with the fascist New Swedish Movement several years after the end of the war and was friends with its leader Per Engdahl, whom he, in 2010, still referred to as "a great person." When the exposé made the rounds of the Swedish media, Kamprad apologized to his employees, appealing to them to recall their own youth and any stupid things they might themselves be guilty of. "In hindsight I know that I've forgotten to mention this among my fiascos, but that is now spilled milk!"[22]

Ingvar Kamprad's grandfather, Achim Kamprad, grew up in a German castle, and was related to Paul von Hindenburg, German commander during the First World War, later Germany's president and an active participant in the process that brought Adolf Hitler to power. In 1896 Achim Kamprad emigrated to Sweden, and the farm where his grandson grew up was by far the largest in the area.[23]

Yet in the media, Ingvar Kamprad largely managed to portray himself as a simple, down-to-earth *smålänning*,[24] with strong social pathos and socialist sympathies. News of his dubious past did little to change his hero-like status in Sweden. In 2008, IKEA topped the list of societal institutions that Swedes trust the most, surpassing institutions like the Swedish Parliament and the Swedish Church.[25]

FUCKING OSBY

Mother has decided to relocate to fucking Osby. Chang can't think of a worse place. It's more than ten times the size of Killeberg—7,000 people instead of 600—but somehow it feels even more like the backwaters of Skåne. His new, bigger school is a squared, Soviet-style building lacking both rural charm and big-city flair. They rent an apartment in downtown Osby. Chang's new room is plain and Spartan with a bed, but little else in the way of furnishings. He tries to stay out as much as possible.

One night, Chang learns that Arnold and his friends have stolen a riding lawnmower and driven it through the ice of Osby Lake. He rushes to the lake, where Arnold excitedly presents the rest of their contraband. Among the booty, there is a chainsaw. Chang picks it up and joins Arnold and his friends on their late-night adventure. As they walk past his school, Chang takes one look at his brother and smiles. Arnold smiles back. Chang fires up the chainsaw.

He starts by sawing his way into the building. One of the hated school benches catches his eye first. Something about the way it sits, obediently, in the middle of the room provokes him. The wood chips fill the air. It's intoxicating. Chang proceeds to saw the neat rows of chairs to pieces. Then he makes holes in the walls. There's a painting made of particleboard honoring the local hockey team. It depicts two crossed hockey sticks behind what looks like a wild boar. Chang stops for a moment to look at it, then drives the chainsaw through with all his might.

* * *

"Chang, there's a phone call for you," the Social Services lady informs him. It's a beautiful summer's day. Chang is in Neustrelitz, northern Germany, at a camp for troubled teens. He shares a tent with another Swedish boy who compulsively labels all his belongings as though he were still in daycare. These boys are all characters, each in their own way. The tent next to Chang's is filled with so much stolen liquor and cigarettes that its occupants no longer fit, but have to squeeze in with their newfound friends.

Although Chang's attendance at the camp is a consequence of his chainsaw extravaganza, he is genuinely having a good time. Just being away from Mother fills him with an almost intoxicating sense of freedom. He even smiles at the Social Services lady as she hands him the cell phone. "Yes, Chang here." The voice on the other end informs him that his father has been killed in a hit-and-run.

Chang hangs up. Rays of sunshine trickle down through the branches of the tall pine trees that surround him. He has no idea to whom he just spoke. All he can think of is the video of his father that he never had time to shoot.

Later he will learn that the driver has been caught, but he is never convicted. If there is a funeral, Chang is not informed of when or where it will take place. He doesn't bother to look up his different siblings. He doesn't even know how many there are. As far as he's concerned, Arnold is his only brother.

THE RISE OF THE MORAL SUPERPOWER

Perhaps fueled by the guilt of having escaped the war unharmed, humanitarian ideals and openness to the world began to shape the Swedish self-image after the Second World War. In 1953, Olof Palme, then head of the Swedish National Union of Students, gave an important speech in Lund outlining the role as "world conscience" that Sweden would later take on under his lead as prime minister from 1969.

In his speech, Palme presented atonement through action as an alternative to the painful self-examination and lingering sense of guilt over Sweden's restrictive refugee policy and support for Nazi Germany. Through humanitarian aid, support for democracy movements, and active refugee assistance, Sweden could restore its moral honor.[1]

With its extensive financial and political commitment to international organizations such as the UN—where the Swede Dag Hammarskjöld was secretary-general from 1953 until his death in 1961—Sweden became a self-professed moral superpower. The country was fiercely critical of racism and colonial oppression in third world countries, implying that Swedes were, and always had been, above such evils. As such, it became natural also to take the lead when it came to fulfilling the UN conventions regarding rights of refugees and asylum seekers.[2]

In the 1940s, Sweden was one of the most homogenous countries in the world. Not only had 99 per cent of the population been born in Sweden, but the combination of uniformity of language, experience, and social engineering helped ensure that Swedes even thought as one collective Unimind. However, in the post-war decades, booming Swedish industry welcomed hundreds of thousands of immigrant workers.[3] At this point, the expectation on immigrants was assimilation. Of all political parties, the Social Democrats opposed the concept of multiculturalism the longest, and emphasized the need to "Swedify" immigrants. "They must become Swedes or move on," said Foreign Minister Torsten Nilsson at a 1964 meeting with a student association in Stockholm. MP Hilding Johansson summarized the party's position in 1967: "To avoid unnecessary antagonism in the society where one is [living], those who have immigrated need to adjust socially and culturally to Swedish circumstances. One should avoid linguistic and cultural isolates within Swedish society."[4]

The military coup in Chile in 1973 and the revolution in Iran in 1979 created new types of arrivals. Previously, most immigrants to Sweden had been European, and more than half of Nordic descent—mainly Finnish—which meant a partly shared cultural and linguistic history. But the 1970s saw a shift: fewer economic migrants and more refugees. Politically, a shift of consensus was also taking place. One by one, the political parties, including the Social Democrats, began to argue that immigrants should not have to give up their culture. Instead, they must be helped to preserve it and to develop their knowledge of their native language.[5]

In 1974, the first extensive research measuring the Swedes' attitudes towards immigration was conducted. The study showed significant resistance to it among the population. Author Arne Trankell wrote that he hoped the Swedish people would eventually be freed from their "superstition and ignorance" by traveling abroad more.[6] Ignoring public opinion, the Swedish leadership decided that Sweden ought to do more to be a role model in the area of immigration policy. In 1975, a unanimous Parliament decided that Swedish immigration policy should strive for a multicultural society, where immigrants and minorities should decide for themselves to what extent they wished to be assimilated. The aim was to enable Sweden's transformation from a homogenous society to a multicultural one.[7]

The new policy meant that immigrants were to be given increased opportunities to preserve their culture and develop their native languages. Funds were set aside to enable native language training, cultural association grants, and news broadcasts in other languages.[8] Immigrants were granted unprecedented rights. For example, Sweden was the first country in the world to grant non-citizens the right to vote in municipal and regional elections. It was also first in offering all pupils state-financed education in their native languages.[9]

When asked if he believed the Swedish population supported the policies enacted by the government and Parliament at this time, Prime Minister Olof Palme replied: "We were ahead of the public opinion, I won't deny that." The key to preventing the rise of right-wing extremism in the wake of the new policies was to stick to reasonable, regulated quotas, and to politics that promoted equality, Palme said. "If any of these two prerequisites gives way we risk difficult problems."[10]

The leadership had made its decision; now consensus around it would have to be engineered—Swedish-style.

In 1980, Immigration Minister Karin Andersson, of the Centre Party, emphasized the importance of educating the Swedish people on the benefits of immigration:

"It is immensely important to place more weight on really making it clear to the population that immigration is positive for Sweden. We have to speak about the positive significance of immigrants in our country, how great they are as laborers, how they enrich our culture."[11]

Meanwhile, there was widespread arrogance when it came to interpreting culture clashes. When Assyrian parents objected to daycare personnel wearing bikinis on the job, their criticism was dismissed with the argument that they were simply threatened by the temptation "nudity" might pose to their men.[12]

At this point, few people considered immigration a threat to Swedish values. The culture of these "Others" was deemed backward and inferior; it was self-evident that the immigrants, once they developed enough, would adopt the more evolved Swedish way.

MAKING IT HAPPEN

Samvel can smell the gas, but the stove won't light. He leans in, squinting to see what's wrong. Then suddenly: whoosh! The flame shoots up and he feels the heat on his face. His thick glasses protect his long, white lashes, but he can tell from the smell of burnt hair that his eyebrows have been singed. Good thing his mother didn't see that. She is convinced he will never make it on his own. He, on the other hand, is determined to prove her wrong. It's 3 a.m. and Samvel is practicing frying eggs and chicken dippers. He hates eggs, but it's the easiest thing to cook, and if he's going to live on his own he has to be able to feed himself.

What started as a vague idea has turned into an obsession: Samvel is moving to Sweden. Applying to a university was easy. All he had to do was submit his choices to the Swedish admissions authorities. Unlike in the US, where one submits separate applications for each university, in Sweden it is all centralized. Tuition is free. And to apply for a scholarship, he simply has to tick a box. It can all be achieved with one form. No essays to write, no opportunity to argue one's case. Either one's grades hold up or they don't. The tough part is waiting for the outcome.

Samvel has only applied to the prestigious University of Lund in southern Sweden, where he wants to study EU politics.

Tomorrow morning is when the admission authorities will communicate their verdict. All Samvel has to do is log in to the portal. But morning doesn't seem to want to come. The minutes drag by and Samvel can't sleep.

For good luck, he is wearing the Viking t-shirt that cousin Armen bought for him. It is white, with a blonde Viking in the center, framed by the slogan "Sweden—the land of Vikings" in a semi-circle. His cousin is an engineer who went to Sweden on a Scania corporate exchange and decided to remain. Samvel doesn't know him too well, but the stories he has heard during Armen's brief visits back home confirm his perception of Sweden as a civilized and developed utopia. People are nice and honest, in sharp contrast to Armenia, where one must constantly keep one's guard up so as not to be taken advantage of. "If you forget your wallet in a public place in Sweden, someone will immediately come rushing to hand it to you," his cousin had bragged.

Samvel checks his watch again. Four hours and 43 minutes left until he can log in. He carefully wipes all the oil splatter from the white tiles behind the stove. Leaving them greasy was his giveaway the first time he secretly practiced cooking. He knows it's the first place his mother will check in the morning.

Samvel cleans the kitchen carefully, and then sits down to wait. He feels nauseous. Perhaps he didn't cook the chicken dippers properly. Perhaps he is just nervous. He has never wanted anything this much in his life.

When morning finally comes, Samvel is still sitting in his chair. He hasn't slept, but he is no longer nervous. Instead he feels an odd sense of peace as he logs in to the system.

He knows this is meant to be.

THE SWEDISH MODEL II

THE CONTRACT

Increasing affluence meant that citizens' expectations were constantly growing. In a parliamentary speech in January 1956, Prime Minister Tage Erlander first introduced the idea that unmet expectations would be the greatest challenge of the future. The role of the political class, he argued, was no longer merely to protect people from unemployment, illness, and poverty, but increasingly to respond to their demands for more spacious housing, their own car, modern kitchens, better education, increased opportunities, and greater individual freedom. The good times and technological progress provided the state with opportunities to do more. Individual advancement did not have to come at the expense of collective security; it was simply the next step in the development of society. If the Sweden of the 1930s had been built on standardized solutions for the betterment of the whole, Erlander's speech heralded a new era: it was now time for social engineers to enable self-realization through more individualized solutions.[1]

With the rise of the New Left, known in Sweden as the '68 Left, came fierce criticism of centralism, technocracy, materialism, and alienation—the ills that modern society was believed to cause. Reforming and modernizing Sweden was no longer considered an honorable mission, but rather a negative endeavor; an escape from moral responsibility. The bureaucrats of modernity went from being heroes to villains. By selling out to the capitalists, the Social Democrats were accused of having created a cold society populated by soulless citizens.[2]

The Social Democrat patriarchy struggled with how to handle this mounting pressure from the radical left. The solution was a change of leadership.

By 1969, Tage Erlander had served as prime minister for 23 years (1946–69), making him one of the longest ruling heads of government in any democratic state.[3] He was eager to hand over to his protégé, the political prodigy Olof Palme, who had rapidly ascended the Social Democrat ranks.

Palme was a convinced anti-communist and had never been attracted to Marxism, but he was more radical than Erlander and the older generation of party leaders. He was also gifted in rhetoric and a fierce debater. He was just what was needed to appease the radical left. In 1969, Palme was elected leader of the Social Democratic Party.[4]

Palme was of aristocratic pedigree, brought up in an elite military family in the wealthy Stockholm neighborhood of Östermalm. Well-educated, well-traveled, and multi-lingual, he could have used his exceptional intelligence and abundance of opportunity to add to the family wealth. Instead, he gave up his privilege to live modestly in a terraced house in Vällingby, the first socially engineered Stockholm suburb. He wanted to lead by example in pursuit of his vision of a classless society.

Palme was committed to a solid, inclusive welfare state and a foreign policy driven by idealism, morality, and solidarity, especially with the third world. Internationally, Palme personified Sweden's righteous leftwing internationalism. A fierce critic of the Vietnam War, apartheid, and repressive governments throughout the world, he had plenty of admirers, as well as adversaries. Without regard for the diplomatic consequences, Palme would publicly condemn any perceived injustice. He could be very critical of American policy, but still had a profound fondness for the continent, where he had first developed an interest in leftwing liberalism and socialism during his Political Science studies at Kenyon College in the late 1940s. As a student, he had spent a summer hitchhiking across the United States with almost no money in his pocket. The experience exposed him to the realities of poor America, a stark contrast to his hitherto sheltered existence.[5]

Palme opposed any kind of human submission, whether in the shape of colonial oppression, injustices in the workplace, or inequality in the family. He regarded all forms of dependency as a threat to freedom. Nations, as well as individuals, should be sovereign and independent. Socialism, he argued, meant liberation from the dependency of the class society.[6]

In the 1970s, the unquestioning loyalty and obedience of the workers was beginning to waver and wildcat strikes became more frequent. Many were no longer convinced that national growth was of prime importance. Rationalizations had been the prerequisite for progress since the 1930s, but as workers began to question modernity and its consequences, they also began to question rationalizations. The Saltsjöbaden agreements were no longer sufficient. The all-powerful trade union organization demanded stronger labor security and rights.

The government listened and passed laws to improve workers' protection and influence. It became a lot more difficult for employers to dismiss employees and, during a couple of exceptional years in the mid-70s, companies' salary costs increased by 45 per cent. These laws were the first deviations from the previous Swedish model in which parties had sought to solve differences of opinion through agreements, not laws.[7] While increasing conflicts in the workplace shattered the Swedish model that had been the country's claim to fame, a new model—a social contract of sorts—developed under Palme's leadership. His vision was of a classless Sweden populated by independent and equal citizens.

The idea, as such, was far from new. As early as 1838, author Carl Jonas Love Almqvist published a novel called *Det går an* (It Is Acceptable) that was both highly influential and highly provocative. The plot is set on a steamboat where the heroine, Sara Videbeck, a glassmaker's daughter, falls in love with the officer Albert. The two become romantically involved and have sex but, to Albert's dismay, Sara refuses to marry him. She wants complete independence as a woman and intends to run her own business. Albert is allowed to rent a room in her house, but she only wants them to meet when they truly feel like it. They should share love, not property. Almqvist had used his story to argue that true love is only possible between people who are completely, financially independent of one another.[8]

It was a radical suggestion at a time when women lacked most rights, including the right to vote and provide for themselves, but it had gone on to influence many Swedish intellectuals, including the renowned feminist and author, Ellen Key (1849–1926). Both Almqvist and Key had argued that an intricate web of financial, legal, social, and cultural dependencies tied people together far more than true feelings. Real love, as opposed to submission and exploitation, had to build on financial and legal independence. Almqvist and Key had both drafted suggestions for reforms, radical for the era, whereby the state would assume the financial burden of all children in order to liberate women from their dependency on men.[9]

Alva Myrdal was influenced by these ideas. She was an enthusiastic reader of Ellen Key and a great advocate for liberating children from their parents. The state was to act in loco parentis; its responsibility was to each individual, not the family.[10] By the late 1950s, the standard family constellation—with a male provider and a female housewife—was increasingly under intellectual attack, and this was reflected in the way social policies were drafted. "A precondition for equality between the sexes is that women become completely financially and socially independent of the men," wrote Eva Moberg, journalist and editor of the magazine *Hertha*, in 1961. "Motherly love is the most exploited feeling in history."[11]

Moberg, Almqvist, and Key were all liberals, not socialists, but they were prepared to give the state great influence in order to realize their vision of emancipating the citizen from all forms of dependency and subordination.

Marriage as a way to provide for oneself had to be eliminated, Moberg argued, as it constituted prostitution: "It is very odd that we condemn free prostitution while at the same time sanctioning it in marriage." She emphasized that men must do their half of housework and childcare, but also called for more preschools and daycare centers.[12]

According to these authors, the state had far-reaching responsibility for the wellbeing of all citizens, but also the right to override conventional ties. After all, the traditional family couldn't be considered a democratic institution, as family members typically had varying degrees of power and influence. Family was an old-fashioned institution governed by hierarchical and patriarchal structures. Even from a market perspective, the concept of family was a problem. In the workplace, love and dependence between family members could easily turn to nepotism and corruption.[13] Even Plato had wanted to abolish the family. When he outlined his ideal society in *Republic*, he argued that a citizen putting their spouse, children, or parents above the state couldn't be trusted by the nation. The family was the state's greatest rival in the fight for the loyalty of the citizen.[14]

More and more, the Social Democrats began to consider it their mission to free individuals from their families and thereby from the unequal, unjust, relationships of dependency that characterized traditional societies.[15] During his first term as prime minister (1969–76), Palme carried out a series of reforms to that effect. His government deprived the Swedish monarchy of all its remaining powers, save for the purely ceremonial. "Nothing but a plume remains, a decoration, and it is easy to implement a republic if one so wishes ... all it takes is the stroke of a pen," Palme said at the Social Democratic Congress of 1972.[16]

In 1971, joint taxation was abolished so that families would benefit more from having two providers.[17] The commissioners concluded: "In a society where the individual is guaranteed security at old age, and in case of illness, invalidity, or unemployment, the financial dependency on relatives is lessened. The only sustainable principle is to tax the separate individual without considering their burden of provision or the possible household of which the individual is a part."[18] Then, in 1972, the Social Democrats launched a manifesto called "The Family of the Future: Socialist Family Politics." The goal was to build a society on foundations of solidary co-operation between independent citizens. "All adults shall be financially independent of their next of kin," it stated. Citizens were to be freed from the old-fashioned family structures that trapped them in dependencies. True independence and freedom of choice was only possible if each individual was truly financially self-reliant. This was no longer just about freeing women from their men, and children from their parents, but also vice versa.[19]

As the independence of women increased and the state's ability to provide for its citizens improved, men were no longer considered breadwinners. In 1973, the duty to pay alimony to a former spouse was abolished, and in 1974 paid parental leave was introduced along with free abortion.[20] During the first half of the 1970s, the number of divorces skyrocketed, peaking in 1974, while the number of marriages decreased.[21] The Swedish housewife was virtually made extinct and the number of daycare places more than quadrupled in the decade between 1975 and 1985.[22]

Access to higher education also increased significantly. By regarding children and youth as independent individuals with their own rights, and guaranteeing them free education and healthcare, the state had freed them from the strong dependency on their parents that characterizes many cultures. By providing subsidized childcare, separate taxation, and governmental child support, women no longer needed a male provider. And while the state had robbed the man of his patriarchal power as head of the family, it had also freed him from the responsibility this entailed.[23] The Swedish family policy reforms introduced in the late 1960s to the mid-70s account for some of the most far-reaching examples of public policy that the world has ever seen when it comes to the individualization of society.[24] The safety net was big enough for everyone. There was no need to submit to anyone but the impersonal power of the state.

From the 1960s to the 1980s, Sweden had some of the highest taxes of any country—but in return it boasted the lowest levels of inequality in the world.[25]

SAMVEL ARRIVES IN UTOPIA

Samvel wanders the streets of Södermalm, Stockholm's trendy, bohemian quarter. It's a balmy evening in late August. The light lingers, but has none of the strength or heat that Samvel has spent his life avoiding. From Bastugatan he takes the stairs up to Monteliusvägen with its stunning views of the Old Town and Riddarfjärden Bay. He traces the winding Bellmansgatan down the hill from Mariaberget, passing Mariahissen on his way to the pedestrian bridge that will take him across the bay to the island of Stadsholmen, home to the Old Town—one of the largest and best-preserved medieval city centers in Europe.

Many people are out for a stroll on this pleasant summer's night and, for the first time in his life, Samvel feels like he fits right in. Nobody even turns to look at him.

Reaching the Old Town, he makes his way along the narrow, winding cobblestone streets, lined by medieval buildings. Västerlånggatan is too packed with tourists for his taste, but running in parallel he finds Prästgatan almost deserted. There are fewer stores and restaurants on this street, and hence less to draw the crowds. He can get lost in its maze of alleyways and admire the terracotta-red and mustard-yellow medieval townhouses at his own pace.

The neighborhood dates back to the thirteenth century, but most buildings are from the 1700s and 1800s. This used to be a slum where filth collected amidst the uneven cobbles and odors from dung, food, fish, and spices filled the air. Now it has surpassed the gentrification phase and become touristy and overpriced, but Samvel can tell there are still hidden gems amongst the nooks and crannies.

Through the narrow Kåkbrinken alleyway he turns onto Stortorget, the oldest square in Stockholm and site of the infamous Stockholm Bloodbath in 1520. Arriving there is like taking a journey back in time; its colorful, historic, old merchants' houses are so different from the concrete blocks of Yerevan.

From Stortorget, many tourists make their way towards the Royal Palace, but Samvel heads in the opposite direction towards the old German Church. There are plenty of impressive palaces and court buildings in this neighborhood, but he is not interested in the markers of bureaucracy. He yearns for the oddly shaped, the bent, and the twisted, not the squared and city-planned.

* * *

Waking up in his cousin Armen's apartment on Förlandagränd 12, in the southern suburb of Östberga, Samvel feels much more at home. This neighborhood is far removed from the unique and colorful buildings of the Old Town. The gray apartment building is a square box of prefabricated concrete, that would easily fit in any Soviet or post-Soviet landscape.

Armen is only 5 years older than Samvel, but his rounded belly and slight double chin create the impression that they are nearly a generation apart. The feeling is reinforced by Armen's assertive way of explaining the Swedish system and how things work. "Even though you are a newcomer, you are safer here than you were in Armenia when it comes to rights and such," Armen informs him. "You may not be a Swedish citizen—you've just arrived—but that doesn't mean that you have fewer rights than Swedes. If anything should happen to you, you're entitled to a great deal of protection. It's not like in Armenia where, even though you are a citizen, nobody cares about your rights."

Samvel nods. He is a little overwhelmed by it all. But here, in the apartment that his cousin shares with a friend, he feels like he is still in Armenia. There are three beds in his cousin's bedroom and he gets the impression that Armen is constantly hosting guests and extended family members. Samvel is eager to get out; to start exploring. "Can we go for a walk?" he wonders. Armen's protruding belly and unenthusiastic look suggest he prefers talking about Sweden while sitting on the sofa eating dates, but he is a good host and agrees.

As they exit the building—a monolithic structure of tanned stucco on concrete—a minibus pulls up by the front door, where a man in a wheelchair is waiting. The driver gets out to assist him. "Should we offer to help?" Samvel turns to his cousin. Armen shakes his head and points to the text on the side of the vehicle: *färdtjänst*. "It's the mobility services," he says, and explains that this is a special type of public transportation that municipalities are obliged to provide for people with disabilities who have difficulties using conventional public transport.

"This man has a legal right to be picked up and driven to his work each and every morning? At no cost?" Samvel asks incredulously.

"Yup, all for free. Imagine if Armenians had access to this."

Samvel is amazed. This idea of individual autonomy is completely new to him, and when he and Armen return home later that day he immediately goes online to learn more about it. In Armenia, anyone who is ill, incapacitated, or otherwise unable to fend for himself has to be cared for by family members. But here, such responsibilities have been assumed by the state. No one is forced to depend on the goodwill of their relatives and, more importantly, no one is made to feel like a burden. In Sweden, traditional breadwinners have no leverage over weaker or more vulnerable family members. Citizens are free from the traditional ties of community and family that are so strong in Armenia. In Sweden, one can leave at any moment, safe in the knowledge that if one is not able to meet one's own needs, or the needs of one's family members, the state will. As an individual no one is subordinate to anyone else. What, if not that, constitutes true freedom?

The Swedes have arrived; *he* has arrived. He is finally home.

AGENTS OF THE UNIMIND

"All the media seem to be of one mind, advocating the same consensus, professing the same slogans, always, it seems, following the convolution of some party line. They give the impression of existing, not to question authority, but to avoid disturbing the public peace of mind; not to criticize, but to indoctrinate with a certain point of view."

Roland Huntford, *The New Totalitarians*

A balding man in yellow pajamas is lying in bed. "Give yourself three wake-up minutes," the voiceover instructs. "Lay on your back. Stretch out! Twist from side to side." The man in yellow pajamas obediently follows the instructions provided by the invisible voice.

It's the mid-70s and the Swedish Health Authorities have put together a series of instructional videos broadcast on primetime television. This one is called "The Health Authorities' Advice: how to get started in the mornings." The video coaches citizens on suitable morning routines.

"Sit up, pull your legs towards your chin. Lean back, again and again," continues the voice, while the man, in his IKEA-furnished bedroom, does sit-ups in bed.

"And then onto the floor. Pretend you're skiing by swinging your arms back and forth." The man in yellow illustrates how it's done. "Doesn't it feel good? And not very difficult!"

After completing the gymnastics program, the voiceover provides the viewer with five acceptable alternatives for a healthy, nutritious breakfast: oatmeal, sour milk, gruel, hot chocolate with a sandwich, or eggs. "Set the table the evening before to save time in the mornings," the voice advises.

Testimonials follow. An attractive young woman sitting by her breakfast table confesses: "I used to skip breakfast, but then I ended up buying candy at the concession stands and oh, how fat I got. Now I take my time, eat in peace and quiet; most often this..." The camera zooms in on a plate filled with sour milk with raisins, Swedish rye bread, and fruit. "Then I bike to work and get fresh air while I'm at it," she continues. A pie chart appears on screen to illustrate all the important aspects of a balanced meal: vitamins, minerals, fibers, and so on. The routine is meant to ensure that citizens show up for work rested and well fed, so that they can be healthy and productive.

* * *

It wasn't until the 1960s, that television first made its way into the average Swedish home. Few Swedes understood the potential of the new medium better than Olof Palme. As a student, he had worked as a journalist, and he had lived in the United States in the late 1940s when television had its breakthrough.

In 1965, Palme was named minister of communication, responsible for radio and television policies. Televised appearances quickly became part of his everyday routine, and the media, above all television, became his pulpit. When Palme became minister of education in 1967, he brought the responsibility for radio and television with him.[1] Television was meant to educate the population and convey the correct opinions—which meant that its content could not be disseminated without filters.[2]

State-controlled television played an important role in streamlining people's views and habits. Initially, there was only one state-run channel, but in 1969, a second, TV2, was introduced. People watched the same shows, received the same government-approved information, and were taught to appreciate the same aesthetics. This likely contributed to what ethnologist Åke Daun calls "the Swedish homogeneity-syndrome," whereby Swedes, to a greater extent than other nationalities, "prefer conversations with people who share their opinions, support their viewpoints, and laugh at the same jokes."[3]

In his book *The New Totalitarians* (1971), British journalist Roland Huntford managed to get some very candid quotes from the top echelons of Swedish television at the time. Örjan Wallquist, then head of TV2, as well as a socialist and part of the intellectual leadership of the labor movement, admitted that the primary goal of broadcasting was to shape opinion: "Swedes are intellectually primitive and underdeveloped. And TV works in this way: it creates emotions and intellectual life, and therefore it creates opinions. It is an opinion-making medium ... TV is a very powerful indoctrinating medium, and one has to be extremely careful in using it." Other officials were more specific, claiming that the aims of this indoctrination were "to persuade the Swedes that they live in the best of all possible worlds, and to condition them to the ideology of the sitting government."[4]

"In reporting from abroad, the Swedish radio and TV are concerned, not so much to show how other people live, but to illuminate the superiority of all things Swedish," Huntford argued.

> They concentrate on the defects of foreign countries, drawing comparisons to the advantage of Sweden. Viewers are invited to see how difficult life is for people in other countries and to consider how fortunate they are. Press and periodicals portray the same sensibility. It is not only that the Swede is told that they have the highest standard of living, and the best social security, but that they really are superior in all things, most particularly in politics and culture.[5]

The programs of the era were rarely uplifting. They frequently featured struggling workers or had titles like "A Year of Subsistence Farming in Lapland," "Fire in the Name of Jesus" (about religious violence), or "Knapsack poisoned city," about industrial pollution in capitalist West Germany. Much time was devoted to educational programs such as how to file one's taxes, how to carve wooden bowls, or how to play the accordion. Television was a channel for instruction and guidance, not superficial entertainment.[6]

The state decided when people should watch television—typically in the evenings after work. During the day people were expected either to work or to engage in sports, the outdoors, or other activities with health benefits. Consequently, there were no daytime broadcasts. Initially, Wednesday nights were completely TV-free.

As journalists Filip Hammar and Fredrik Wikingsson so fittingly put it, back then, the television consumption of Swedes revolved around the following hopes:

1) That a t-shirt we had donated to Ethiopia would be worn by a scrawny 14-year-old in a broadcast from Addis Ababa.
2) That the urban center in which we lived would be mentioned on television, which was most likely to occur when The Notice Board threatened "Upcoming TV-license inspections in the following areas..."[7]

Everyone who owned a television had to pay a license fee to finance the state programs; much effort was devoted to informing the public of where license fee inspections were currently taking place, and of the consequences of failing to pay one's share.

At school, children were taught that advertisements were the products of capitalists with evil agendas. Consequently, they were banned. On the other hand, the many government "information campaigns" to which citizens were constantly subjected were not to be questioned. They were true, necessary, and disseminated for the good of the people. Swedes were drowned in catchy slogans meant to convince them to stop drinking ("Go Dry!"), stop bullying ("Don't Touch My Buddy!"), and appreciate their wonderful homeland ("Sweden is Fantastic!").

Few Western governments were as troubled as Swedish leaders by the possibility of direct TV transmissions from satellites. The potential influence foreign broadcasts could have on their citizens was so concerning to the political leadership that, when the rest of the world was deregulating, Sweden preferred to follow the example of the South African apartheid regime, working nationally to prohibit private ownership of satellite dishes[8] and internationally to have satellite broadcasting banned.[9]

In 1766, Sweden had become the first country in the world to abolish censorship and enshrine freedom of the press in its constitution.[10] The Swedish Freedom of the Press Act also introduced the principle of public access to information, which made it legal to publish and read public documents.[11] But despite pioneering such progressive legislation, in practice Swedish media outlets were far from free. Huntford noted:

> Anxious only to expound what their colleagues believe, the Swedish communicators need no compulsion to toe the party line. In their mental world, departure from the accepted norm is a kind of treachery. It is part of conditioning to group thinking, which makes personal divergence a sin, and acceptance of the collective opinion a cardinal virtue. They have an urge to think as everybody else does. In consequence, they have developed a kind of inhibition, what the Russians call the 'inner censor', that tailors the expression of their thoughts to prevailing views. Since they act corporately, by conditioned reflex, it is relatively easy to harness them to a particular ideology. It suffices to convert a select few at the top of the hierarchy, the rest following obediently.[12]

This means that, for the people, "There is only one 'objective' truth to fit given data. This attitude serves to outlaw opposition.

Rejection of the approved viewpoint becomes, not valid criticism to be judged on its merits, but error. The critic becomes a heretic, and is thereby neutralized." Huntford pointed to an extensive list of principles that cannot be questioned, encompassing everything upon which the system rests, including the national principle of consensus.[13]

In an unusually candid interview, Olof Lagercrantz, then editor-in-chief of leading daily *Dagens Nyheter*, admitted: "News must be used to change society and influence people. If it is objective, and designed only to inform, then it is conservative. Now in a small country like Sweden, a newspaper of *Dagens Nyheter*'s size has tremendous power. Single-handed, we can change public opinion." As he put it, "A small country cannot afford to have individuals getting up and taking a stand on their own. There has to be a group. And, of course, since Swedes react in groups, they are easily influenced."[14]

Though the co-ordination between the media and the ruling elites produces a result similar to totalitarian states, the system in Sweden is unique in its lack of direct political coercion. Privately-owned media, such as newspapers, have their liberty guaranteed by law—yet are compelled by their sense of duty to serve as agents of the Unimind, educating and protecting the children.

SMITTEN

Samvel checks the little peephole in his front door one last time before he heads outside. His gaze continues across the open-air hallway that connects the exterior doors of the dorms on his floor. Through the odd wooden slats that rise up from the ground to the flat roof above, he sees only fragments of lush green trees; not a person in sight.

In Armenia, his family thought his obsessive peeping a strange habit, but in Sweden it's normal, and it has nothing to do with safety. Samvel is thrilled to learn that, just like him, many Swedes check the hole not so much when the doorbell rings, but mainly to make sure no neighbor is nearby before leaving their apartment. This culture of avoiding social contact seems like it has been designed specifically for him.

Samvel opens the door and walks to his red Crescent bike, parked right outside the building. Every time he mounts his brand-new bike on his way to class, he has to fight the urge to pinch his arm. He is finally living in Sweden, enrolled at the prestigious Lund University, where he intends to earn his Master's in European Affairs. The university, founded in 1666, and its more than 40,000 students—nearly half the city's population—lend an academic atmosphere to almost every aspect of life in this quaint historic town. The mere thought that Samvel's favorite Swedish novelist and playwright, August Strindberg, lived and worked in Lund as a young student is mind-blowing. Perhaps he biked these same paths that Samvel now traverses every day. Not to mention the fact that Lund is the destination of Professor Isak Borg in one of Samvel's favorite Bergman movies: *Wild Strawberries*. Smaller and more manageable than Stockholm, Lund nevertheless shares the cobblestoned romanticism and old architecture of the capital. Many prominent Swedish intellectuals have at some point made this their home. For Samvel, it's like being encapsulated in a fairytale.

Most days, on his way to university, Samvel bikes past Monument Park, with its horseshoe-shaped lawn, surrounded by flowerbeds, paths, and sculptured lindens. It is reminiscent of an ancient horseracing track and designed to resemble Piazza Navona in Rome. But today he doesn't need to visit the main campus. He just needs peace and quiet, so he opts instead to cut through town to the university park, Lundagård. He finds the park lined with majestic chestnut trees whose autumn leaves have amassed to cover the paths with a colorful carpet. A feeling of bliss fills him as he bikes on to the university's main library. It can be hard to find a seat, but it is still early; he should be fine.

There are twenty-six libraries tied to Lund University and Samvel loves the endless options for inspirational workspaces. Each faculty has its own library and he is intent on trying them all. His favorite so far is the law library, with its tall ceilings and fancy leather chairs. Samvel visited the public library downtown once and never intends to go back. Its squared, Soviet-style design smells of socialism and Brutalism, a far cry from the atmosphere of independent thought and achievement that characterizes the legal faculty library.

Even just approaching the main library brings him joy. The imposing, castle-like building is encased in ivy, radiating the deep, vibrant colors of fall. Samvel parks his bike and walks to the entrance, all the while keeping his gaze fixed on the building's highly stylized brick patterns, perfectly framed and softened by the greenery. The inside is even more breathtaking. He stops to admire the vaulted, wooden ceilings, the delicately carved wooden poles, the details of the wooden chairs, the warm light from the green table lamps. It's so beautiful, Samvel wonders how anyone can stay focused on their work.

THE MURDER OF THE PROPHET

"The future, when it arrives, changes the past as well, and cuts us off from the past that we actually lived in, which could only make sense from the vantage of a future that has disappeared."

Andrew Brown, *Fishing in Utopia*

It's 11:21 p.m. on a Friday evening, 28 February 1986. Two shots are fired at the corner of Sveavägen and Tunnelgatan in downtown Stockholm.[1] A woman is bent down over a man's lifeless body. Several witnesses call 911. The police officers arriving on the scene ask to see the woman's identification. "Can't you see who it is? I'm Lisbet Palme. This is my husband Olof."[2]

A witness waves down an ambulance in the street. The driver, Peter Nordström, and his colleague are informed that a man has been shot. They perform CPR, but the man is badly injured, so they decide to transport him to the hospital. As they are about to load him into the ambulance, the paramedic turns to the driver and says: "Can't you see who it is?"

"No," Peter replies. "Who is it?"

"It's Olof Palme."[3]

At 6 minutes past midnight, Prime Minister Palme is declared dead at Sabbatsberg hospital.[4]

Jan Eliasson, director general for political affairs at the Foreign Ministry, is about to go to bed when he receives a phone call from a colleague at the UN in New York City: "There's breaking news in the media here that your prime minister, Olof Palme, has been assassinated."

"No, I don't think so," Eliasson replies calmly. "If that were the case I ought to know about it."[5]

"The prime minister of Sweden, Olof Palme, a long-time campaigner for world peace, has been assassinated," reports CNN. In the United States and the United Kingdom, the murder of Olof Palme is top news. Meanwhile, Swedish media is silent. The radio plays pop. And when the last Friday night movie has ended on state television, the broadcast is over for the day and a test screen takes its place.[6]

When Deputy Prime Minister Ingvar Carlsson is informed in the middle of night, he takes a taxi to Rosenbad, the seat of the Swedish government, to attend an emergency meeting. Knowing that the assassin is still on the loose, he hunkers down in the backseat. As he arrives at Rosenbad, Carlsson peeks out through the cab window but sees neither police officers nor roadblocks. The total lack of reaction by the security forces leads him to believe that perhaps it's all a misunderstanding; perhaps Palme isn't dead after all.[7]

Ewonne Winblad, reporter at Swedish Television (SVT), is asleep when her daughter Ylva calls. Ylva, who works at a restaurant in London, informs her mother that customers at the restaurant are talking about the murder of Olof Palme. The following morning, at 4 a.m., Winblad informs the Swedish public in SVT's first broadcast of the day.[8]

The entire country awakens to a fog of despondency and shattered security so deep that it manifests itself as stunned disbelief. "It can't be. Not in Sweden," is the common reaction among members of the public. "I didn't believe it," says Minister Thage G. Peterson. In the taxi heading to Rosenbad, he's convinced there has been some mistake. "We all lived with the belief that

Sweden was a calm and peaceful country where there were no bandits or terrorists," he says. "We thought it was impossible that a Swedish prime minister could be murdered in the street."[9]

Olof Palme and his wife Lisbet had been walking home from the cinema on Friday night, unescorted as usual, when an unknown assailant stepped out from the shadows and shot the Prime Minister twice in the chest.[10] Just as Kennedy's assassination served as life-long marker for every living American—and many others in the Western world—every Swede old enough to remember knows exactly where they were when they learned Palme had been killed. Many residents of Stockholm made their way to the scene of the murder, which still hadn't been properly cordoned off, and put down red roses. In other parts of the country, families congregated around the TV, crying. Business ceased to function. Like the early loss of a beloved parent to an unforeseen tragedy, the recovery was very long and very painful.

As though to emphasize the inconceivability of the event, the subsequent murder investigation became a textbook study in police incompetence. It took 5 hours to put up roadblocks. The married chief of police could not be reached as he was off in the countryside having an affair with a subordinate colleague. The tragedy was so utterly unexpected that nobody seemed to know what to do. The last political assassination in Sweden had taken place in 1792, when King Gustav III was killed at a masquerade ball.[11] Events like these simply did not occur in Sweden.

There were leads pointing both inside and outside of Sweden. Hans Holmér, former head of the Swedish National Security Service, SÄPO, became the self-designated chief of the investigation. He was convinced that the Kurdish liberation movement the PKK, which Palme had labeled a terrorist organization, was behind the attack. Until he was forced to resign in 1987, Holmér almost exclusively pursued this lead, at the expense of all others.[12]

In 1989, Christer Pettersson, an alcoholic and drug addict with a history of violence, was tried for the murder and sentenced to life in jail. However, in spite of clear identification by Lisbet Palme, who stood 1.5 meters from the perpetrator at the time of the shooting, his conviction was later overturned. Pettersson was released and paid significant compensation for wrongful arrest.[13]

The gross mismanagement of the investigation by the police has inspired countless private investigators to conduct their own inquiries, fueled by various conspiracy theories. Some thought the CIA was involved. Others pointed to Swedish police or the Swedish military. South Africa's apartheid regime was also suspected. Palme was an outspoken critic of apartheid and the Swedish government did what it could to support the ANC financially, as well as morally. Sources within MI6 pointed to South Africa, as would the subsequent testimony of Eugene de Kock, former commanding officer of C10, an infamous counter-insurgency unit of the South African police that "liquidated" numerous anti-apartheid activists in the 1980s and 1990s.[14]

In 2010, the twenty-five-year statute of limitations for murder was removed in Sweden.[15] The move signaled persistence, but few Swedes have any faith there will ever be resolution.

Palme had been leader of the Social Democratic Party for seventeen years. He was also prime minister twice, from 1969 to 1976, and again from 1982 until his death in 1986. This did not compare to his mentor Tage Erlander's twenty-three years in power, but in many ways Palme had arguably been much more influential. Erlander had passed away just a few months previous, at 84 years of age. On 21 June 1985, Palme had led the funeral procession through Stockholm along Sveavägen, past the very spot where he would himself be murdered.

"Now you alone are left," Palme's wife Lisbet had told him when he worked on his eulogy for Erlander. The speech would be one of Palme's best, at once a summary of the two men's common ideology and a tribute to a close friend: "You have said that society must be strong so that people don't have to be weak. For you, the strong society was never an expression of authority or financial superiority directing people's lives..."[16]

By the start of 1986, Palme seemed to have recovered from his grief and had regained his bright outlook on the future. In his last interview, published in the magazine *Statsanställd*, Palme called 1986 "the year of possibilities." Sweden was financially strong, inflation was decreasing, salaries were going up and there was room for even more reforms promoting equality. The rest of the world was also trending in the right direction. "The international situation has brightened," Palme said, referring to Gorbachev's glasnost endeavors. "The distrust is dissipating like the fog on an early spring morning."[17]

A few hours later he was dead.

Anna Lindh, the first female president of the Social Democratic Youth League, gave a speech at Palme's funeral: "A person can be murdered, but not ideas. Your ideas live on through us," she said.[18] Lindh would go on to serve the Social Democrats as minister of the environment and later as minister of foreign affairs. She was considered the top contender to take over from Göran Persson as party leader,[19] which would likely have made her Sweden's first female prime minister.

On 10 September 2003, she was stabbed to death in a clothing store in Stockholm.

* * *

The murder of Palme was the first in a series of events that would forever change Sweden. It wasn't just his death that people mourned, but the death of the Sweden that Palme had personified: a safe place where nobody, not even the prime minister, needed bodyguards; where he could ride the subway by himself or with his family like any other citizen; where everybody knew where he lived (and far too many knew that he kept his key in a wooden clog under his doorstep), and his phone number was still listed in the public directory; a virtually crime-free society where one didn't have to lock one's bike, or one's home, and where murders only happened in movies—and even then much of the gore was cut by state censors.

Less than two months after Palme's assassination, disaster struck again. On 26 April 1986, a reactor exploded at the Chernobyl Nuclear Power Plant in what was then part of the Ukrainian Soviet Socialist Republic of the Soviet Union. Freed caesium-137 particles entered into the atmosphere and traveled with the wind across the Baltic Sea to unsuspecting Sweden. Five per cent of the particles released during the accident gathered in clouds above the High Coast and northern Svealand province. Then the sky opened and days of heavy rain deposited highly radioactive material all along Sweden's northeastern shores.

The incident served as confirmation of all the sentiments that Palme's murder had unleashed: Sweden was not immune from the evils and tragedies afflicting the rest of the world; the universe did not end at our borders.

Then, not unlike the former Soviet republics, in the early 1990s, Sweden was hit by a severe financial crisis. The housing market collapsed, and consumption came to a screeching halt. Unemployment quintupled as more than half a million Swedes lost their jobs. It was the worst economic crisis since the 1930s.[20] In order to prevent capital flight and currency speculation, in the fall of 1992 the Central Bank raised the interest rate to an unprecedented 500 per cent. This helped temporarily, but the government soon realized much more would be needed to maintain a fixed currency exchange rate.[21]

On 19 November 1992, the Central Bank decided to decouple the Swedish krona's value from the basket of currencies to which it was fixed. It immediately lost 25 per cent against the German Mark and 40 per cent against the dollar. The government had to bail out a series of banks that were deep under water as a result of the weakened national currency and the collapse of the real estate industry.[22]

It constituted yet another blow to the insular Swede. Like teenagers coming to realize the imperfections in their parents, crisis after crisis began to pick away at Swedes' confidence and faith. The state could not be counted on to protect them from all the dangers of a chaotic world.

SAMVEL AND SWEDISH ANGST

"Ångest, ångest *is my heritage*
The wound of my throat
My heart's cry in the world"

Ångest (Anguish), Pär Lagerkvist, 1916[1]

Samvel and his friend Henrik stand before a seemingly endless isle of potato chips in the grocery store ICA Malmborg in downtown Lund. While Samvel feels nearly paralyzed by the amount of choice, Henrik paces impatiently back and forth. He walks a few meters down the aisle, scrutinizing the options, then turns around and scurries back, agitatedly. He pulls his hand through his light-brown bangs, shakes his head, looks at Samvel with eyes tormented by distress, then exclaims: *"Beslutsångest!"*

Ångest means anxiety or angst. Like ice cream in America, in Sweden *ångest* comes in a near-infinite number of flavors. *Beslutsångest* is new to Samvel but he catches its meaning instantly: decision anxiety.

For Samvel it's a moment of bliss. To think that there is a word to express the simple frustration experienced when one feels unable to reach a trivial decision, such as whether to pick sour cream or cheese and onion chips.

The first time Samvel heard the word *ångest* he thought it was the most beautiful Swedish word he had ever come across. *"Ååå-*

ngest," he said aloud, over and over. But its beauty went beyond its poetic sound, extending deep into its semantic roots. A lover of linguistics and a fluent speaker of vastly different languages such as Russian, Armenian, and English, Samvel had never before found a word that could not quite be translated.

It took a while before he deciphered the full meaning of *ångest*. While Russians are infamous for being lugubrious, as far as Samvel knows they do not experience the type of *ångest* that Swedes seem to harbor. The dictionary says that it means "anxiety, angst, or anguish," but Samvel soon learns it has much broader connotations. It can also mean depression, stress, melancholy, discomfort, and a plethora of other unpleasant emotions. It is intimately integrated into everyday life and people's thoughts. And it exists in countless compound variations, from trivial matters such as *bakisångest* (the anxiety experienced during a bad hangover), to more existential feelings of anguish such as *livsångest* (angst about life and its meaning), or *dödsångest* (a crippling fear of death). It can express itself as acute pain in the form of *panikångest* (panic attacks), or be attached to any day of the week, like *söndagsångest* (Sunday anguish), which is different from *måndagsångest* (Monday anguish).

Ångest is constantly used to express everything, from mundane concerns to the various types of deep, existential pain that seem to accompany Swedes through life. Samvel embraces them all. He senses that he has discovered an important key to the Swedish soul. And now, here's a new one to add to his collection. Samvel's blue eyes, magnified by the convex lenses of his glasses, sparkle as he turns to Henrik and echoes enthusiastically: "*Beslutsångest!*"

So much of a culture is conveyed or hidden in its language! Suddenly Samvel is overcome by the urge to *absorb* Swedish. Communicating is not enough. He wants to *belong*—to interact without ever being perceived as an outsider. He is going to have to study the history, read all the classics, pick up as many obscure cultural references as possible—old television shows, out-of-print magazines, poems, expressions, and jokes...

"What are you smiling at?" asks Henrik, who is now staring at Samvel bemusedly through his own rimless glasses.

"I'm learning to be Swedish!" replies Samvel, as much to himself as to his friend.

* * *

Samvel slides comfortably into the new routines of his life in Sweden. During the week, there is school, and on Saturdays he likes to sit around with his new friends and complain about the weather. He can't believe his luck. In Armenia, people would be off to enjoy the sunshine on the weekend, and Samvel would be left alone at home with his books. Not in Sweden. Here, he can participate. Sitting in coffee shops listening to the rain or bitching about the latest snowstorm requires no skin pigment.

Then comes Sunday. In Armenia, Sunday is a busy day of church visits and encounters with relatives. It's a family day meant to nurture relationships and spend time with loved ones. In Sweden, however, Sunday is the day for loneliness and *ångest*. With the exceptions of laundry, cleaning, and watching television, there are few socially accepted activities that can be carried out on a Sunday. Nobody goes to church. That's a non-starter. Fridays and Saturdays people head to the bars and nightclubs, but drinking the night before a workday is socially taboo. As is doing anything spontaneous. For some strange reason (Samvel suspects that the unions are to blame), on Sundays most cafés close at 4 p.m., or don't open at all. It's like a vacuum in the state-regulated existence. One can't just call someone up and suggest something. Samvel has tried that and been immediately brought in line. "Tomorrow is also a day," the expression goes. At first Samvel didn't get it. That statement seemed self-evident. But what it's meant to convey is the necessity of resting and getting ready for the following day's work.

One might as well accept it, Samvel figures: Sunday is a day when nobody cares about you and you aren't meant to care about anyone else. It's a day for deep, existential *ångest*, a day to ponder the passing of time and regret the squandered opportunities. Then, Monday morning will arrive with the familiar dread that accompanies the start of a new week. The *söndagsånges*t will vanish, only to be replaced by *måndagsångest*.

SWEDISH GLASNOST

On 31 December 1987, the Swedish media monopoly officially ended; a new channel, TV3, started broadcasts via satellite from London in order to circumvent Scandinavian legislation. The government fought competition in the terrestrial network for another few decades, but it was too late. American sitcoms and Hollywood productions replaced Soviet-style state productions. A new world opened up. There was more talk about freedom and individualism than of solidarity and collective solutions.

In the 1960s, the mass media had assumed the role previously held by the social engineers of the 1930s, developing the homogeneity and shared experience that was fundamental for the continued existence of the Swedish Unimind. Through television, information had been disseminated about the right way to decorate one's home, spend one's free time, or raise one's children. With glasnost came the divorce between the state and the media, but it was a very Swedish divorce: the parties went their separate ways, but they remained on friendly terms, in full agreement about what was best for the children.

In 1989 the Berlin Wall fell, and with it the Iron Curtain, signaling the imminent demise of the Soviet superpower. The map of Europe was redrawn and Sweden's turn to the West reinforced. There was more criticism of the state and more praise for market-based solutions. Ronald Reagan's United States and Margaret Thatcher's Britain became sources of inspiration. The leftist hegemony that had been prevalent throughout the 1960s and 1970s was slowly starting to crack.[1]

In 1991, a new political party appeared on the scene. New Democracy was founded by the wealthy businessman Count Ian Wachtmeister and the self-made entrepreneur Bert Karlsson. Karlsson was a record producer and the founder of one of Sweden's first amusement parks who had made his fortune in the Swedish dance band industry. While the cultural elite laughed at him, he grew rich investing in the spandex-clad bands that had been widely popular in rural Sweden since the 1950s. Shunned by critics, these bands were nevertheless loved by the common man. And it was this "common man" whom Karlsson claimed to represent.

One day, gossip magazine *Hänt-i-veckan* reached out to Karlsson asking him to name his dream government as a joke for their next edition. Karlsson played along and submitted a list with celebrities such as Queen Silvia and IKEA founder Ingvar Kamprad as ministers. A friend told him about "a funny count" he'd seen on television and, on impulse, Karlsson crossed out his own name as prime minister and wrote Count Ian Wachtmeister instead.[2]

In 1985, Wachtmeister had published a popular satire of Swedish politics called *The Duck Pond*. Afterwards, he conducted a book tour where he expressed his disdain for the political establishment and openly mocked the leadership. Many found his disrespect refreshing and funny.[3] Here was an outsider who was wealthy and successful enough to dare criticize the establishment.

Wachtmeister found out about Karlsson's list when people began jokingly greeting him as "Mr Prime Minister." He phoned up Karlsson and they agreed to meet for coffee. *Hänt-i-veckan* showed up and wrote a half-ironical story about the encounter: "Noble Wachtmeister arrived at the meeting wearing a snappy hat, flowery tie and an exclusive briefcase. The man of the people wore sensible shoes, a leather jacket, and a plastic bag from Sparbanken in which he stored his important papers."[4]

Then, *Dagens Nyheter* got in touch with the two and asked them to write an editorial. A few days later they sent in a text entitled "This is our party program," and, just like that, New Democracy was born. The media loved this renegade party that wanted to outlaw meter maids, lower the tax on liquor, and bring the fun back into politics. Opinion polls showed a significant portion of the electorate would consider voting for the party, and this fueled the media circus even more, resulting in much airtime for the two showmen.[5]

Much like Donald Trump, the duo appealed to business and industry by advocating for drastic tax cuts while also being firmly anti-establishment, claiming to represent the interests of the working class. Then, six months after its creation by the media, New Democracy was voted into Parliament. The financial crisis of the time had forced drastic cutbacks of government-financed welfare. Meanwhile, war had erupted in the Balkans. It quickly turned into the most serious armed conflict on European territory since the Second World War, creating a stream of refugees. In Sweden, the number of asylum seekers more than tripled in a year, from 27,000 in 1991 to 84,000 in 1992.[6]

Financial crises, massive unemployment, and high levels of immigration are a volatile combination anywhere. Now in Parliament, New Democracy began to emphasize its anti-immigration rhetoric. Why should the citizens' hard-earned tax go to pay for this new mass influx of immigrants? The New Democrats' message was clear: most immigrants are criminals. Cut back on immigration and Sweden's economy will once again flourish.

UNINTENDED VICTIMS OF THE UNIMIND

He was only 3 or 4 years old at the time, but Wolfgang Zaugg still remembers it clearly. He was sitting alone with his pail and bucket in a corner of the sandbox. The dark-haired son of a German mother and a Swiss father, Wolfgang had recently moved with his family to the suburb of Vällingby, especially designed for the new, modern Swede. A group of blond boys were playing together further afield. Wolfgang approached to join them, but one of the boys dismissively shouted out: "Blackie!" Then he started a chant and the other boys joined in: "Blackie can't play with us, Blackie can't play with us!"[1]

Fast-forward a few years to the early 1960s. Wolfgang had recently started at Kungsholm's *folkskola*, one of Sweden's largest schools at the time. A few weeks into the semester, he bumped into a group of older kids in the hallway.

"Get out of the way you fucking nigger!" one of the boys exclaimed. Wolfgang looked around for the black face, but no one else was there. Stunned, he realized the comment had been meant for him.

"There were almost 2,000 students at Kungsholm's school. And I was the only one with black hair. It made me think," Wolfgang recalled in an interview more than forty years later.[2]

Despite being white, as well as born and raised in Sweden, Wolfgang always felt that his dark-brown hair set him apart, signaling that he was not a biological Swede. Håkan Henriksson, who lived next door to the family when Wolfgang was a child, remembers how he would say things like: "I'm tired of being German. I want to become Swedish. I want to be like everyone else. I want to feel at home. I don't want people to think of me as that black-haired German."[3]

In 1978 Wolfgang started the process of becoming "a real Swede." He changed his name to John Stannerman, applied to become a Swedish citizen and to carry out his military service.[4] Despite undergoing psychological treatment at the time, he was enrolled in a program for non-commissioned officers and taught to handle weapons such as machine-guns and mortars.[5]

A few years later, John changed his last name once again, this time to Ausonius, and started dying his hair and eyebrows blond. "I've always had a complex about my hair. It's way too black. It doesn't look Swedish," he told the hairdresser. In April 1991, he also started wearing baby blue contacts to cover his brown, foreign-looking eyes.[6]

A few months later, on 3 August 1991, John launched a series of attacks aiming to cleanse Sweden of other non-Swedes like himself.[7]

During the course of seven months, John shot eleven dark-haired or dark-skinned individuals, one of whom died. Several received injuries that would cripple them for life. John became known as the Laser Man because survivors of the first attacks noticed a red laser beam an instant before being hit. On 12 June 1992, the Laser Man was finally arrested when attempting to rob a bank. He was sentenced to life in prison.

Later, in an interview from prison, he explained his actions: "I felt there were too many immigrants in Sweden who simply didn't belong, because they were so many and so culturally different. They couldn't find work, they drifted about, living off of welfare benefits."[8] "The xenophobia of New Democracy resonated with me and strengthened my self-confidence."[9]

Ulf Åsgård, an expert psychiatrist in the investigation, believed John's actions were in part due to the fact that, as the child of immigrants, he was excluded and marginalized, causing a lack of self-esteem so strong that he wanted to destroy himself. "Then murdering, or attempting to murder, other immigrants becomes a kind of execution of his own self-image. That way the supposed suicide is repeated over and over."[10]

MEDIA HANGOVER

At the beginning of the 1990s, a wave of racially-related violence swept across Sweden. In addition to the attacks carried out by the Laser Man, during 1990 and 1991 there were fifty-two attacks on refugee camps involving petrol bombs, arson, and explosives.[1] Neo-Nazi groups declared war on the Swedish state. VAM, modeled after its American namesake White Aryan Resistance, became the first Swedish terror organization based on racial ideology to establish itself in the country.[2]

"How long until our Swedish children will be forced to turn their faces to Mecca?" New Democracy Deputy Party Leader Vivianne Franzén asked in one of her summer speeches.[3] Shortly thereafter, a few young men burnt down the mosque in Trollhättan. One of them quoted Franzén during the police interrogation.[4]

Appalled by the apparent impact of New Democracy's platform on the masses, the media turned off the microphone, placing the party in shadow, and only giving it attention when scrutinizing its facts or exposing New Democrats' racist remarks. The approach worked. In the election of 1994, New Democracy received a mere 1 per cent of the vote, falling out of Parliament and imploding shortly thereafter.[5]

Meanwhile, the media was left with a painful hangover. The days of monopoly might be over, but those working in media had discovered they had to be very careful with what they published, as the Swedish public apparently lacked the critical thinking skills necessary to separate opinion from fact; the good guys from the bad, and good ideas from bad ones. Used to regarding TV as a medium of instruction, disseminating "truth" that citizens should internalize and put into practice, the media concluded that the public still had to be protected from the potentially destructive influence of unfiltered debate.

The media had made New Democracy's parliamentary term possible. If they weren't aware of their power before, this experience certainly served as a reminder. The rise and fall of ND demonstrated that the media could both make a party, and break it. Consequently, it mattered greatly not only to whom they handed the microphone, but how they interpreted what was said. In practice, this meant that the openness that Swedish glasnost could have brought was instead cut short, at least as far as domestic affairs were concerned. The media resumed their role as guardians; sheltering the children from opinions and facts they weren't deemed mature enough to handle.

While racist currents, and the polarized climate of the time, have been heavily emphasized as explanations for the actions of the Laser Man, the role of social pressure has received much less attention—perhaps because it hits closer to home and makes all Swedes who fit the norm complicit. Much more than a product of New Democracy, the Laser Man was a bastard of the People's Home. It was the narrowness and imposed uniformity of Swedishness that had made him an outsider to begin with. Born and raised in Sweden, he could tap into the Unimind as easily as any Swede, but all it did was reinforce his suspicion that he constituted The Other; that he, and people like him, did not belong. Sweden's unparalleled pressure to conform, especially among those whose physical appearance ensured they never fully could, often had brutal consequences, and resulted in some unlikely alliances.

THE BLACK NAZIS

BASTARDS OF THE PEOPLE'S HOME

"Call me Nigger-Lasse!" The black boy behind the wheel turns and smiles. It is 1992 in the rural north and he has just offered two teenage girls a ride home in his blue EPA tractor.[1] A green, scented spruce, the trademark of cruisers, hangs around his rear-view mirror. The stereo is playing Ultima Thule (Farthest North), the Swedish Viking rock band of the era, known for its politically nationalist, reactionary right-wing music. They ride in silence. He lets them off in the little cul-de-sac by their apartment building. Puzzled, they look at each other. They've just met one of the driving forces behind the local branch of VAM: White Aryan Resistance.

* * *

Lars, or "Nigger-Lasse" as he called himself, was born in Bangladesh in 1976 and adopted by Swedish farmers when he was a baby. His dad told him that when he had first started daycare, he'd had to stand at the gate and physically keep people out, as they had traveled from all over to get a glimpse of the black boy. His parents named him Lars Henrik Mazud Murla Johnsson, integrating his original Bangladeshi name with his new Swedish one, so that from the very start he was equipped with dual identities.

179

My first thought when I entered puberty and started going in search of my identity was that it was simple. I am Swedish. I live in Sweden, will remain in Sweden, and die in Sweden. That's it. And that works well until one looks oneself in the mirror. I've been called a fucking nigger my whole life, from every possible and impossible direction.

So Lars began to introduce himself as Nigger-Lasse. "If that's your name there's not a whole lot worse they can call you," he says.

When asked about why he became a right-wing extremist, Lars replies: "I was trying to become an ultra-Swede." And he claims he was far from alone. "There are quite a few right-wing extremists who have been adopted from abroad. It's a way of reinforcing their assumed identity." Lars believes the reason for such self-deception is the pain involved in taking the next step:

> I remember it so vividly: Lasse, this will not work. No one buys it. You look in the mirror; you look at your dad. I am a nigger. I will always be a nigger in the eyes of others. I will never become Swedish. I will never be accepted as such. It's a very painful realization.

As an adult, Lars began to interchange his names. Sometimes he'd go by Lars, other times by Mazud. This acted as a constant reminder of the hidden racism in Swedish society. Noticing how much faster and easier it was to deal with Swedish authorities and companies using a Swedish name, he decided to conduct a test. He created two identical CVs; one under his Bangladeshi name and one under his Swedish name. He published them on the same site, on the same day. After a month, Mazud Murla had thirty-six viewings, while Lars Johnsson had some 4,500. "That says a lot about how Sweden works," says Lars. "Deep down inside Swedes are convinced that anything not Swedish is mere crap. That attitude remains very ingrained."[2]

But despite these types of testimonies from non-native Swedes, Swedish society refused to regard itself as a place where structural, racial discrimination occurred. In the three main cities of Stockholm, Gothenburg, and Malmö, there were ninety-one complaints filed for discrimination between 1992 and 1994. Only one of them went to court, while police dismissed the remaining ninety. In 1996, polls showed that two out of three black Swedes had been denied entrance to a bar or restaurant because of the color of their skin. Swedes of Iranian or Turkish origin were also frequently denied entrance. Two out of three black Swedes, as well as two out of three Iranian Swedes, also claimed they had at one point or another been denied a job because of the color of their skin.[3]

In 1991, Sweden was criticized by the UN for lacking laws against ethnic discrimination in the workplace. Despite having signed the convention against racial discrimination in 1971, it wasn't until 1994 that Sweden finally introduced such legislation. However, by the end of the millennium there had still not been a single conviction. The courts seemed to agree with the national consensus: structural, ethnic discrimination did not occur in Sweden.[4] Racism was a fringe phenomenon perpetrated by small groups of skinheads or other misguided individuals.

Professor Benjamin Teitelbaum, an expert on Nordic national-ism, believes Swedish society needs the fringe parties to serve as an alibi for Swedish society at large, assuming the very important role of scapegoat: "The role so-called organized racists tend to play in Western societies is that they allow people to say, 'I'm not racist. You mean racist like them? They are the racists!' If there is any other kind of tacit, structural racism at play in a society, the explicit racists are there to mask that—to allow some sort of quiet racism to perpetuate itself."[5]

* * *

Storuman Lake in the far north of Sweden is a place of dense forests, populated by tough men and even tougher women, like eleven-time world arm wrestling champion Heidi Andersson. Or her mother, who carried so much cement when Heidi was in her belly that she ruptured her spleen, thereby finding out she was pregnant. Plagued by mosquitoes and ruled by the Law of Jante, this is a place with little, if any, room for weakness. For most of his childhood, it was also the home of Jackie Arklöf, a black boy adopted from Liberia.

It was 1975 when a local chicken farmer brought Jackie back to this remote part of northern Sweden. He caused a stir. Many locals had never before seen a black person. At school, he was the obvious outcast. "Microphone head!" "Black skull!" "Fucking nigger!" "Swamp nigger!" the kids would taunt him. Jackie pretended not to care. Sometimes he even referred to himself as a "fucking nigger."[6] But it took its toll. At an early age, Jackie became aggressive, difficult to control and frequently in trouble.

In high school, Jackie got into a fight with Christer, a young Nazi. Not long after, Jackie bumped into Christer and a group of his Nazi friends. Jackie was alone and convinced he would be beaten senseless. He wasn't. Instead, he and the Nazis somehow managed to forge an unlikely friendship. Joined by their hatred and disdain of the society from which they felt excluded, they banded together to engage in vandalism and hooliganism. Another member of the local Nazi group was also a black, adopted boy.[7]

Most of the local young men were avid hunters, but Jackie's interest in weapons was extreme from an early age. He loved to read about warfare and was eager to do his military service. With one year left until graduation, he dropped out of high school and enlisted with a commando unit. The army did not disappoint. For the first time, Jackie felt treated like an equal. He wanted to continue to become an officer, but the commanders didn't deem him suitable.[8] When his ten-month-long service ended, Jackie was left with a sense of emptiness. Eager to engage in real combat, he decided to head to former Yugoslavia, where war had recently broken out. Jackie sympathized with the Croatian side of the Balkan wars. Croatia was one of Nazi Germany's allies during the Second World War, and Jackie had read a great deal about the Croatian Nazi militia Ustasja active during that period. He believed that Croatian culture and religion were more "civilized" and "Western" than their Muslim counterparts in the region.[9]

Jackie traveled to Bosnia and enlisted with the infamous Croatian paramilitary unit Ludvig Pavlovic. In its name he carried out countless atrocities against both armed and civilian Muslims. He regularly beat and tortured prisoners. According to his own diary, later confiscated by police, he ransacked, humiliated, and killed. On 24 August 1993, he and his comrades-in-arms launched a surprise attack on a Muslim village near Mostar: "We throw hand grenades through the windows, then rush in and liquidate all living," Jackie summarized the day in his diary. On 27 August, he wrote:

> A terrible stench of corpses surrounds us. There are rumors that the UN might come to make controls, as well as the humanitarian aid and the Red Cross. Our Colonel gives the order to immediately dispose of all civilian bodies. Burn or bury, a dirty job without equal. The stench sticks to the uniform, especially from half-burned bodies.[10]

On 4 May 1995, Jackie's time as a mercenary came to an abrupt end when he was surprised by Bosnian military police in Mostar. They found a swastika in his wallet and discovered that he was wanted for war crimes. Jackie spent a month in military prison, during which time he was systematically beaten until the Swedish State Department learnt of his incarceration. At his trial Jackie admitted to most of the crimes of which he stood accused. In September 1995, he was sentenced to thirteen years in prison for war crimes, involving several cases of abuse and torture of civilians as well as prisoners of war. A psychiatrist appointed by the court of Mostar examined Jackie and concluded that, while he did not suffer from a psychological illness, he did have a psychopathic personality structure, involving aggression and deviating morals. According to the psychiatrist, the root cause of this was the fact that he grew up as the only person of color in a small village where he was not accepted.[11]

After the signing of the Dayton agreement, the war in Bosnia finally came to an end. In September 1996, Jackie was released in an exchange of prisoners and able to return to Sweden. As he had only served a year of his sentence, the Swedish prosecution service also decided to press charges against him. But Jackie changed his story, pled not guilty to any of the crimes that he had previously confessed to before both the Bosnian court and several Swedish journalists. Unable to locate Bosnian witnesses, the head prosecutor Jan Danielsson decided to release Jackie, who walked out of jail less than a month after returning to Sweden, along with 27,000 SEK from the Swedish state as compensation for his month in detention.[12]

His return garnered a great deal of attention in Swedish media. Many expressed their resentment, but there was one person whose reaction was the opposite. In Tidaholm prison, Nazi Tony Olsson was serving time for conspiracy to commit murder. He realized that Jackie could be a valuable soldier in the Nazi liberation war that he dreamt of launching in Sweden, and decided to write him a letter. Jackie's response was immediate, and the two men began to correspond.[13]

Back in Swedish society, Jackie's Nazi convictions grew. He left Storuman for Östersund, where he joined the local Nazi group, NS Östersund. They decided to accept him despite his color as long as he shared their ideology. "But when we came to power he would have to be castrated," adds a local Nazi who describes Jackie as a close, loyal, and reliable friend.[14]

In February 1998, Olsson finally revealed his plans for Jackie. He had founded his own militant Nazi organization, modeled after the IRA, with the goal of overthrowing the parliamentary system. In a letter, Olsson expressed admiration for the military knowledge and experience that Jackie had acquired in former Yugoslavia and asked if he was interested in helping to build up the organization's military capabilities. He signed off: "I hope that we can meet in the future and regard each other as participants in a struggle that mutually bonds us together as brothers for a noble cause. Your Friend. Tony Olsson."[15]

Jackie and Olsson continued to correspond throughout the spring and summer of 1998. Jackie also communicated his convictions elsewhere, for example in the party magazine *The True National Socialist*, drawing on his experiences from the Balkans to argue against multiculturalism:

> The civil war lasted 5 bloody years. The bloodiest part of which took place in Bosnia, because it was home to Croats, Serbs, and Muslims. They all wanted their own republic or religion, and no one would give in! The price for the multicultural society of Yugoslavia was high, more than 700,000 dead and more than a million homeless and on the run. So, what then have "our" politicians learnt from this? Nothing! They continue to pack non-Swedes into every corner of this country.[16]

In his letters, Olsson began to stress how important sound finances were for the struggle to be successful. As soon as he was granted leave from prison, the two men met in person. Throughout the fall of 1998, Olsson and a fellow Nazi prisoner, Mats Nilsson, were granted regular leave from prison under the pretext of being involved in a play. They introduced Jackie to another Nazi on the outside, Andreas Axelsson. While Olsson was on leave, he and Axelsson robbed a supermarket. It was Jackie's turn to join forces with Axelsson on the next one. During the winter and spring of 1998–9, the men carried out a series of robberies to fund their struggle.[17]

On 28 May 1999, they executed their biggest hit yet. Olsson, Jackie, and Axelsson robbed the bank Östgöta Enskilda in Kisa, southeastern Sweden. They managed to get out with 2.6 million SEK, but were closely pursued by police. In nearby Malexander, a shootout took place. The two pursuing police officers were gunned down, and Axelsson injured. Before continuing their escape, Jackie walked up to the police vehicle to make sure the policemen were both dead. He found Officer Olle Borén lying face down in a ditch, and shot him in the neck. The other officer, Robert Karlström, was lying on his back behind the police car. Jackie put a bullet in his forehead.[18]

Axelsson's injuries were such that he was forced to seek medical attention. The hospital notified police. A few days after arresting Axelsson, police tracked down and captured Olsson and Jackie. The three men were eventually sentenced to life in prison for murder.[19]

Years later, journalist Magnus Sandelin interviewed Jackie in prison. When asked why a black man wants to become a Nazi, Jackie replied: "Many believe that it stems from self-contempt on my part, but it didn't. It was much more about the fact that I wanted to be like all other Swedes, and to really show that, I turned to Nazism."[20]

* * *

While the vast majority of adopted children obviously don't become violent Nazis, there is a widespread sentiment of exclusion among adoptees; of never being fully accepted as a "real" Swede. With 60,000 adopted children, Sweden has the most foreign-born adopted children per capita in the world. Sixty-five per cent of them arrived in the 1970s.[21] And, in the past few years, increasing numbers have begun to speak out about their experiences. On social media, in documentaries, and news programs, their testimonies share a common plight.

A local Green Party politician living in Varberg, but adopted from Sri Lanka, expressed it well in his editorial titled "I became your monster" (*Jag blev ert monster*):

My name is Martin Öberg. Yes, I know, I don't look like a Martin Öberg. I've heard that before. Many seem to find it important to let me know that I deviate, that there is something wrong with my Swedishness. Coming out as gay was a piece of cake compared to coming out as Swedish.

Öberg goes on to talk about the feelings that many adoptees share: feelings of not belonging, of being "too brown to be Swedish, but too Swedish to be anything else," and the constant demands for displays of gratitude over the amazing opportunity to be raised in safe and affluent Sweden. "I would have loved to be Swedish. But you've never allowed me to be, and for as long as I live that will remain as a hard, sharp thorn in my heart."

The most striking part of Öberg's text is when he, not unlike Lars or Jackie, catches that same prejudice in himself: "Still to this day I can feel contempt when I see someone else who is black. A cold, split second before the shame overcomes me and I realize that I'm a white man under my brown skin, a white man with the white man's gaze."[22]

* * *

Foreign-born adoptees are more likely to be unemployed as adults and more dependent on social allowances. They also suffer more than Swedish-born residents from drug and alcohol abuse as well as psychiatric conditions. They are also less likely to start a family, and many have low incomes as adults despite having been adopted by middle-class or upper-class Swedes. According to the Swedish health authorities, rates of suicide are 3.5 to 4 times higher for this group than for the Swedish-born population. Among adoptees from Korea, it is the most common cause of death.[23]

In a 2017 documentary about the shared experiences of adopted children, Patrik Lundberg, of Korean origin, speaks about his childhood: "I didn't walk around the school hallways and perform perfunctory *heils*. I didn't do that, but perhaps I used expressions that I shouldn't have, especially when it came to pinpointing other immigrants as 'The Other' while stressing that I was a part of the Swedish collective."[24]

PART THREE

THE DISSIDENT, THE IMMIGRANT,
AND THE FIGHT FOR THE UNIMIND

CHANG MAKES A FRIEND

It starts with the sound of a revving engine. Someone is speeding up and down the street outside Chang's house. Chang steps out to see what's going on when an older boy comes rushing past again on his moped. He screeches to a halt in front of Chang. "Is it tuned?" Chang asks.

"Of course." Legally, mopeds aren't meant to go very fast, so manufacturers have to install restricting devices. Luckily, they are easy to bypass.

"So, what did you do to it?" Chang asks.

"I just unscrewed these bolts on the air intake case. Then I removed the case and drilled holes in it. You want to be careful to only place the holes on the side that faces outwards." Chang knows all this very well, but he also knows that asking is part of the expected small talk.

"What's your name?"

"Dan." Chang studies Dan as he points at the upgrades on the bike. He's tall, blond, and fairly strong-looking. Chang figures he must be a couple of years older. Chang is 14, but he already has a moped of his own. He brings it out and, after a few minutes of comparing carburetors and cylinders, he knows he and Dan will be friends.

Dan lives in the forest with his mother, who smokes yellow Blend cigarettes under the kitchen fan. His room is a battlefield of empty beer cans, cigarette butts, and dirty laundry. He listens to nationalist Viking rock and on the walls are posters promoting both the nationalist Sweden Democrats and their predecessors Bevara Sverige Svenskt (Keep Sweden Swedish), along with racist propaganda.

Chang has heard about New Democracy, but this is his first exposure to the Sweden Democrats and the Keep Sweden Swedish movement. He can't recall having seen anything about them in the media.

Chang notices a sticker depicting a caricature of a black man with big lips and a bone in his hands. "Is this the future of the Swedish race?" the text reads. Chang finds the image a little crude, but who is he to judge. Dan could be rightwing, leftwing, Arab, or Jew for all he cares; he has finally found a friend. They have fun together, riding around on their mopeds, stealing apples from backyards, and catching crayfish.

* * *

One evening Chang ends up at a party with skinheads. Not one to shy away from confrontation, he immediately puts his cards on the table: "You know I'm both a Jew and a gypsy, right?"

The room falls silent. The skinheads eye Chang, exchange glances, then one of them says: "Okay. Do you want a beer or what?" Chang is intrigued. People who say they are open shun him. Now people who are known to shun others are accepting him. What do they want?

Chang has been taking more of an interest in politics lately, and has recently joined the youth branch of the Moderate Party in an attempt to increase opposition to the Social Democrats. The society they built—the People's Home, the "open" society accepting of all—is a lie. His brother. The Travelers. The Different. What they have, they've clawed out for themselves. They're on their own.

CHANG MAKES A FRIEND

Chang spends a long time chatting with a nerdy-looking guy named Jimmie, who has recently been elected president of the Sweden Democrats' Youth League. Jimmie is convinced one day the party will enter Parliament. Chang thinks that Jimmie must be smoking something.

Ten years later, Jimmie will be proven right.

* * *

By the start of the new millennium, the neo-Nazi skinhead culture was unraveling. In part, this was due to stricter enforcement of hate speech laws, but an equally important part was the advent of online file sharing.[1] When white-power music made its breakthrough in 1993, many of the radical nationalist groups advocating militant struggle had reinvented themselves as production companies in order to finance their movement.[2] When their music could be accessed for free on the Internet, giants such as Nordland and Ragnarock Records, some of the biggest producers of white-power music and hate propaganda in the world, went bankrupt or dormant. Desperate for other sources of income, an increasing number of skinheads turned to crime. It wasn't long before many high-profile members had ended up behind bars. All the commotion aside, they could show little in the way of political achievements. Crude racism was increasingly considered both unpalatable and inefficient. In the post-skinhead era, many patriots yearned for a more civilized form of nationalism.[3]

Founded in 1988, the first leader of the Sweden Democrats was Anders Klarström, formerly linked to the far-right Nordic Reich Party and convicted for anti-Semitic death threats.[4] While he had distanced himself from his past, Klarström did not want to ban Nazis from attending the party's demonstrations, and the image of rowdy skinheads would continue to haunt the Sweden Democrats for years to come. Mikael Jansson, formerly active in the Center Party, took over as leader in 1995. He began the process of cleaning out all visible signs of racism and Nazism, but the party rhetoric was still harsh. For example, the party's 1996 program stated that any immigrant who had arrived in Sweden after 1970 should be repatriated to their home country, even if they were married to a Swede.[5]

Jimmie Åkesson joined the party in 1995, the same year that the party leadership transferred from Klarström to Jansson. He believed that the extremist rhetoric of many Sweden Democrats prevented the party's further expansion. In order to create a wider public appeal, any remaining racists and Nazi followers would have to be purged. This required new, firm leadership. In 2000, Åkesson was elected head of the Youth League, and in 2005 he was named party leader. In 2001, the more radical factions of the party broke away to form the National Democrats. Åkesson continued to purge the party of any symbols and rhetoric that were keeping it from crossing the 4 per cent vote share threshold for entering Parliament.[6]

The new leadership distanced itself from the ethnic nationalism of the past and launched the notion of "open Swedishness," which in theory meant that immigrants could very well be considered Swedish—if they assimilated, learning Sweden's language, culture, and traditions.

SWEDISH PSEUDO-CONFLICT

"I just found this in the recycling bin today." Alexander holds up an empty yoghurt container and accusingly looks around at the students gathered in the dorm kitchen.

Samvel glances at his Kurdish hallmate, Gurbet, and sees his own failure to comprehend reflected in her face. "Was it in the wrong compartment?" he finally asks.

"No, but it hadn't been rinsed out," Alex replies, his voice breaking under the pressure of restrained anger. "Containers like these will remain at the recycling stations for weeks. Imagine the stench something like this would create had I not caught it and rinsed it out properly!" He puts it back in the recycling box and storms out of the kitchen.

Alex is the self-declared controller of Samvel's dorm. He is a longhaired, fashionably bearded, vegetarian hipster, who is noticeably embarrassed by his Stockholm accent and the fact that he was raised in an upper middle-class home. Roaming through other people's garbage, on the other hand, apparently does not embarrass him. It turns out this behavior is not uncommon in Swedish neighborhoods.

Twelve students share a corridor and a kitchen, about half of them Swedes and the other half international students like Samvel. The Swedes are eager to show the internationals how things are done. But it's the way they go about it that fascinates Samvel. He has come to regard them, particularly Alex, as a litmus test of Swedishness.

One day an African student has put a frozen fish in the blender, causing it to break. Alex calls a meeting to go over kitchen rules. The girl who broke the blender is not present. "It is not allowed to put fish in the blender," Alex informs the students gathered. Just as he finishes his sentence, the offender strolls into the kitchen. Alex turns and watches her enter, nodding in stern greeting. She nods back, but then walks past him to retrieve something from her cupboard.

She apparently didn't come for the meeting.

Alex tries to recover. He turns back to the group, nodding. Behind him the girl closes the cupboard and turns around to leave. Several students, including Alex, saw her break the blender, yet nobody asks her to stay. Samvel looks at the girl, then at his fellow students. It's as though they are trying not to look, pretending they haven't noticed her. Samvel wants to say something. Is no one going to say anything? Is nobody going to tell her that a meeting is underway and that she ought to attend since she is the cause of it?

The girl leaves.

"It is not allowed to put fish in the blender," Alex repeats.

"But we didn't..." one of the other students tries to protest.

"It's not about assigning blame." Alex cuts him off and pauses, raising his hand and lowering his gaze like a disappointed father collecting himself. He takes an audible breath. "We are simply here to go over and clarify the rules of the kitchen," Alex continues, with the passive-aggressive restraint that Samvel has come to associate with Swedish pseudo-conflict.

CHANG AT HOME AT THE SCRAPYARD

From his office window, Niklas watches as another truckload full of metal turns into his scrapyard on the outskirts of the southern town of Kristianstad. It's Georg's boys and their friend Jonny again. As usual, Chang is driving. Niklas suspects he's the only one of them who still has his license.

Niklas walks down the stairs and steps outside to greet them. Large mountains of colorful scrap metal surround him on all sides. Cords, cables, and massive sheets of metal are stacked taller than the surrounding buildings. To most people it probably looks like garbage, but Niklas knows what it's worth. He has built a recycling empire on scraps. Eventually it all gets sorted and processed; old Christmas lights are stripped of their copper, batteries of their lead. Beneath a surface of junk run blood vessels of gold. Every day is like a treasure hunt. One never knows what people, particularly Georg's boys, will bring by.

Niklas is himself a Traveler, and a very successful entrepreneur. In addition to his scrapyard, he owns and runs a motel, and a restaurant. As such, he is always working, but he tries also to set aside time for the things that matter most, like family and his horses. And he takes pride in the Travelers' tradition of being hospitable and looking after his kind. He'd like to help Georg's boys, but Arnold makes him weary. He suspects that the metal he brings by hasn't always been acquired honestly. Convicted of multiple crimes, Arnold has been in and out of different institutions since the age of fifteen. His friend Jonny is on a similar path. But Chang is different. After graduating from high school, he immediately left Osby, and his mother, behind. Now in his early twenties, he has completed his military service and studies mechanical engineering at Kristianstad University. Niklas considers him a smart kid. There has to be a better way for him.

* * *

"When are you going to stop delivering your brother's stolen metals and come work for me?" Niklas jokes. They've just unloaded the latest heap of scraps and are sealing their deal with a cup of coffee.

Chang laughs, but one morning when school's out for summer, Niklas finds him out on the scrapyard picking away at self-assigned tasks. The next morning he shows up again. And the next. There's been no agreement or salary discussion, but the boy does good work. Niklas figures he ought to start paying him.

The last generation of traditional Travelers is still doing the rounds in Sweden. Old men of quirky appearance show up at the scrapyard with pickup trucks filled to the brim with scrap metals, collected from the back roads and farms of southern Sweden. Quite a few of the men are already in their seventies; some have passed eighty. Wearing dirty jeans with a cash-stacked wallet in the back pocket, checkered flannel shirts that rarely covered their bellies, and pointy shoes, they stop by every day and stay for hours, drinking many cups of coffee and telling their colorful stories of life on the road.

When he isn't too busy, Niklas likes to share a story or two himself: "'So do you have any money or assets for us today?' the debt collector asks. 'Sure, I keep all my savings in here,' the man—let's call him Conny—replies.'" The old men giggle. They all know Conny. And they've probably heard this story before, but no one interrupts. Niklas has the floor.

"'Are you joking?' the debt collector wonders. 'Hell no. Come on in and I'll show you.' So Conny brings the debt collector around to his backyard and walks him over to the sewage tank. He lifts the lid, points down at the brown liquid and says, 'That's where I keep them.' The collector shines his flashlight into the tank. 'You hide your money down there?' 'Yup, it's right there,' Conny replies. 'Can't you see it?' 'What do you mean?' the debt collector asks, bewildered, covering his nose now because the stench is so bad."

Niklas stops for effect and has a sip of coffee. "'Well,' says Conny ..." Niklas puts his cup down and leans back in his chair. "'I've spent all my money on food and then I shat it all out!'" The old men fold over laughing, their round bellies hanging out from underneath their short, wrinkly shirts.

Chang is right there with them, soaking it all up. He's hungry for the legends and Niklas likes that they seem to give him a sense of context and belonging. Sometimes he has to remind the boy that they contain a great deal of bullshit. Niklas has grown up with these stories and he knows that a new layer of exaggeration is added with every season. What started as a scratch becomes a life-threatening wound in less than a decade. These tales aren't meant to be taken literally; they are meant to be entertaining and build the common mythology that creates a sense of shared destiny.

Except for the hospitality, the legends, and the language, not much of the Traveler culture has survived into the new millennium. Niklas considers himself lucky to have such regular contact with the last generation that hasn't assimilated. And he likes that Chang is now able to spend time with these old men as well. In the process of learning about the Travelers, Chang also learns more about his father.

Georg was known for his uncanny way of walking into an establishment and immediately knowing if it was worth his time. Was there someone there who'd take a cut on the side, someone who'd be willing to strike a mutually beneficial deal? He'd travel and get to know people across the country so that when someone needed something, he'd always know just who could deliver. Niklas can tell that Chang has his father's eye for good business, but he is by no means perfect. On numerous occasions Niklas finds himself outside Chang's student dorm, physically banging on his door, because calling doesn't seem to wake him up. Anybody else would be fired for tardiness, but Niklas is determined to see Chang live up to his potential.

When Chang finally does get out of bed and isn't too busy drinking coffee while listening to the old men's tales, he has a great deal to contribute. When Niklas decides to ensure his scrapyard is environmentally friendly and ISO-certified, Chang is able to put his academic knowledge to use. He manages the process flawlessly, saving Niklas a great deal of money.

Chang spends Christmas and other public holidays with Niklas and his family. Before long, it feels like that's the way it has always been.

* * *

Chang sits in his barren office overlooking the scrapyard. The walls are brown and the desk dusty. He's in his work overalls, phoning his way through a list of all the municipal energy companies in the country. He knows new government policies will soon force these companies to get rid of all electricity meters that can't be read remotely. That means they will soon have a great deal of metal waste to dispose of, and Chang figures few of them know how much all that metal is worth. "Have you considered how to dispose of your electronic waste? I work at a recycling company and if you can gather large enough quantities, you don't have to pay anything to get rid of it," Chang repeats over and over.

At Tekniska verken in Linköping, he strikes gold. It turns out they have already replaced a great quantity of meters. The old ones sit idly in a massive warehouse.

"We have huge quantities. Take it all," is the reply. By offering to collect and scrap them for free, Chang is able to gather hundreds of tons of metal scrap. He and a truck driver go to pick it up and transport it all the way down to Denmark, where they sell the metal by the kilogram, making a substantial profit for Niklas.

* * *

Miles and miles of obsolete overhead wires line the roads like sagging laundry lines. After the massive Cyclone Gudrun in 2005, large parts of southern Sweden are left without power. Energy companies are pressured by the government to weatherproof their cables, causing them to shift to underground cables. Left above ground are the remnants of outdated technology. The overhead wires are ideal for scrapping, as they only need to be cut in order to more or less fall apart into their components, requiring very little sorting. Chang learns that the costly job of tearing down the wires is open to the lowest bidder. He decides this is the business he needs to be in, but Niklas is not interested in branching out. He feels it's too risky, so Chang resigns from the scrapyard and starts his own company. By negotiating to keep the scrap metal afterwards, he is able to outbid any competitors and achieve a turnover of more than 3 million SEK in his first year.

Overnight, Chang becomes a success story. The local media love him, featuring stories with titles like "Chang Frick Brightens the Atmosphere." They write about Chang's sponsorship of the local ice hockey team and about the fact that he often plays the trumpet at local sports events. The young newcomer can do no wrong. On 23 October 2008, the day before his twenty-fifth birthday, Chang is selected as Kristianstad's Young Entrepreneur of the Year.

* * *

"What the hell are they doing roaming about in the middle of the day, sitting about in cafés? Where do they get their money?" Roland comments, stubbing out another one of his cigarettes in a tin container.

"And where are their women? At home by the stove?" one of the younger guys comments, spitting his snuff out the window of the excavator.

In his new line of business, Chang interacts with a variety of working-class Swedes across the south. Out on their excavators in the forest, or behind the wheels of their trucks, they are increasingly, but cautiously, opening up about their fears. They've had enough of immigration. They are worried the increased cost to the system threatens their pensions. What will happen if they fall ill, or become unemployed? Will the state be able to afford to help them with all these immigrants coming in? Sweden is changing at a speed that terrifies many. Chang feels some fears are exaggerated, but others he can understand. Regardless of the opinions expressed, what troubles him is the reticence with which they are expressed.

"I don't vote for the Social Democrats, nor the Moderates," says Roland, flashing Chang a crooked smile.

"Okay, so who do you vote for?"

"Who do you think?"

Chang shrugs his shoulders. How the hell should he know, and why does this guy think he even cares? Roland remains silent for a while, then whispers: "The Sweden Democrats." He locks Chang's gaze, waiting for a reaction.

"Why are you whispering?" Chang asks.

CHANG AT HOME AT THE SCRAPYARD

"It's sensitive stuff. One has to be careful, especially around that guy," Roland says and motions with his head to indicate another worker. "He's active in the union."

Fearing that they will be branded as racist, many of the workers only dare express their opinions at home or deep in the forest surrounded by like-minded friends. Some say they even lie to the opinion polls, but there is no doubt; the silent support for the Sweden Democrats keeps growing. Even so, when someone does muster the courage to speak up more boldly, the feared consequences often materialize. Chang has heard of truck drivers being excluded from their unions. People have their windows smashed in. Some even lose their jobs because of their political opinions, though the latter is often hard to prove, as officially it's always pinned on something else.

In Chang's mind it is clear and simple—it is bullying. These aren't evil people, nor are the majority of them racist. They are just afraid about the impact of the immigration policies, and have lost faith in the elites to protect their interests. But somehow the discussion is taboo and any criticism of the national position off limits. When Chang tries to raise the topic with his Moderate Party comrades, the conversation is immediately shut down. Whether people agree or not, the subject is apparently too sensitive to even discuss.

The week before the 2002 general election, a team of undercover investigative journalists from Swedish Television travelled the far reaches of the country, visiting local campaign offices for each of the political parties. Posing as concerned citizens wanting to discuss immigration, they filmed their interactions with a hidden camera and caught several local members of the Moderate Party making xenophobic or racist statements. Christer Ewe, a Moderate representative on Kristianstad City Council, said, "Muslims are good at having many children and abusing our system." According to Swedish Television, all seventeen Moderate politicians filmed candidly had expressed strong support for a more restrictive immigration policy.[1]

The report caused a media frenzy. Whatever their feelings on the subject, henceforth Moderate politicians watched their tongues carefully. When the 2006 election came around, no one wanted anything to do with ideas that could in any way be interpreted as xenophobic.

Under the leadership of Fredrik Reinfeldt, the conservative Moderate Party had successfully rebranded itself as the new "Worker's Party," claiming to be the only party to represent citizens who actually worked, as opposed to those who depended on welfare. This earned them 26 per cent of the vote in 2006, a drastic increase from the 15 per cent they had managed to scrape together in 2002. Together with the Liberals, the Center Party, and the Christian Democrats, the Moderates formed a right-of-center coalition with Reinfeldt as the new prime minister.

Nyamko Sabuni of the Liberal Party became the new minister for integration. She introduced a series of proposals she believed would support integration. One of Sabuni's proposals questioned why Sweden granted paid parental leave retroactively to immigrant families arriving with children. In Sweden, the state grants parents 480 days of paid leave to care for each child. The bulk of these days are obviously used when the child is a baby. However, at the time, parents could distribute them as they wished until the child reached 8 years of age. Since many immigrant families arrived with several young children, the parents could add up all their parental days and be paid to stay at home caring for their children for long periods of time. Sabuni's argument was that this was to the detriment of both children and parents, especially women, as it prevented them from learning the language and delayed their entry into the workforce. Children who did not go to preschool did not learn Swedish and consequently had greater difficulties when the time came to start elementary school at age seven.[2]

The proposal to remove retroactive parental pay for immigrants was met with fierce rejection by the media and politicians alike. Meanwhile, Sabuni, herself a Burundian-born black woman who had arrived in Sweden as an immigrant, was branded a racist and intensely criticized by political opponents and comrades alike. "This is a move that should not come from a minister for integration and equality, so from now on she'll have to call herself minister of segregation, because that is what she is," left-wing MP Kalle Larsson said on Swedish Television. "Sabuni crawls through the populist mud," wrote Social Democrat Evin Cetin in an *Aftonbladet* editorial. "What will be her next proposal—separate benches for whites?"[3] In *Dagens Nyheter*, Sabuni was accused of "reinforcing racism and discrimination."[4] Even members of Sabuni's own party objected. On Swedish Radio, Liberal Party member Mikael Trolin said: "She has taken what we call an Uncle Tom role ... pandering to the prejudice we believe flourishes among great parts of the population and the middle class."[5] The media eagerly extended the microphone to anyone who had something critical or derogatory to say of Sabuni, who was eventually replaced as minister for integration against her own wishes.[6]

When Minister for Migration and Asylum Tobias Billström used the expression "volumes" while talking about the number of refugees traveling to Sweden, he too was publicly scolded—on Swedish Television, by his own party leader, Prime Minister Reinfeldt: "We don't use that kind of language. Immigration enriches Sweden."[7] Billström was now labeled xenophobic, despite the fact that he had overseen some of the most extensive liberalizations of immigration policy that Sweden had seen since the 1960s.[8]

Regardless of source, nuance, or intent, the Unimind allowed for only one, binary opinion—accepting refugees of any kind and in any amount was the right thing to do.

SWEDISH IMMERSION

It is Saturday afternoon and Samvel has just been invited to have dinner with his friends Henrik and Gurbet. He wants to bring a bottle of their favorite Amarone wine, but by the time he stands beneath the green and yellow sign that marks the entrance to Systembolaget (literally "The System Company"), it has already closed. It is only 3 p.m., but as Sweden has an alcohol monopoly, only the government-run chain of stores is allowed to sell alcoholic beverages, and they try to avoid doing so. Through a combination of limited opening hours, exorbitant alcohol tax, and odd rules, they aim to decrease consumption.

Samvel can't quite get used to the bizarreness of shopping in a place where the salespeople are meant to dissuade you from buying more than you intended; where there are never any special deals, ads, or promotions; and where you are always made to feel a little bit guilty for contributing to the deterioration of the *folkhälsa* (people's health). "Try alcohol-free," is the only spontaneous recommendation staff are allowed to make, as they must "sell responsibly" and inform shoppers about the risks.

Restaurants, bars, and nightclubs are Samvel's other options, but they are so expensive that, for a student like him, drinking out is not feasible. Consequently, he arrives apologetically empty-handed at Henrik's place. It's a bright, one-bedroom apartment arranged in a very Swedish manner, with an IKEA Billy bookcase juxtaposed beside an exclusive Norrgavel sofa, with its characteristic wooden frame. As Samvel takes a seat on the fine, off-white fabric, he is reminded of all the times he has helped Henrik carry this family heirloom to different student dorms and temporary housing options. "I tried to get some wine, but Systembolaget was closed," he comments sheepishly.

"As it should be," Henrik immediately counters. "Alcohol is a huge drain on society. It costs taxpayers tens of billions every year—addiction, disease, violence, accidents, deaths..." he pontificates.

"Sure, but it's a question of freedom," Samvel replies. "Shouldn't it be up to me if I want to drink myself to death?"

"Not when society has to pay for it. Do you know what would happen if the state abolished its alcohol monopoly? I was just reading this. Every year there would be an additional 29,000 cases of physical abuse, and many thousands more cases of DUI and alcohol-related deaths. It's important for the *folkhälsa*."

That word *folk*, again... Samvel sighs wearily. In a society where the unhealthy choices of individuals are billed to the taxpayer, the state will naturally want to keep you from making sub-optimal choices, but freedom, and choice, suffer in the process.

"We're having tacos," Gurbet exclaims as she and Henrik bring out the bowls of carefully chopped up vegetables.

"And it's not even Friday," Henrik adds with a smirk that accentuates his dimples.

"Very *osvenskt* [un-Swedish]," Samvel smiles back.

Having first Swedified Chinese food beyond recognition in the 1970s, a couple of decades later, the Swedes took on Mexican food, and turned "tacos" into the national Friday staple in many homes. Having stripped them of their beans and most of the spices—and so most of the flavor—the average Swede can now enjoy the exotic feeling of experiencing a foreign dish without challenging the palette. With each ingredient served in a separate bowl, everyone is free to pick and choose what they like, composing their own ideal "taco." Individual choice from a limited range of options, a contemporary *smörgåsbord* of sorts—in many ways, a culinary expression of state individualism.

Over the last decade or so, the taco has become intimately associated with the concept of *fredagsmys* ("Friday coziness"), the Swedish tradition of celebrating the end of the working week with a predictable meal and some downtime in front of the TV. This causes the trend-sensitive Swedes to feel unconventional, a little wild and crazy, even, if they consume Friday-night tacos on a different day of the week.

But there are limits to how far off the beaten track one can stray, in mind and spirit. "If consumers could buy alcohol at grocery stores, the number of venues would multiply, and opening hours would increase by 76 per cent," Henrik says, returning to the subject of the state's monopoly on alcoholic beverages. "76 per cent! Privatization, in any form, would increase competition, which would lead to lower prices, and increased availability ... and so on ... things we know would increase drinking."

Samvel is baffled. Every Swede he knows seems like a hologram of the entire Swedish system. How does one even begin to argue with someone who just spits facts at you and writes off any emotional argument as irrational? Henrik is Samvel's best friend, but whenever certain topics come up, it's like a robot takes his place and begins to play a propaganda recording. Even among friends, there is this bureaucratic approach to solving problems. And there is a routine for everything. To meet people, Samvel has tried joining clubs and associations, but the strict administrative procedures for how everything has to be done—meetings held, receipts scanned and copied—soon kills any joy he gets from it. Everything is not about facts and logic.

"It's not like Swedes drink any less than other nationalities," Samvel counters.

At least Henrik is open to an argument, more than can be said for most Swedes. Usually they just sit with unlistening eyes, waiting for their turn to talk. Not once has Samvel been able to persuade a Swede to change their mind on any given issue. It's hard to keep track of all the things one has to do, say, and believe. Pro-life? Don't even go there. Attempting to argue against free abortion will get you socially ostracized in an instant. Israel versus Palestine? No point discussing it: Israel is the bad guy. The "zero-tolerance" drug policy... Samvel can think of countless examples where there is only one acceptable answer.

But hardest of all are the many unspoken rules and expectations that characterize Swedish society. This is not an area where Samvel can simply ask someone and receive a straight-up answer. Officially there is no "right way" to behave in Sweden. Diversity is supposedly valued and multiculturalism constitutionally enshrined, but socially, nothing is further from the truth. Being different is not appreciated, and even someone as introverted as Samvel has to learn greater self-restraint. Hold back, observe, and imitate.

The greatest source of anxiety is never quite knowing if he is behaving in the right way or not. It doesn't help that both the political leadership and the media insist there is no such thing as Swedish culture. This only means that no one corrects or points out his faux pas; instead he'll simply feel their quiet disapproval without knowing exactly what he has done wrong. The unwillingness of Swedes to openly admit they believe there is a "right way" of doing things makes integration very difficult.

It made Samvel feel a little bit better when he learned that the self-perception of being cultureless is actually a typical Swedish characteristic. According to ethnologists such as Åke Daun, Swedes tend to look down on people who are governed by their culture, traditions, or religion, dismissing them as not yet having reached the Swedish level of modernity, democracy, equality, and rationality. Somehow, Swedes fail to realize that this is as ethno-centric a viewpoint as any other.[1] Swedishness, they seem to think, is not a culture but an ideal end state, a sort of Nirvana that even less developed people like Samvel can eventually reach.

Henrik interrupts his train of thought: "Swedes definitely don't drink as much as most nationalities."

"Sure you do. You guys get wasted all the time," Samvel insists.

"But we don't drink very often."

"No less than other people."

"Yeah, way less!"

"Cut it out and eat already," Gurbet interjects, shoving a bowl of chopped, red onions in Henrik's direction. Samvel sprinkles minced meat over his soft tortilla and focuses on being grateful for the fact that his friends are unconventional enough to have him over for "Friday tacos" on a Saturday.

* * *

"In our relations with other people we mainly discuss and evaluate their character and behavior. That is why I have voluntarily withdrawn from nearly all so-called relations. This has made my old age rather lonely."

Professor Isak Borg sits crouched over his desk in his old-fashioned office. He has his back turned to the camera as his inner monologue plays. His voice sounds very unfamiliar to Samvel. He is used to watching the dubbed Russian version of Bergman's *Wild Strawberries*. This is the first time he has taken on the original in Swedish. The protagonist, Professor Borg, sounds nothing like what Samvel is used to, speaking an old-fashioned Swedish filled with expressions with which he is not acquainted. Perhaps he isn't ready. He considers switching back to the familiar Russian version, but decides against it. He has to power through.

He is rewarded about forty minutes in, when he suddenly feels it click. It is the scene where Professor Borg is having lunch with the young hitchhikers: "I believe that modern man looks his own meaninglessness in the eye, believing only in himself and his own biological death. Anything else is nonsense," says Borg's young acquaintance Viktor, who is studying to become a doctor.

"Modern man is a figment of your imagination. Man regards his death with horror and can't stand the meaninglessness," replies theology student Anders.

Viktor: "So be it; religion for the people; opium for the aching limb." The phrase echoes in Samvel's head: "*För all del, religionen åt folket; opium åt den värkande lemmen.*" The language has taken on a life of its own. Samvel finds himself no longer fighting to translate each phrase. The dialogue, in all its eloquence, hits him straight in the chest. The nuance and beauty that was lost in translation is found.

Not until the credits begin to roll does Samvel snap out of Bergman's universe. He becomes aware once again of his surroundings: the narrow bed, the barren student dorm. A sense of accomplishment and satisfaction fills him as he looks around the room at nothing in particular. He did it.

THE UNIMIND ENFORCES ITS BOUNDARIES

Eggs, bottles, and rotten fruit fly through the air. The noise from multiple megaphones embedded in the crowd is so loud it drowns out the speeches of the Sweden Democrats. The campaign ahead of the 2010 election is a heated affair across the entire country. Now convinced that the Sweden Democrats are needed to counterbalance Sweden's political correctness, lack of honest discussion, and false self-image as some kind of multicultural utopia, Chang has left the Moderate Party, joined the Sweden Democrats, and agreed to run for office on Kristianstad City Council. As it turns out, making himself heard is more challenging than it was to write his speech. At many of the party's rallies, such large numbers of counter-demonstrators show up booing and blowing whistles that the party's speakers are unable to get their message across.

Sometimes their opponents throw rocks, and venues are so frequently vandalized that they begin to have trouble renting meeting sites.[1]

When they finally decide to end the event, Chang heads straight for his car. He leans back in his seat and takes a minute to collect himself before starting the drive back to Kristianstad. He can't shake the feeling of having just been cornered by a pack of wild dogs. He turns the ignition. The radio fires up, but he immediately turns it off. What he craves now is silence.

These small-town rallies all feel the same. A few dozen Sweden Democrats; hundreds, if not thousands of counter-demonstrators with their noisemakers. It's exhausting. He feels a headache coming on and reaches for his water bottle.

He already knows what the media coverage will say in the morning. In their description of the turmoil at the campaign event, the media will portray the party supporters as the villains, the unrest as their fault; while the violent counter-demonstrators can do no wrong. There is certain to be at least one editorial suggesting that the Sweden Democrats should pay for the increased cost of policing their political rallies, as though it's their fault that they are being attacked. It's like arguing that a woman in a short dress has herself to blame for being sexually assaulted. He takes a sip of water and turns out onto the main road leading from town.

Deep in thought, his hands choose the long way home—his biological autopilot. The hum of the engine, the sound of the road, and the familiar scenery of red houses and open fields begin to slide past. He can't help feeling that he's driving through a lie. The peaceful, pastoral beauty that surrounds him now has surrounded him his whole life. But, like a teenager who slips their porn in between the covers of a hollowed-out *National Geographic*, the surface is a fraud. The mainstream media presents as fact a reality that he sees contradicted every day, as though their job is to preach the way the world should be, not how it actually is.

The road is almost empty. Chang loves driving in Skåne in the summertime. He sticks to the coast as much as possible and prefers smaller roads to highways, even if it means the drive takes longer. His mind slides back to the rally. Events like today are nearly pointless. Almost no supporters come, and certainly no undecided people who might be open to the message. He navigates a few gentle bends, and slows for the one speed camera his foot knows is active.

THE UNIMIND ENFORCES ITS BOUNDARIES

The only thing that will matter, the only impact from today, will be what the media says about it. They interpret events for the masses, spinning them into their pre-ordained narrative. Or not covering them at all. Without access to their microphones, it is impossible for him, or any idea outside the confines of the narrow Swedish mindset, to ever truly address the nation.

Chang watches the open fields of red poppies and yellow rape-seed go past. Their dense, solid colors contrast against the green of the grass and the blue of the sky, making them resemble the bands of a flag. This really is a fairytale landscape. And, like all fairytales, it has a clear cast of heroes and villains.

MOTHER'S FROWN

For as long as opinion polls have been conducted to measure attitudes towards immigration amongst the Swedish population, at least 40 per cent of respondents have stated that they believe Sweden takes in too many immigrants. More than 80 per cent believe that immigrants "have a duty to adjust to our customs."[1]

Meanwhile, by the start of the 2010s, the political parties had become increasingly generous and liberal in their views on immigration, and less open to any counter-demands or deviations from the official standpoint. Half of all parties represented in Parliament had aspirations striving towards free immigration. The Sweden Democrats were the only party to argue for decreased immigration, and the other parties and the media did their best to shut them out.[2]

Ahead of the 2010 election, the Sweden Democrats were banned from the final party leader debates on state-financed Swedish Television. The commercial channel TV4 refused to broadcast a party advert in which a pensioner with a squeaky walking frame and a group of burka-clad women pushing strollers rush towards two emergency brakes: one marked "pensions" and the other marked "immigration." The voiceover announced: "All politics is about prioritization. Now you have a choice. On 19 September, you can choose the immigration brake before the pension brake." The channel's refusal to broadcast the advert stirred a great deal of attention, and soon the video received hundreds of thousands of views on YouTube.[3]

On election day, most of the major media outlets were outright shouting direct commands to the public. The front page of leading tabloid *Aftonbladet* featured a raised hand, signaling, "Stop!" The text written on the hand's palm reminded Swedes that they like diversity and must not vote for the Sweden Democrats.

Expressen, the competing tabloid and political opponent of *Aftonbladet*, took its imagery one step further. Its front page featured an image of a Sweden Democrat ballot, crumpled-up, in the gutter, next to a cigarette butt. The word "NO" was printed in big, block letters, followed by an instruction not to vote for the party.

In Sweden, each political party has their own ballot paper, and members of the electorate vote by placing this paper in a special envelope that is then placed in the ballot box. All parties' ballots are available at the polling station on the day, but parties also distribute them via post. To maintain secrecy, voters must either bring their ballot paper with them, or take one of each at the polling station and make their choice behind a screen. However, ballots are frequently placed near the entrance, and most people only pick one, allowing others around them to see their choice. International election observers have criticized Sweden for not doing enough to protect the secrecy of the vote, warning that lack of privacy may create peer pressure to vote for a certain party.[4]

The Sweden Democrats have reported many instances of sabotage resulting from this system: polling station staff refusing to provide SD ballots, SD ballots being stolen or hidden behind those of other parties, or SD ballots being separated from the rest to hamper the possibility of voting for the party in secret.[5] Those convicted for tampering with ballots in a deliberate attempt to influence the electoral outcome include elected politicians, such as Monika Rydin of the Social Democrats.[6]

Despite these and many other efforts, the Sweden Democrats received 5.7 per cent of the vote, well over the 4 per cent needed to enter Parliament. The following day, *Expressen*'s first page was printed in all black. The reason for the mourning was explained with the text "Yesterday, 781,120 Swedes voted for..." followed by the blue anemone, symbol of the Sweden Democrats. The same shame and disgust was apparent across all media. At least this time no one could say they didn't try. The official election night party of the winning Moderates had felt more like a wake. Re-elected Prime Minister Reinfeldt came out on stage and suggested that due to the growth of the Sweden Democrats, there was no reason to celebrate.

Mom was disgusted. Dad was disappointed. The rules needed to be tightened.

HOMELAND

Samvel is wearing his best white shirt as he stands before the intimidating gray block that constitutes the offices of the Migration Authorities in the Stockholm suburb of Solna. His current visa is about to expire and he has decided to take the leap and apply for permanent residency. It has been six years since he first arrived in Sweden, and when he tells people that he is not from here, few believe him. Any last remnants of an accent are entirely gone and he knows and loves the country more than most Swedes. This is his true homeland, and he is anxious to start the process of making it formal.

The lady at the reception provides him with all the forms to fill out. Samvel takes a seat in the anonymous waiting room, where light, pine-framed chairs line the walls. There are many people before him and Samvel prepares himself for a long wait. Most people look like they are of Middle Eastern or African descent. Some could be Eastern European, Samvel figures. He assumes most of them have come to seek asylum. After a few hours, his number is called.

"You're a Skåning, just like I am," the immigration services officer remarks, pleasantly surprised. He's a fairly young man with a thin beard and glasses. Samvel likes him immediately. "I lived in Helsingborg for many years," the officer continues. "But you sound like you're from somewhere closer to Lund."

"Yes, that's where I lived before moving to Stockholm," Samvel replies.

"Beautiful place, but I have to say I prefer Helsingborg. It has the flair of continental Europe."

Samvel lights up as he remembers his own visits to Helsingborg. They begin to reminisce about favorite places and cafés, until the officer catches himself and returns to the matter at hand. "I have to warn you that this will probably take a while. We have many applications to process."

After all the formalities are squared away, Samvel is photographed and fingerprinted. He has to leave his passport with the Migration Authorities, but he receives a confirmation of his application—a sheet of paper, which he carefully folds and puts away with his important documents.

Samvel leaves the Migration Authorities feeling lighthearted. That wasn't as bad as he had expected.

THE FIGHT FOR CONTROL OF THE UNIMIND BEGINS

"The French Revolution would not have been possible without the Enlightenment. Before any Lenin, there must always be a preceding Marx."

Alain de Benoist, *Against Democracy and Equality*[1]

It is 24 November 2010—such a cold winter evening that journalists would later report the ink in their pens had frozen.[2] The ground is white and the awnings of the nearby 7-Eleven are weighed down with heavy snow. In between two speakers hangs a banner with the words *Svensk Strävan* (Swedish Quest), the title of a famous poem by national icon Vilhelm Moberg. Chang is standing outside the Royal Dramatic Theater, in the heart of trendy Östermalm. Wearing a thin, black leather jacket, with no mittens or hat, he is ill prepared for the Arctic winds blowing through him. But, he can hardly leave in the middle of a duel.

"Once from the depths of Swedish hearts..." he sings together with a group of young people from the Sweden Democrats' Youth League (SDU). They are performing the Swedish royal anthem. Two police vans down, counter-demonstrator Magnus William-Olssons begins to recite Gunnar Ekelöf's poem *Non Serviam*, Latin for "I will not serve."

Inside the Royal Dramatic Theater, Stockholm's yearly poetry festival is underway. The theme is diversity and, in their promotion of the event, the organizers had targeted the Sweden Democrats by featuring a picture of a woman tearing up a Nazi flag, accompanied by the text: "Cover your ears, Jimmie Åkesson." By this point, Chang has learned that no mainstream media outlet would print any kind of reasonable rebuttal, let alone a counter-attack on the monocultural past of the Social Democratic Party, with its racial hygiene, sterilization policies, and covert support for Hitler. The Sweden Democrats would need to pull some kind of media stunt to get their point across. So Chang organized this protest reading of Swedish poetry in the cold winter night outside the venue.[3]

The works of Vilhelm Moberg, Viktor Rydberg, and Verner von Heidenstam are read aloud in protest of the cultural elite. As always, counter-demonstrators have mobilized, and what is now underway is more reminiscent of a poetic duel than a protest. But the tactic turns out to be a media jackpot. At a time when coverage of the Sweden Democrats is almost exclusively negative, Chang succeeds in showing a new side of the party.

Encouraged by the success, two weeks later, he forms The Cultural Association for Young Swedes, aiming to spur debate and disseminate the Sweden Democrats' view of reality. On his blog Chang writes: "An appropriate name for the association could be 'The Culture War,' because that should be a close description of the plans I'm forging. May the self-denying, pompous establishment shiver as the SDU aims its arrow to puncture their last watered-down argument!"[4]

* * *

Among the intellectual leadership of the party, there has been increasing talk about Italian philosopher and neo-Marxist Antonio Gramsci, who had a tremendous influence on the

Swedish movement The '68 Left. Gramsci argued that a metamorphosis of the cultural sphere had to occur before there could be any real political or economic change. Consequently, any attempt to change the political landscape must commence in culture. Gramsci's thinking inspired members of the French political movement Nouvelle Droite (the New Right), who concluded that the dominance of liberalism in the West, under left- and rightwing rule alike, evolved from its prior dominance in the cultural sphere. This dominance had eventually caused liberalism to be considered common sense, rather than political ideology.

Waging culture wars to win people's hearts and minds was thus more important than winning political power, if one wanted to achieve long-term change. Subsequently, Nouvelle Droite activists began devoting themselves to the dissemination of ideas and values with the goal of achieving long-term political transformation. They saw themselves as intellectual soldiers fighting their battles in the arenas of cultural production, such as film, literature, art, theater, education, and music.[5]

Many in the Sweden Democrat leadership were amazed by how the ideological left had succeeded in taking over institutions they felt should oppose them, such as the Church, the Local Heritage Federation, and the folk music movement. It was time to take back such institutions, deploying the same strategy that the left had used so successfully in Sweden to gain cultural dominance—and, ultimately, control over what constituted common sense. Party leaders began referring to this methodological approach as "metapolitics."[6]

SAMVEL STARES INTO THE VOID

Samvel is exhausted. An aching molar on the right side of his mouth has kept him up most of the night. "Even in toothache there is enjoyment," wrote Dostoevsky, "if he did not feel enjoyment ... he would not moan." While he admires Dostoevsky, Samvel feels that such lines are not best appreciated when one is suffering from toothache oneself. He desperately needs to see a dentist. The obvious choice is Folktandvården (The People's Dentistry). Launched in 1938, Folktandvården provides most Swedes with dental care. Private dentists have been allowed since the 1990s, but Folktandvården remains the incumbent. Being from a former Soviet state, Samvel has an aversion towards any institution that contains the word *folk*. In his ears, it rings socialist and authoritarian. Consequently, he decides to go elsewhere.

He takes a seat on the beige sofa of his current Stockholm home. The living room is full of plants. Colorful, abstract art covers the walls. He is only renting a bedroom, but he's allowed to use his landlord's living room. After learning that his landlord works as a car salesman, Samvel did not expect to share his tastes in interior design, but now, as he looks around the room, he is embarrassed by his own prejudice; he wouldn't change a thing. Better still is the fact that the landlord is hardly ever at home. Samvel feels like he has his very own pad. This morning, however, the toothache is keeping him from enjoying it. He curls up on the sofa and fires up his laptop to go in search of a private dentist.

Samvel does extensive research, reading many reviews of various practices. In Armenia, he never felt the need to research things this thoroughly, but here every independent decision that deviates from the state-prescribed norm causes him stress. Finally, he settles on a multicultural practice with dentists from all over the world. He phones them up and speaks to a pleasant and confidence-inspiring lady who books him an appointment for the following day. It's short notice, so he won't be able to cancel, she warns. "No problem," Samvel assures her. He has every intention of showing up.

Samvel hangs up and stretches out on the sofa. He reaches for his copy of Herman Hesse's *Steppenwolf* to take his mind off things, but he struggles to focus. Has he made the right choice? There has to be a reason Folktandvården is the state-prescribed practice. If it's state-approved, it has to be good.

As the hours go by, Samvel's anxiety grows. After another night of pain, now mixed with anxiety, Samvel's resistance to the word *folk* has been completely worn down. He knows it's too late to cancel his appointment, but by now he's so overcome with suspicion towards the private alternative that he doesn't care if he's double-billed. He grabs his phone and makes an appointment with Folktandvården.

* * *

While his self-imposed indoctrination has resulted in mastery of the language, it has also brought about changes that go beyond the mere linguistic. Samvel isn't sure it's always a good thing. The new, Swedish Samvel finds himself more prone to minimize risks and follow instructions. He adheres to the recommendations of the various state agencies. When in doubt about the right answer, he'll simply turn to the relevant authority to check the official position on any given issue.

SAMVEL STARES INTO THE VOID

While he accepts that this is the way to order and health, he simultaneously experiences feelings of loss that he struggles to understand. As a person who is passionate about freedom of choice, he's sad to note that his ability to make choices has deteriorated. The welfare state has made him passive. There's always a ready-made answer for everything; a recommended best practice for any curve ball life might throw you.

Too often he'll simply lean back against the comfortable cushion of his existence and surrender his choice to the trusted judgment of governmental experts or institutions. Increasingly reluctant to take initiatives of his own, Samvel has begun to second-guess any impulse that is not in line with the established order. The experts in any given area surely know better, so best just to follow their recommendations. There's a kind of forced harmony, a relief, that comes with surrendering to the collective will.

Samvel used to like to provoke, to spur a debate, to question rules rather than follow them blindly. That approach does not work in Sweden. The most depressing part is that, when he does rebel, taking the time to really question something, he still finds himself reaching the same conclusion as the one already arrived at by experts. All that stress and anxiety for nothing. It's like all problems have already been pondered and taken to their most reasonable, logical conclusion. Everything has been solved. What is he to contribute? When he debates with other foreigners, he even finds himself arguing that the Swedish approach to the given topic is the only reasonable one.

This has been his goal all along, after all. But rather than rejoice, Samvel begins to feel strangely empty.

* * *

In Armenia, most people turn to God for answers. And non-believers like Samvel typically turn to dreams of some far away utopia where politicians aren't quite so corrupt and where opportunities abound. The daily struggle to make ends meet consumes the bulk of people's time there. In Sweden, society runs pretty seamlessly, leaving too much time for existential quandaries with no ready answers.

Struggling with this strange, newfound emptiness, Samvel grabs his light blue windbreaker and heads out for a walk. He likes to listen to podcasts when he walks. His favorites are from a radio show called *The Philosophical Room*. Yesterday, he listened to a very interesting episode on euthanasia, of which he is a strong supporter, but today he needs something more uplifting. He flips through the options and settles on an episode dealing with Swedes and their ambivalent take on religion. While the country consistently rates as one of the most secular countries in the world, this is yet another example of an area where the Swedish self-image doesn't quite line up with reality.

Samvel takes Odelbergsvägen to Bägerstavägen, where he turns right past Linde Park. When he reaches Gullmarsplan, he turns left towards Årstaviken Bay, where he continues his walk along the water. It's a gray day so the walking path is pretty quiet. If any birds are out, Samvel can't hear them. In his ears, the podcast features historian Inga Sanner in conversation with David Thurfjell, professor of religious studies at Södertörn University, about his book *A Godless People*. Thurfjell names a number of famous Swedes who have recently "come out" as Christian. "These are people we look up to and respect!" the host Peter Sandberg exclaims incredulously. In Sweden, to be a Christian is something almost shameful, something to be embarrassed about, as it goes against the national religion of rationality. Thurfjell testifies to the fact that many of the priests he has interviewed for his book are embarrassed to tell people about their faith because they know it is associated with a deficient intellectual ability.

When asked if they believe there is a God, only one in five Swedes say yes (compared to the European average of 52 per cent).

Despite this, 79 per cent of the Swedish population belongs to a religious organization, and a full 66 per cent are still members of the state Church. This means that almost half of the Swedish population are paying members of a religious institution without believing in God or considering themselves religious. Research shows that on a random weekend, just over 1 per cent of the population—or 3.3 per cent of members of the Church—attend a church service.[1]

The loyalty of Swedes towards the Swedish state Church is apparently more an expression of national identity than an expression of faith. Many Swedes celebrate Easter and Christmas, baptize their children, get married and are buried in church, yet would never dream of calling themselves Christians. According to Thurfjell, religion is something Swedes like to believe they have liberated themselves from; something for other, less modern people, who, again, have not yet reached the same level of development. Thus, the Christian customs celebrated by most Swedes are not to be considered religious, but rather traditions or habits. Referring to Christian rituals as religious would require secular Swedes to label themselves religious, which would be contrary to their self-image.[2]

The episode comes to an end, but Samvel doesn't feel like going home. Beautiful surroundings tend to lift his spirits, so he walks across the bridge into the heart of Södermalm, where he continues to wander the little side streets for hours. He strolls the familiar Monteliusvägen and admires the Old Town and Riddarfjärden Bay in the distance. He makes his way down the Mariaberget hill along the winding, cobblestoned Bellmansgatan. He crosses over to Stadsholmen and the Old Town with its stunning medieval buildings. These are the same streets that hypnotized him with their beauty and mystery when he first arrived. But today, their presence leaves him unmoved. In the process of becoming Swedish, Samvel seems to have been infected with

Swedish melancholy. There's a hollowness that he can't quite explain, and with no faith except rationality, that existential void is hard to fill.

Many Swedes seem to experience the same thing, he thinks to himself. Materialistically everything is fine; all their needs are met. So why aren't they happy?

THE CONSEQUENCES OF DISOBEDIENCE

On the wall outside Chang's apartment in Kristianstad, "Die Frick" has been spray-painted alongside an anarchist "A."

While he isn't the type to be intimidated, ever since being elected to the city council, Chang's everyday life has taken a drastic turn for the worse. It wasn't long ago that he was named young entrepreneur of the year and considered a local role model; Chang Frick, the kid with an immigrant background who had made it. His company delivered a healthy profit. His logo was on every hockey jersey of the local team. Now, all that has changed. As he stands outside his door, looking at the asymmetrical "A" inside a circle—the mark of the anarchists—he makes a mental list of all the recent strikes against him.

In the wake of the financial crisis, Chang's business slowed. As power companies downsized, some of his customers went bankrupt before they could pay him for services rendered. Before long, he had depleted his entire reserves. He had to start letting people go and selling off his equipment. But in the end, it wasn't enough. Then, his girlfriend left him. Chang's not sure if it was because he lost his job, or because he joined the Sweden Democrats. He doesn't know which would be worse. Though he had been a member of the Moderates for years, the fact that he is now with the Sweden Democrats seems to overshadow everything. He can't help but reflect on the irony of his situation. First, he grew up shunned as the "immigrant" who should "go home." Now here he is, still shunned, but for being "a racist."

Chang takes a seat on the ground outside his front door, leaning his back against the cold concrete. He is used to feeling like an outcast, but the steep social price tag has come as a surprise even to him. Still, compared with many of his fellow party comrades, Chang knows he can consider himself lucky.

* * *

On 23 September, a few days after the 2010 election, five boulders shattered the windows of the kitchen, living room, and bedroom of Sweden Democrat Issa Issa's apartment in Gothenburg. Outside, someone shouted: "Fucking Christian, fucking Sweden Democrat, come down!"[1]

While Issa's mother, sister, and sister's children hid under the tables, Issa, a fairly big and strong man who worked as a security guard, decided to pursue the two teenage assailants he could spot from his window. When he stepped outside, the young men began to run. Issa followed them, but as he rounded the second corner, he realized he had run into a trap. A larger group of men awaited him. Issa was beaten, kicked, and stabbed. When he regained consciousness, he was in the hospital with eighteen stab wounds, including two to the head and ten in the back. He had narrowly escaped death, but his right arm had been permanently damaged and his right hand paralyzed.[2]

Issa had first arrived in Sweden from Syria as a Christian refugee. In 2005, he joined the Sweden Democrats. "I feel that the SD has the best politics to preserve the beautiful society that Sweden is. Too many immigrants have arrived in too short a time-span. And they have brought along traditions and customs that reject the Swedish way. It divides society and creates insecurity," he told Christian newspaper *Dagen*.[3]

THE CONSEQUENCES OF DISOBEDIENCE

A few days before the election, Issa had been distributing campaign literature in the immigration-dense suburb of Hjällbo, when two young men threatened to kill him. He didn't take them seriously. In hindsight, he wished he had. The investigation was classified, but three months after the assault, no arrests had been made. Issa and his family received new identities and were forced to leave Gothenburg, their home for seventeen years, behind.[4] "There is no democracy in Sweden," Issa told newspaper *Expo*. "You are not allowed to express your opinion and so I have left the party. The country cannot guarantee our safety."[5]

Around the same time, Kristina Winberg, a Sweden Democrat from Jönköping who would later go on to represent the party in the European Parliament, was subjected to repeated threats. Following the 2010 election, Winberg was notified by the extreme-left organization Antifascist Action that, unless she quit politics, a "campaign" would be launched against her. What followed was a series of threatening letters, spray-painted walls and smashed windows. Once, Winberg even had an axe driven into her front door.[6]

The Swedish National Intelligence Service, Säpo, confirmed the elevated threat level facing active Sweden Democrats. Party leader Jimmie Åkesson and the top brass of the party had been assigned bodyguards, but this had not stopped the threats, the attempts to do him physical harm, or the recurring vandalism of his home.[7]

* * *

A loud bang startles Chang, interrupting his thought process.

It's just one of his neighbors slamming their front door. He hopes this experience won't make him jumpy. He doesn't think so. Ever since his brother Arnold turned into a living weapon of a man, there is little in the way of physical danger that he fears. But he also knows he is not representative of most people.

He has friends in the party who struggle on a daily basis with their own anxiety and fear, not infrequently turning to sedatives or alcohol for relief. Having now lived it from the inside, it isn't hard to understand why so many Sweden Democrats prefer to keep a clenched fist in their pocket over taking a public stand. Or why so many who do take a stand eventually balk under the pressure and drop out; why the party struggles to fill its seats and keep them manned.

Understanding is easy; knowing what to do about it is harder. If the social price for being involved with the party remains this high, it will never be able to attract enough supporters. Only people like him—people with nothing to lose—will take up the cause. At least, until the party's values are considered socially acceptable. But, in order for that to happen, the Sweden Democrats would need to be able to change what constitutes "socially acceptable" ideas.

Chang stands back up and begins to trace the outlines of the anarchist "A" with his fingers. What made the actions of these vandals socially acceptable to society? Why was it that they could insert an axe into someone's door and get away with it, while it would create a media frenzy should a Sweden Democrat supporter decide to pull a similar stunt?

The week before the 2010 election, another SD politician reported that two members of the extreme left had assaulted him and carved a swastika into his forehead. Commenting on the incident, Prime Minister Reinfeldt had said: "I distance myself from all types of violence and threats, but would like to point out that those who live on promoting an 'us and them' way of thinking, and a hateful way of looking at the relationship between people, should not be surprised if this happens."[8] Meanwhile, several media outlets asserted that the injuries were likely self-inflicted.[9]

Chang sits back down. The cold of the ground begins to wear through his pants, giving him a chill, but he doesn't want to move just yet. His ass is near numb by the time it dawns on him: he's been focused on the wrong things, so distracted by all the battles that he has lost sight of the war. He stands up and heads determinedly towards his apartment.

The ideological left has something the Sweden Democrats, and any other alternative opinions, lack: control over the narrative. Influencing the portrayal of reality is more important than winning parliamentary seats. There has to be a more effective way for him to engage in the battle of ideas.

HUSBY RIOTS

Whoosh! A car explodes in flames. Police in riot gear group together behind their shields and begin to advance towards a mob of young men, but they are cut short as fire crackers and rocks rain down on them. "Let's not go any closer," Chang shouts to his friend who is holding the microphone. "Rocks incoming!" Chang lowers his camera to protect the lens and it registers the sound of rocks hitting the pavement all around them.

It's the night of 20 May 2013, and the immigration-dense Stockholm suburb of Husby is alight with riots. The turmoil had started the previous night, when the suburb's center was vandalized. Gangs of youth broke off pieces of pavement that were then used to smash windows and launched at police, injuring several officers. Around 100 cars were set ablaze, and some fifty people had to be evacuated from an apartment building following the arson of a nearby garage.[1] Betting this wouldn't be the end of it, tonight, Chang has come with his video camera.

Another car catches fire. As it goes up in flames members of the crowd begin to ululate and cheer. People stand around filming on their phones, apparently unfazed by the prospect of being associated with the arson. Bobbing like reality TV, Chang's footage alternates between groups of young, hoodie-clad men, riot police, countless vehicles, and, occasionally, the gray concrete

239

ground beneath him, as he is forced to change position or protect the camera from rocks.

As the mob begins to charge them, both journalists and police officers run in the opposite direction. In spite of the massive police presence, they fail to bring the situation under control and advise Chang and other journalists to leave Husby.

Chang retreats from the heart of the action and goes in search of a local resident to interview. He finds a concerned teacher who doesn't want to be filmed, but who agrees to talk to him, as she feels it is important that the media acknowledges the ongoing radicalization of the suburbs. She tells Chang that she has heard youth screaming "Allahu Akbar!" as they launch their rocks at police. She is herself a Muslim and is very concerned that the riots and vandalism are being enacted in the name of religion.

Chang also manages to get an interview with Diana Sundin, a middle-aged, serious-looking police officer with blonde hair and black-framed glasses. She says that, in addition to the car burnings, there have been many other, smaller fires. As if to prove her point, a nearby recycling station goes up in flames. "The fires are meant to attract the fire department," Sundin says. She explains that, when the firefighters arrive, the mob proceeds to steal their water hoses and pelt them with rocks. "So now they won't enter unless we accompany them," she adds. Instead, riot police patrol the area with fire extinguishers, attempting to put out the lesser flames.

"We hope things will calm down. That people will feel the need to go home and get some rest. So that we can try again, using the good forces to help bring this to an end tomorrow, because this does not feel good," Sundin tells Chang.

Rather than wind down, the riots begin to spread to other areas. By Saturday morning more than a dozen Stockholm suburbs have been rocked by the turmoil. Some 200 cars have been set aflame and fires have been reported in schools, at police stations, and in restaurants. Then the disorder spreads to other cities such as Uppsala, Södertälje, Linköping, and Örebro.[2] Meanwhile, the UK and the US issue travel warnings discouraging their citizens from visiting the problem-ridden suburbs.[3]

*　*　*

As soon as he gets home, Chang posts his footage on YouTube. Sitting by his computer, he's amazed to watch the likes and views stream in. People are sharing and linking to his video, creating a snowball effect that cascades into an avalanche. The response is intoxicating; he's not even a journalist. All he did was turn on his video camera and let reality speak for itself.

As the numbers on his monitor climb, he reflects on the changes the past year has brought. Disaffected by the limited impact of his political activities, he has given up his seat in the Kristianstad municipal council, ceased to be politically active in the Sweden Democrats, and moved to the capital. Not long after settling in Stockholm, he met Polina, a pretty, redheaded Russian film student with an air of somber austerity. An unplanned pregnancy caused the couple to kick-start family life. While this wasn't what Chang had in mind, he had no intention of repeating his father's pattern of stray children.

Finding affordable housing in Stockholm hasn't been easy, and like many others, the couple had to move around, taking on different short-term leases. In need of more space after the birth of their daughter Malou, they ended up in Hallunda, one of Stockholm's southwestern suburbs, where they were able to find a lease on a two-bedroom apartment off the books. Chang looks around at the dated design and worn furniture that surround him. It's a far step down from his swanky loft apartment in downtown Kristianstad. But that was before he joined the party and his business sank. He is certainly in a worse financial position now, but somehow he feels better off.

*　*　*

Chang is lying on the couch when Sweden Democrat MP Kent Ekeroth calls him up and suggests that he start a news site. While he is suspicious of Ekeroth's motives, the idea of launching his own thing has been on Chang's mind for some time. By now, his video of the Husby riots has more than 150,000 views and he has produced a number of other video blogs that have been widely shared.

As Chang listens to Kent stress the importance of creating an alternative media landscape, he does a quick search for available domains. "*Nyheter Idag* [News Today] is free," Chang comments. The idea excites him. Though he'd already been thinking about it, his conversation with Kent somehow makes it more concrete. If the mainstream media refuse to show the truth, then he will. He has no full-time job. No status. His Sweden Democrat ties make him a pariah. He truly has nothing to lose.

Chang begins to read up on media legislation and the journalistic code of conduct. If he is going to play, he is going to play by the same rules as the incumbents, and beat them at their own game. Unlike the vast majority of alternative news sites, Chang decides to affiliate *Nyheter Idag* with the Swedish Press Council, the body responsible for determining whether or not the actions of a newspaper are in line with good journalistic practices. This voluntary commitment means his site will be bound by the same ethical guidelines as mainstream media, and suffer the same penalties should he violate them.

THE LONELY HOLOGRAM

Sweden is the loneliest country in the world. About half the population live alone—in Stockholm it is 60 per cent[1]—and one in four die alone.

Samvel is not surprised by the depressing message. He is watching the documentary *The Swedish Theory of Love* on his laptop, sitting at his tiny wooden table, alone in the small single room studio he now rents in Stockholm. Film director Erik Gandini accompanies Swedish government officials as they deal with the deaths of people whose passing has gone unnoticed. Sometimes, the corpses have been rotting for years before they are discovered. A neighbor phones the landlord complaining about the smell coming from the deceased's apartment, or the automatic rent payment eventually fails as the funds of the deceased have run dry. Officials then begin the process of tracking down next-of-kin whom nobody has heard from in years. If they are unsuccessful, the state simply lays claim to anything of value and arranges for the rest to be transported to the nearest dump. It's not unusual and, according to the officials interviewed, the number of cases is growing by the year.[2]

The movie unsettles Samvel. He looks around at his miniature room: the small wooden table, the one wooden chair, the single bed, and the closet. A large, triangular window is the room's saving grace; it's the reason he picked this room over more spacious options. It's so big that the curtains are neither long nor wide enough to keep out the light. Outside the sun is beginning to set over the budding trees. It's beautiful, but somehow it feels far away, like he is trapped in a snow globe with an invisible screen separating him from the sounds and smells of spring. He looks up at the slanted ceilings. Only the very center is tall enough to hang a noose from. Standing on the little wooden chair would be enough to reach. Samvel wonders if these are the types of thoughts that lonely people ponder—until one day they find themselves too old to climb the chair, and are left having to wait for death to come for them. The documentary portrays this solitude as the ultimate outcome of the kind of state individualism that characterizes Sweden. To be Swedish, historians Henrik Berggren and Lars Trägårdh argue, is to strive for independence, freedom, and individual self-realization, at the expense of community, intimacy, and traditional duties.[3] But, Samvel muses, that is also how one becomes a forgotten, rotting corpse.

It's easy for Samvel to picture himself ending up in a similar situation. He leads a very desolate existence. At first he justified his isolation by the fact that he needed to focus on his studies. But after a while he grew used to it. Most of the friends he had when studying for his masters have graduated and left and he has given up on trying to build a new social network. He has accepted his solitude and, with time, has even come to enjoy it. He is aware that his Swedish lifestyle would probably concern his mother. Sometimes he doesn't even answer the phone or contact anyone; he just stays in his bubble, wrestling the anguish. Armenia does not lend itself well to existential *ångest*, but Sweden is made for it; the darkness, the cold, the fact that people like to light so many candles at home. A normal Swedish home looks like a home in mourning to the average Armenian.

Samvel's passion for books remains unabated and he finds himself returning to Berggren and Trägårdh, whose book *Is the*

Swede Human? inspired Gandini's documentary. While he appreciates their intellect, it's not exactly cheerful reading. When they talk of individualism, Berggren and Trägårdh don't mean it in the positive sense of independent thought, or the courage to forge one's own path. Rather, they mean individualism as French political scientist Alexis de Tocqueville first defined it: the atomic culture that results from elimination of the undemocratic ties or duties of family, religion, and community that used to unite human beings.[4]

Samvel googles de Tocqueville. In the early 1800s, he expressed his belief that radical individualism could mean the end of humanity, as it would inevitably lead to atomism: the destruction of all that binds human beings together and all that distinguishes them from one another. An atomistic world is one populated by many equally insignificant, identical, isolated selves, each of whom is free from all external duties and restraints that might determine the purpose and direction of their existence. Tocqueville argued that such individuals were anxious, melancholic, restless, and dissatisfied even in the midst of abundance. This was, he argued, because the individual knew that they could not truly satisfy their own deepest longings, yet individualism remained the only option.

To Samvel, this sounds precisely like the average Swede. He follows some links and ends up at *The Problem of Democratic Individualism*. Professor Peter Augustine Lawler interprets Tocqueville thus:

> The very perception of unlimited freedom by a human being is dizzying and terrifying. It is something from which the apparently radically liberated self desires above all to escape. Without communal resources to shape and limit self-determination, the democratic self chooses not to determine itself, i.e., not to exercise its freedom. It passively defers to public opinion, Tocqueville says. But this opinion itself is determined by no self in particular. The democratic self really

seems to defer to some principle of impersonal materialism. It has no point of view from which to differentiate itself from its "environment." Radical individualism makes individual distinctiveness—individuality in any meaningful sense—impossible.[5]

Samvel lowers his computer lid and looks up at the peak in his ceiling. He wonders how many Swedes have hanged themselves here, or thought of it. He shakes his head, and heads down the hall to the shared toilet to brush his teeth and get ready for bed.

BLINDSPOTS OF THE UNIMIND

"Allahu Akbar," shouts Chang as he enters his local tobacco store in Hallunda commercial center. The building is squeezed in between the subway station and a rock wall, just a few minutes away from where he lives. It is similar to other suburban cores around Stockholm's satellite communities, but its offerings are quite different. Instead of the big brand stores, there are second-hand shops, pawnshops, and jewelers. The type of food offered, as well as the style of fashion displayed, creates an atmosphere that is more Middle Eastern than Swedish.

"*Inshallah*, *ostfralla* [cheese sandwich]," Anwar, the owner, replies, lighting up when he sees Chang, who always comes here to buy his snuff. Anwar pulls out a couple of stools from the back corner of the store and tells Chang to help himself to coffee from his vending machine. Out here in the suburbs, life happens at a different pace.

Anwar is a Lebanese Christian and very anti-Muslim. He fought in the Lebanese Civil War before coming to Sweden in 1984. Physically, he only lost a finger, but mentally the war lives on. He believes that Swedes are very naïve and have very little concept of what it means to fight for your values. He has spent the past thirty-odd years in suburbs like Hallunda, Alby, and Fittja, and he feels society is trending in the wrong direction.

While more and more immigrants are arriving, the Swedes are leaving, he says. And the ones who stay are afraid to go out at night for fear of being mugged. The police are powerless. Tougher tactics are needed to fight crime.

Recently, four masked robbers drove a Jeep into the commercial center and rammed it into the jewelry store a few shops over from Anwar's. But he is not worried about himself. "Nobody dares rob me. My kids would get them within 24 hours. That's the way it should be ... My son told the kids who were burning cars in Fittja that whoever burns my car will burn inside a car."

Close to Anwar's little shop is Direkten, a betting and tobacco establishment, also owned by a Lebanese immigrant. It recently fell victim to an attempted robbery. The owner's cousin, an infamous bodybuilder, happened to be at the store when two masked men pulled out a gun. By the time Chang arrived to cover the event, police were busy examining a blood trail, an abandoned robber's mask, and a pistol that had been found on the scene. The robber had been taken to the emergency room.

* * *

Chang's new neighborhood, Hallunda-Norsborg, is one of the Stockholm suburbs that the authorities characterize as "particularly vulnerable." According to a 2015 report by the police authorities, Sweden has fifty-three so-called "vulnerable areas." Fifteen of these are considered "particularly vulnerable,"[1] or what some police officers and international media have referred to as "no-go zones."[2] According to the police, a "particularly vulnerable area" is a place of low socio-economic status, with high levels of crime and a general unwillingness to participate in the administration of justice. Here, the police are prevented from doing their job, and as a result parallel societal structures have developed where local power players offer protection or enforce their own rules. These areas also tend to be a breeding ground for violent religious extremists, as the vast majority of Swedish ISIS fighters reside or have resided here.[3]

Most of the areas that are today characterized as vulnerable were built between 1965 and 1975 as part of the state's goal of building 1 million modern, affordable homes within a decade.[4] The ambitious "Million Program" was the culmination of several decades of housing reform that had started in the 1930s, when Sweden had amongst the most deplorable living standards in all of Europe. Homes were dark, damp, drafty, over-priced, and small. As a result, people fell ill as sickness and vermin spread.[5]

Journalist Ludvig Nordström traveled the country interviewing a multitude of district doctors and pastors about people's living conditions. In his classic 1938 book *Lort-Sverige* (Filthy Sweden), he concluded that

> Sweden has filth within its borders, more filth than can be calmly tolerated ... this filth must be got rid of as quickly and thoroughly as possible, and not just for the sake of national prestige, but also, far more important, for the sake of national effectiveness. We cannot afford to have so much filth in our national machinery."[6]

The Myrdals and other social engineers agreed: if a healthier population was the goal, more and better homes were needed. Consequently, hygiene became a state responsibility.[7] Modern living was not just meant for the few; the vision of a uniform, modern lifestyle included everyone.

Between 1945 and 1960, several hundred thousand homes were torn down across Sweden and replaced with 822,000 new, modern apartments.[8] The reconstruction of Stockholm city center in the 1960s was one of Europe's largest and most radical urban development projects. At a time when the rest of Europe was struggling to build up what had been destroyed during the war, the municipal officials of Stockholm were systematically tearing down much of the downtown core. Old historic buildings and entire neighborhoods in the heart of many Swedish cities were demolished. The argument against anyone who objected was that everyone had the right to the same high standards. In practice, that meant that old standards had been outlawed, and alternatives that were considered substandard had to be eliminated. Campaigns to save threatened buildings were weak, ineffectual, or non-existent.[9] No price was too high for progress. Besides, nostalgia was not rational. During a Stockholm City Council debate in 1963, City Commissioner Joakim Garpe said that the city center was to become "a display window for Sweden, a worthy reflection of the modern welfare state."[10]

On the outskirts of Stockholm, so-called "ABC Cities" were constructed. The acronym stood for *arbete* (work), *bostad* (housing), and *centrum* (center). Modern metro stations would tie the ABC satellites to the main city center, but the idea was that they would be self-sufficient; residents should be able to work and have access to public services in their own neighborhood without having to venture into the downtown core. Planning was to be carried out in a way that optimized access to welfare resources. If homes were too spread out, the supply of public services would become too expensive. As a consequence, many communities were built as tower blocks of flats near a central core, housing government agencies. Further out in the periphery, low-rises with terraced houses were located.[11] The guidelines were very specific. The plan from 1952 stipulated that the center should be 450 meters from the first blocks of flats, 900 meters from low-rise town homes, and 600 meters from the local industries.[12] To ensure efficient use of resources, rooms were small and ceilings low, but they were well-built, with proper insulation and ventilation, and all the necessary amenities.[13]

Still, more homes were needed, so in 1965 the government launched the "Million Program," aiming to provide the whole population with "healthy, spacious, well-planned and functional homes of good quality at a reasonable cost."[14] The vast majority of the new homes consisted of multi-story housing blocks in new working-class suburbs. Functional and mass-produced, the buildings resembled IKEA furniture, in that they consisted of a series of small boxes with walls that could be removed and relocated.[15] Mass-produced functionality was cost-effective, but also had the benefit of contributing to equality and the elimination of class difference, as everyone got the same standard. Housing co-operatives took on ownership and administration of most of the new homes. When the program was complete, there were hundreds of thousands of nearly identical flats across Sweden.

In the Soviet Union, citizens were housed in large blocks primarily because collective surroundings were believed to encourage collective thought. It also facilitated surveillance and control. In a not dissimilar way, Sweden redesigned its living space to facilitate the development of a collective mentality and the creation of the unsentimental, egalitarian man for its new, modern society.[16]

In the interests of equality, the population should live mixed, which meant larger housing estates were preferable to smaller ones. Lennart Holm, who was appointed director general of the National Board of Urban Planning in 1969, said: "Estates of small houses are bad. They encourage social stratification, and this is what we want to avoid. ... We cannot allow people to preserve their differences. People will have to give up the right to choose their own neighbors."[17]

Construction of these functional, new homes went ahead regardless of whether anyone wanted to live in them or not. Near the big cities, people typically did, but in the rest of the country the new satellite towns orbited the solitude of already half-deserted communities. Within a few years of the Program launching, the housing deficit had turned to surplus in several areas, but the government still insisted on sticking to the plan of 1 million new homes; a significant number given that the total population of the time was no more than 8 million.[18] During the

1970s, the number of apartment vacancies in these engineered communities grew, even in the bigger cities. Most who could afford to leave did so. Those who were left behind were frequently immigrants, the poor, or the socially excluded. Ever since, these areas have been plagued by ethnic segregation, unemployment, low socio-economic status, and exclusion from society. Among youths, there is a widespread feeling of marginalization and alienation.[19]

The engineered suburbs were designed to have an inner green zone as well as traffic-free zones. Circular roads feeding the major highways were constructed around the areas for the benefit of commuters. Underneath the roads were pedestrian tunnels so that residents would be able to walk to centrally located services and schools without coming into contact with traffic. This design made the communities fairly closed off from their surroundings. According to the police, this now makes them particularly hard to work in, as there are no roads that police can use to retreat.[20] The fact that officers are more concerned about their ability to escape than about deterring criminals in these areas says a great deal about the prevailing power balance.

In its 2015 report, Swedish police described many of these communities as areas where democratic structures have been allowed to disintegrate, only to be replaced by alternative power structures that challenge the Swedish legal system. Residents won't testify to crimes for fear of retaliation. The judicial system is not believed to function, and residents don't trust in the ability of the police to serve and protect them. The victims of crime in these areas often express a feeling of abandonment; that society and its institutions have turned their backs on them. This further fuels the tendency not to report crime or contribute to the enforcement of justice.[21]

The social control that does exist is tied to criminal networks that take the law into their own hands, enforcing their own rules. Conflicts are solved outside the democratic system as local power players sometimes mediate between families, or clans, and administer justice. It is not uncommon for criminals to inflict their terror on local entrepreneurs, who are sometimes forced to pay for protection. As a result, there is frequent turnover of ownership, and some have even opted to close their businesses. Criminal youths have been known to physically attack or threaten local schoolteachers, residents, and police officers. There is extensive drug dealing taking place in the open. Many residents avoid the public squares or refrain from going out at night for fear of becoming a victim.[22]

Daytime shootings have become more common, and even occur in the vicinity of preschools and schools. There have been shootouts in the central squares and other public areas, in which innocent passersby have been injured.[23] Since 2008, deadly shootings have more than doubled from fourteen in 2008 to thirty-one in 2015,[24] and the number keeps rising.[25] In the rankings of European countries, Sweden is now near the top when it comes to the number of shootings per capita, in parity with certain regions of southern Italy. There are four to five times as many deadly shootings per capita in Sweden as in Norway or Germany. Perpetrators of gang-related violence are younger than ever and using heavier weapons than has been customary.[26] For example, a 2017 study showed that the number of hand grenade attacks per capita since 2011 was similar to the number in Mexico during the same period.[27]

Compared with worldwide levels of violence, or countries such as the US where thousands of people are shot to death every year, numbers are still low, but it is a disturbing trend, and many residents of afflicted areas are frustrated, as they feel there are no consequences for those who commit crimes. Many fear to speak openly with police and are reluctant to report crime or participate in legal processes, for fear of reprisals. Young people claim they prefer to look the other way when crimes take place so as not to risk being subjected to violence.[28]

Violent religious extremism has been identified in a third of the vulnerable areas. The definition of this problem ranges from the mere presence of sympathizers and facilities where their beliefs are propagated, to the presence of people who actually travel back and forth between Sweden and conflict areas to participate in combat, most commonly as ISIS volunteers. The vast majority of the identified individuals who have gone to fight for ISIS have come from officially vulnerable areas.[29] In 2010, Sweden had 200 known Islamist extremists. By 2017, that number had grown to 2,000.[30] Some 300 Swedish passport holders have traveled to fight for ISIS. About half of them have returned to Sweden. In April 2016, it became illegal to join terror organizations such as ISIS. Before then, individuals could travel back and forth freely, for example to receive medical attention in Sweden, without risking legal ramifications.[31] Sweden is among the three European countries that have provided the most ISIS fighters per capita.[32] Whether or not Sweden truly has a higher rate of youth marginalization than other countries, social exclusion is frequently cited by Swedes as a likely explanation.

In several of these areas of exclusion, the 2015 police report stated, residents are afraid to openly display their religious faith for fear of reprisals by extremists. Secular Muslims who are perceived by power players as being too liberal, or who don't dress in a way that more extreme supporters deem appropriate, have also been victimized.[33]

The police struggle to do their job in these areas, as criminals warn each other when police approach and gangs frequently group together to display their aversion to the presence of officers. A routine vehicle check can draw a massive crowd, which then proceeds to "liberate" suspects or attack the police patrols. "In the more exposed areas an arrest can result in riots with stone-throwing and car fires as a result. For this reason," the report said, "police sometimes have to delay in interfering." Patrolling police officers travel in two cars to minimize the odds of being attacked. They have also had to reinforce their vehicles to protect themselves from rocks and other missiles being launched.[34] But it's not just police officers who struggle to do their job. Ambulance workers and fire fighters are so frequently attacked that they can no longer venture into some of these areas on their own, but are forced to wait for a police escort. This, in turn, causes delays that can cost lives.[35]

A classified police report, leaked to *Aftonbladet*, reveals that in Hallunda-Norsborg, assisted living personnel, estate agents and postal and municipal services have been forced to adjust their operations to deal with their new reality. According to the police report, some caretakers opt to wear helmets to protect themselves from residents throwing things from the balconies. It also flagged signs of political meddling, fraud against the Swedish Social Insurance Agency, and corrupt insiders working at the Unemployment Office.[36] Indeed, in 2016 the head of the Norsborg mall was sentenced to three and a half years in prison for crimes including serious fraud and gross forging of documents; Halef Halef was ordered to repay 3.4 million SEK in damages to the Unemployment Office, and 3.9 million to the Social Insurance Agency. Nine others were convicted, and the mall's entire board was replaced. In total, according to *Expressen*, police investigations in Norsborg—ranging from murder and extortion to drug dealing and money laundering—have resulted in over 160 years' worth of prison sentences, and the state has demanded payment of more than 50 million SEK from tax evaders.[37]

* * *

Not far from Chang's apartment is St Petrus & Paulus Syrian Orthodox Church. Its golden onion domes, resting atop a burgundy roof and beige walls, make for a beautiful addition to a landscape otherwise dominated by concrete and a main highway. Less than a 10-minute walk away is St Georgis, another Syrian Orthodox church. Hallunda-Norsborg is dominated by Christian Assyrians. As far as Chang knows, he does not have a single ethnic Swede among his neighbors in the apartment building. He finds it liberating. Every morning he does the rounds, talking to the local entrepreneurs and shopkeepers. With them, he can spit his snuff and discuss politics without offending anyone. People don't dodge the real issues; they live them. Out here, political correctness does not exist.

Chang has witnessed, and filmed, several attacks on police officers, including attacks with Molotov cocktails and hand grenades. But the Assyrian mafia makes sure life on his block is quiet. While cars can be burning mere streets away, and Chang can film events unfolding from his window, he has never seen a car burn in his own parking lot. If anyone sets the wrong person's vehicle on fire here, they'll get a bullet in the head; of that Chang is convinced. As long as his family is safe, he is fine with that.

* * *

It's a quiet afternoon. After chatting to Anwar at the local tobacco store, Chang decides to drop by to see Mohaned, who runs another tobacco store with his brothers right next to the subway station in nearby Masmo. Unlike Anwar, Mohaned lacks a personal vigilante to fight off thugs. A few months ago, the store was robbed. Mohaned's brother, who tried to stop the robber, was beaten bloody with a hammer. The assailants escaped on a moped.

When Chang arrived to cover the story, Mohaned's brother had been taken to the hospital and police were busy securing blood samples from the floor, where the hammer and a pistol had been left behind. "I am angry with the politicians who make the decisions. Thieves are given permission to stay; they get citizenship and everything. But he who works, pays taxes, and toils is constantly rejected," a defeated Mohaned told Chang.

Mohaned arrived in Sweden ten years ago from Iraq and, two years later, his brother followed. However, the brother has still not been able to gain citizenship.

In addition to publishing the news article, Chang uploaded the audio recording of their conversation to his site, to avoid accusations of fakery. Today, he decides to check in on Mohaned again, but when he arrives at his small store, none of the brothers are present. A friend of theirs is manning the till. He tells Chang the store was robbed again just a few weeks ago. "It's a constant battle," he sighs.

Immigrants in these crime-ridden areas are the main victims of crime. It upsets Chang that it is the people who make an effort to become a part of the Swedish society who end up paying the price for its failed integration policies. It's their cars that go up in flames.

* * *

In 2014, Sweden accepted a record number of asylum seekers. Meanwhile, the country was becoming increasingly segregated. A growing number of areas were plagued by social exclusion and crime. In 1990, Sweden had three so-called "areas of exclusion." By 2012 that number had grown to 186, with a population of 566,000 people made up of predominantly second-generation immigrants.[38]

Four weeks ahead of the 2014 election, Prime Minister Reinfeldt gave a speech in which, instead of proposing solutions, he reminded the Swedish people of the nation's brand promise: "Sweden, my friends, is a humanitarian superpower. Now I appeal to the Swedish people for patience. Open your hearts to people fleeing; fleeing towards Europe, fleeing towards freedom, fleeing towards better conditions."[39] No further social reforms should be expected in the coming years, he explained, since the costs associated with the many refugees were so extensive that there would not be room for anything else.[40]

Reinfeldt and his party lost power. The Moderates' vote share fell from 30.1% in 2010 to 23.3%. Meanwhile, the Sweden Democrats more than doubled theirs, from 5.7% to 12.9%. They were now Sweden's third largest party, but since no others wanted to collaborate with them, it was the Social Democrats—on 31% of the vote—who ended up forming a minority government with the Greens. It was the first time since 1957 that the Social Democrats had been forced to share power while in government.[41]

Stefan Löfven, a former welder and trade unionist, became the new prime minister. He continued Reinfeldt's policy of openness and generosity towards people on the run. But despite the rhetoric and heavy investments, Sweden's integration policies were obviously failing. The country combined the greatest number of refugees per capita with the worst marketplace integration. In 2015 no other OECD country showed a larger gap between foreign and native-born individuals when it came to employment and teenage dropouts.[42] While 82.9% of the Swedish-born population aged 20 to 64 had jobs in 2015, only 59.6% of their foreign-born counterparts did.[43]

Perhaps this is why, paradoxically, support among immigrants for the Sweden Democrats has grown rather remarkably. In 2014, only 1.6% of women and 2.5% of men with foreign backgrounds supported the party. In 2017, those numbers had grown to 10.3% and 15.4% respectively, making the Sweden Democrats the third largest party amongst immigrants.[44] This suits the party well, having long fought its image as a rightwing, xenophobic organization, and claiming rather to take the best from both left and right by combining leftwing wealth redistribution policies with more conservative social values. One of its prioritized target groups has been "blue labor"—conservative workers who prioritize restrictive immigration, law and order, defense and family, while still adhering to traditional Social Democratic values when it comes to support for income equality and a strong welfare state that provides financial and social security for all.[45]

According to the Sweden Democrats, the main conflict is between the people and the political elite, or "the establishment," as Åkesson likes to phrase it. The establishment has betrayed the people and their interests by allowing foreign cultures to take hold in Swedish society. The elites have also forced people to accept new value norms, such as multiculturalism, radical feminism, gender pedagogy, and queer theory, thereby outlawing traditional norms. As the only party that questions the universality of these new norms, the Sweden Democrats argue that they constitute the only true opposition party.[46]

Hence, immigration is not the only area where the Sweden Democrats differ from the rest. It is the only party wanting to restrict the right to free abortion from week eighteen to week twelve, arguing that after twelve weeks abortion should only be allowed under special circumstances, to dissuade people from using it as a form of contraceptive. The party also dislikes compulsory paternity leave and believes that parents should be allowed to decide for themselves who stays at home with the kids and for how long. The Sweden Democrats distance themselves from the commonly accepted norm that gender is a social construction, arguing that differences in gender are natural. These political standpoints have caused the media and the other parties to label the Sweden Democrats extreme not only on immigration, but also on family and gender equality.[47]

"Your politics are quite un-Swedish," argued former Liberal leader Bengt Westerberg in a debate with Jimmie Åkesson. "Swedes don't have any issue with divorces or abortions, but that's the very thing you are trying to fight."[48] In most European countries, however, a twelve-week limit to free abortion is standard. As researcher Andreas Johansson Heinö points out, it is only from a Swedish perspective that such standpoints can be considered extreme. In fact, the values of the party on issues relating to family and equality are closer to those of the average European party than those of any other Swedish party. Interestingly, Johansson Heinö has also suggested that the Sweden Democrats have the values closest to those prevailing in the home countries of the bulk of immigrants to have arrived in the last few decades. According to him, it is common for immigrant voters in general to favor leftwing financial policies in combination with more conservative social values when it comes to lifestyle, law, and order.[49]

According to research projects such as the World Values Survey (WVS), which measures cultural differences, beliefs, values, and motivations of people throughout the world, no other country in the world has a set of values that deviates more from the global norm than Sweden. The WVS, which measures both "traditional" values (related to religion, family, and nation) and "emancipative" values (self-realization and individual autonomy), ranks Sweden as having the most atypical and deviant value profile of all nations. Swedes are the least traditional of all nationalities, according to the WVS, with values that are described as extremely secular-rational.[50] For example, Swedes prioritize personal independence over family or traditional authorities. Swedes are the least religious, the most accepting of divorce, and the most adamant that men and women have the same financial obligations as breadwinners. Few Swedes believe that children must love or respect their parents.[51]

* * *

It's late evening when Chang steps out of the shower. He puts on a ripped tracksuit, and peaks in to see that the kids are asleep. Polina seems to have dozed off beside them while tucking them in. Chang doesn't wake her but steps into a pair of sneakers, and pulls a beanie hat down low over his forehead. He exits his apartment building and walks across the dimly lit parking lot to his light gray Volvo to start patrolling the suburbs. Last night he captured footage of a burning car, as well as the aftermath of a shootout in Norsborg. Most incidents occur between 10 p.m. and 3 a.m., so for the real action, he has to work nights. He begins to circle the neighborhood, looking for little clues to steer him in the right direction. A wet curve on an otherwise dry road, for example, can indicate that a fire truck has recently passed, as their excess water tends to overflow on the bends.

It's still quiet, so Chang pulls over to grab a burger at the local Max hamburger joint. He eats in his car. The parking lot is much larger than the venue itself and most guests seems to congregate in or around their vehicles. Judging from clientele alone, one could easily get the impression of being in the Middle East. The parking lot is filled with men sporting large, immaculately trimmed and groomed beards. While Chang is growing his own, his black wisp comes nowhere near their dense and carefully sculpted creations. It is reminiscent of the horticultural practice of topiary, whereby a shrub is transformed into a piece of art.

But even disregarding areas like his home turf, where the density of immigrants is particularly high, Sweden is quickly becoming a different place. By now, one in five residents of Sweden was born outside of the country, compared with around one in seven in the UK in 2017. If one includes people born in Sweden to at least one foreign-born parent, the proportion is more than 30 per cent, a far cry from the homogenous make-up of the past.[52] In most European countries, the vast majority of immigrants come from neighboring countries or from former colonies, where a common language, partly shared history, and cultural knowledge facilitate integration.[53] In Sweden, Syrians are now the largest immigrant group and there are more Afghans than

Danes or Norwegians.[54] No other European country has such a large non-European portion of its population.[55]

* * *

Politicians were arguing that immigration was necessary to support an aging population; that it would actually financially benefit Sweden in the long run. But they were basing their claims either on international statistics from countries like Canada, which had welcomed many well-educated and highly skilled migrants, or on old data about the foreign workers who had come to Sweden during the post-war industrial boom of the 1950s and 1960s, and who had immediately started to contribute and pay tax. In contrast, many of the refugees who were now arriving lacked the qualifications and skills necessary to be successful in a knowledge economy, while their needs, when it came to education, language training, and health care, were often significant.

In 1998–9, 25 per cent of refugees in Sweden had only a primary education or no schooling. By 2009–10, that segment of the refugee population accounted for 45 per cent and continued to grow.[56] Meanwhile the overall trend in Swedish society has been the opposite, with higher education becoming increasingly common.[57] In a country taking pride in its technical progress and egalitarian salary structures, there are now very few low-cost job opportunities for those who don't speak Swedish or lack marketable skills. Consequently, after eight years in Sweden, only about half of all refugees had secured their first job in 2016. After fifteen years in Sweden, that number was just under 60 per cent, and there it remained over time, with many people permanently excluded from the workforce—trapped by welfare dependency.[58]

As more and more refugees arrived, the media campaigns aimed at generating popular support for the open door policy was becoming increasingly fervent. In September and October of 2015, *Dagens Nyheter* launched a campaign in which 100 Swedish celebrities took a stand for compassion. Under the hashtag

#SwedenRefugees, they also posted daily stories of refugee life, meant to humanize; to show the people behind the numbers; to wear down resistance among the growing number of Swedes who wanted to restrict immigration. The other media outlets did the same. Scandinavia's largest media group, Schibsted, financed two rescue boats in the Mediterranean, where teams of reporters from their newspapers *Svenska Dagbladet* and *Aftonbladet* were working to save refugees from the ocean while covering the crisis at the same time.[59] *Expressen* teamed up with the Red Cross in the #jagvillhjälpa (#Iwanttohelp) campaign.

While the humanitarian efforts were commendable, there were also several examples of manipulation of numbers in an attempt to portray Sweden's current inflow of refugees as financially lucrative for society, contrary to official calculations.[60] One of the most extreme examples appeared in *Dagens Nyheter*, where it was reported that the municipality of Sandviken made a profit of 500 million SEK each year off its foreign-born residents. "It has been debated whether immigration constitutes a cost or an income, and if so, to what extent. That's why the committee ordered this study and it was positive that also an independent report so clearly demonstrate that the plus side of immigration is so much bigger," Leif Jansson of Sandviken municipality told *DN*.[61]

What the article failed to mention was that none of the costs borne by the state had been included in the calculus of expenses. Meanwhile, the personal incomes of the immigrants had been categorized as profit for the municipality.[62] It took ordering a copy of the actual, full report to figure out just how skewed the numbers were.[63] Conducting propaganda was hardly the task of the media, and it was beginning to take its toll on their credibility. A 2015 study showed that more than half the Swedish population believed that "Swedish media don't tell the truth regarding societal problems related to immigration."[64]

* * *

Just as he unwraps his burger, Chang's phone rings. The screen tells him it's Mattias, one of his contacts in nearby Alby. "I just heard a machine gun round being fired!" Mattias exclaims. Chang hangs up and immediately calls the police. He speaks to the duty officer, who confirms that they've received reports of shooting, but there have been no reports of anyone being injured. Chang finishes his burger in one bite, backs out of his parking spot and starts making his way towards Alby to check it out.

He hasn't been on the highway long when a police car with flashing sirens passes him, heading in the other direction. After hesitating for an instant, Chang drops the machine gun lead and turns around to follow the police car. Minutes later, he arrives in Solberga in southern Stockholm. A man in his twenties has been shot; when Chang arrives, heavily armed police officers are searching for the perpetrator, who is still at large. A stretch of the road has been roped off while a K9 officer and his dog are busy examining the bushes and parked cars. A few locals have congregated near the police cordon.

Among them, Chang finds an eyewitness who lives in the nearby building. The middle-aged man tells Chang he saw three people standing around eating take-out food when a gunman approached and started shooting at them. One person was hit, while the other two managed to escape. "They were, excuse the expression, Negroes," he says, in broken and heavily accented Swedish. The witness claims he recognized the victim as one of his neighbors. In his article, Chang does not use his quote, but says that according to the witness, the men involved were "young and of dark complexion."[65] Other media covering the event make no mention of physical descriptions at all.

* * *

"My Europe builds no walls," says Prime Minister Löfven. "We help each other in times of great need." It is 6 September 2015, and 15,000 people have gathered at Medborgarplatsen in Stockholm under the banner "Refugees Welcome." Millions are escaping war-torn Syria, Afghanistan, and Iraq. During the summer, the number of people hoping for a better future in Europe skyrocketed, putting a great strain on the capacity of many countries to provide food and shelter, as well as on the relationships between different European countries. Prime Minister Viktor Orbán announced his intention to close Hungary's borders and build a 4-meter-high fence, resulting in massive criticism from the Swedish government and much of Western Europe. It wasn't long before other nations also claimed they were reaching capacity and needed to enforce their borders, ultimately resulting in legal action by the EU. But Löfven makes it clear that Sweden will continue to welcome those in need. For Sweden there is no limit.

By the fall of 2015, it is clear that the number of refugees will be at least double that of 2014. One week, 8,194 asylum seekers arrive; the next it's 9,258, then 10,175.[66] During the month of October, more asylum seekers enter Sweden every week than the total number of Chilean refugees who arrived in Sweden in the entire decade of the 1970s.[67]

THE PEOPLE'S CONTAINER

Endless rows of pine and spruce trees line the straight, monotonous highway. Chang is heading south; back to his hometown, Killeberg. He stops at his favorite trucker's roadside joint for lunch. Here, servings are large and table manners superfluous. The further he gets from Stockholm and anything reminiscent of pretense, the brighter Chang's mood. He must have driven this road a thousand times.

The small towns that blur past all look alike, but there are hardly any people. It's pastoral, but dead. In 2015, Agunnaryd lost its status as an "urban center" when the population fell below 200 people. Looking around, it's hard to believe this is where the global success story of IKEA was once born. In 1943, 17-year-old Ingvar Kamprad registered the company that would become a beacon of Swedishness worldwide. The name is an acronym consisting of the founder's initials, the first letter of Elmtaryd—the farm where Kamprad grew up—and of this village: Agunnaryd.

About a further 30-minute drive south is Älmhult. With its 9,000 inhabitants, it's the main town in these rural parts and only about a 10-minute drive from the village where Chang grew up. Älmhult's main claim to fame is that it housed the very first IKEA store, opened in 1958. While the corporate head office is now in the Netherlands, Älmhult remains the company's spiritual hub. Today, it is home to the IKEA museum and the base of "IKEA Together," the center for corporate culture where employees from across the world come to study and internalize the brand.[1] As he passes the furniture giant's buildings, Chang stays true to his habit of speeding up. IKEA gives him a migraine.

* * *

"How's Arnold?" Chang asks Lasse. "I've tried phoning, but I guess his service has been shut off." Chang is having coffee on the old, familiar leather couch of Lasse's living room. On every trip down south, he always makes a point to stop by at the car paint and repair shop where he and his brother used to hide out as kids.

"He's out back," Lasse replies, motioning to the far end of his lot. "He lives in an old shipping container back there." Unsure whether or not Lasse is joking, Chang gets up, finds his shoes by the front door, and makes his way around to the back.

Crisscrossing between piles of scrap metal, ashes, and the remnants of burnt garbage, Chang tries to find paths around the muddy puddles scattered across the backyard. At the edge of the property sits a large, white, refrigerated container that someone has begun to paint red.

Imposingly tall, long-haired, with a shirt stretched by the muscles bulging beneath, the adult Arnold resembles the Marvel version of the Norse god Thor. While the brothers share some facial features, Arnold has tied-back, wild blond hair and a blond beard. His giant arms are covered with tattoos. But it's his eyes one remembers. They are the unmistakable, fire-ice blue of a wolf. During one of his many trials, a witness testified to being terrified just by seeing "the blue flame." But today Arnold is on his best behavior; a gentle giant. He shows Chang how he has turned the container into a home. He has put in flooring, painted the walls, installed a fridge, and used random IKEA cabinet doors to build a bed and a makeshift privacy wall. Even the IKEA product names remain. A repurposed Ensvik wardrobe door does its part to create "a better everyday life for many people."

With a small wood stove, Arnold is trying to generate heat. But his attempt to use ductwork instead of a stovepipe to clear the smoke through a hole in the side of the container is not working. While he and Chang sit and talk at his little makeshift table, the container keeps filling up with smoke and Arnold constantly has to get up and open the door for fresh air, thereby also letting out all the heat.

"I'll need some kind of ventilation," he says, "I guess I'll have to make a hole somewhere." He pours accelerant on the fire and throws a handful of napkins with crayfish patterns into the stove.

"You have to seal the pipe to vent the smoke and gas outside," says Chang.

Meanwhile, the stove spews out new clouds of thick smoke into the container.

"I have to sort this out if I'm to make it through the winter. The snow is coming soon, the newspaper said. It's supposed to be a cold one," Arnold comments, as he throws another handful of napkins into the stove and fans the smoke from his face.

Arnold didn't always live in a container. He used to rent an apartment in a terraced house in Delary, 12 kilometers west of Älmhult. But at the end of 2014 he was evicted following a change of ownership.

"What happened?" asks Chang.

"The new owners wanted to convert the building into a home for unaccompanied minors," replies Arnold with a gruff snort. Though they have rented out other facilities to the Migration Authorities, the new owners deny that any such agreement was in place for this building.[2] Either way, Arnold made sure it wouldn't happen. "I dumped garbage, oil, and toxic waste all over the place," he says. "And then I wrote a sign: 'Opening soon—a home for unaccompanied refugee children.'"

Älmhult municipality filed a police report with a long list of serious environmental offences. It contains thirty-four photos illustrating the extent of the damage and confirms that dangerous chemicals have seeped into the ground. The area has been decontaminated, but further efforts may be necessary, the report asserts.

* * *

Chang stops for coffee and a sandwich at a gas station before starting his drive back north to Stockholm. It's his birthday; his least favorite day of the year. It reminds him of all the childhood birthday celebrations that never were. Once again he passes by Älmhult's main claim to fame: IKEA. He thinks of the odd doors and pieces of discarded furniture his brother has used to build his existence. He feels the first signs of a headache coming on.

THE FUSE BLOWS

THE UNIMIND CHANGES ITS MIND

"Recently, we've been having a very difficult discussion within the party about the perception of reality," says Åsa Romson, deputy prime minister and leader of the Greens. Then her voice breaks and she starts to cry: "But in the last couple of weeks, I've become convinced that the best way to help my local Green Party politicians is to actually do something." It is 24 November 2015. Romson and Prime Minister Löfven have called a press conference announcing the reversal of Sweden's open-door policy towards asylum seekers. And it is the Green Party, traditionally advocates of the most liberal immigration policies, that has to break the news.

Samvel is watching the live broadcast of Romson's collapse on his computer, but he struggles to feel any sympathy. Like most Swedes, he's been following the escalating drama around the immigration crisis with increasing interest. He folds his thin legs underneath him as he curls up into a fetal position on the sofa. He pulls the laptop closer.

After having said there was "no limit" to how many asylum seekers Sweden could receive, the six main political parties—not counting the Sweden Democrats or the small Left Party—have suddenly and magically shifted on this question, all at once. On

23 October, they announced the first restrictions to Sweden's immigration policies. For example, adult refugees without children would henceforth be granted temporary instead of permanent residency permits. By 30 October, Foreign Minister Margot Wallström had announced that there was, after all, a limit to how many immigrants Sweden could take in. The system would collapse and the endeavor would lose all popular support.[1]

On 9 November, 1,868 people sought asylum in Sweden in a single day. That was as many as would normally seek asylum in Finland in the course of a whole year. Over thirteen weeks, 23,400 unaccompanied minors arrived. The sheer numbers created chaos in several municipalities, which tried desperately, and frequently unsuccessfully, to rent housing from private providers. Some even filed legal charges against themselves, as they realized they were failing to receive unaccompanied minors in a safe way.[2] In three weeks, the small southern town of Trelleborg (population 40,000) received 1,900 unaccompanied minors, 1,000 of whom never showed up at their assigned housing, but simply went missing.[3] Tent camps were beginning to pop up, in a country that took pride in a safety net so tightly-knit that no one could slip through. Staff at the Migration Authorities were deep under water.[4]

The government's failure to deal with the migration crisis has caused support for the Sweden Democrats to skyrocket. Some opinion polls place them as the second largest party,[5] others as the single largest party.[6/7]

On 10 November, a Sentio Research poll claimed support for the party had reached an all-time high: 26.8 per cent. This would give it a significant lead over the second biggest party, the Social Democrats, who polled at 22 per cent.[8]

Two days later, on 12 November, border controls were reestablished for the first time since 1995. Three days after that, the government announced that Sweden would replace permanent residency permits with temporary ones, and henceforth not accept more refugees than the EU-required minimum.[9]

And now this press conference. When Romson manages to compose herself, she and Löfven outline a number of measures meant to dissuade future refugees from choosing Sweden as their destination. For example, the right of refugees' family members to join their next of kin is to be restricted, and previously criticized medical assessments to determine age will be introduced, to make sure unaccompanied minors are truly minors.[10] It isn't the restrictions per se that bothers Samvel. It's the timing of it that rings false. Now that the Sweden Democrats have surpassed 20 per cent in the polls, the government has suddenly rediscovered its old devotion to a closed welfare model.

In 2015, Sweden took in close to 163,000 asylum seekers, the most in a year in the country's history, and more per capita than any other country in the European Union.[11] Sweden took in 35,369 unaccompanied minors—a third of the total seeking asylum in Europe. Most of them were boys and the vast majority (23,480) were from Afghanistan. Taking care of these minors was expected to set the taxpayers back by 30–5 billion SEK a year. Including the costs for health care and other expenses, it's closer to 45 billion SEK (almost £4 billion) a year—the equivalent of Afghanistan's entire national budget.[12]

While Samvel thinks the headlines of collapsing systems are exaggerations, they reflect a more important truth to him: that the compassion and generosity of the average Swede has reached its limits. With a different, less paternalistic system, he thinks, it could be done. But the majority of Swedes don't want a new Sweden. If anything, they want a return to what they had in the 1960s and '70s. They want their little, safe Sweden back. And migration isn't compatible with the *Folkhem* or the welfare state. It is pretty clear it has come down to immigration, or the Swedish model; us or them.

Samvel closes the lid of his laptop, and stands up to get a drink. He can understand the resistance to multiculturalism in practice. What he can't understand is the simultaneous, continued theoretical commitment to it that has enabled the prime minister to stand in central Stockholm and give a bombastic speech about how his Europe builds no walls, mere weeks before deciding to close the border. Why continue to project the image of Sweden as a humanitarian giant, and continue vocally to welcome people, when he must have known change was coming? 'There is plenty of room,' the leadership had conveyed clearly, loudly, and globally. 'Come and we'll take care of you.'

He opens his landlord's fridge and scans it blankly. Of course that kind of advertisement was going to attract people. It created false expectations, luring people to put their lives in the hands of ruthless human smugglers, just to get to Sweden, thinking they could find happiness here. Now, they've shown up only to find out it was just about branding. There was no real plan. Without warning, the border has been closed.

This quick shift has taken Samvel by surprise. Swedes call it the "opinion corridor;" a kind of metaphor for the limits of what is a commonly accepted belief or topic for debate. In Sweden, that range is narrow; Samvel knows that much. But he always thought of it as more or less constant, and was not prepared for how quickly it could shift. He closes the fridge and grabs a large glass from the cupboard. He runs the tap until it's cold, fills his glass carefully, and leans his hand against the counter as he takes a long, slow drink.

THE OPINION CORRIDOR

In a rare attempt to openly admit and actually put into words the notion of an "opinion corridor," *Aftonbladet* columnist Johan Hakelius explained in 2015:

> It is almost magical and very Swedish. Suddenly the corridor turns. What was considered a suspicious statement a couple of months ago is suddenly common sense at the center of the opinion corridor. The shift is not preceded by any free, bold, and open debate. Publicly, the work of keeping down, stigmatizing, and denying, continues to the very end. It is beneath the surface that preparations happen. There grows the insight of what is unsustainable and unrealistic. Beneath the surface, "open our hearts" has long been written off as naïve student politics. But no one wants to crack the façade on their own.
>
> Instead, the entire house is torn down bit by bit behind the façade, which remains standing. Then comes the decisive moment. At a given signal, the old façade falls. Behind it a new one is already in place. It appears to have always been there. In a blink, everything is changed. Politicians, journalists, everybody follows suit. Now we have a new corridor.

Most Swedes were familiar with this process, Hakelius argued. They had all experienced it firsthand in workplaces, associations, or among friends. As a result, they had learned to sense when it was about to happen, developed a kind of intuition for it—which helped them to prepare so that they would not keep heading in the wrong direction when the sudden shift happened. "But," Hakelius mused, "how in the world do you explain Sweden to a newcomer?"[1]

PART FOUR

ON THE TRAIL OF THE CULPRIT

THURSDAY 7 JANUARY 2016

Hans has a missed call from the *Dagens Nyheter* journalist. At 2:23 p.m., she has left a voicemail: "We spoke in August. Now, after what happened in Cologne, I would like to talk to you again. It got stuck on certain things when we were doing this in August." She has also sent an email: "I'd like to get in touch with you again after what happened in Cologne during the New Year holidays." Hans reads her message and grits his teeth. More than four months have passed, and now she chooses to get in touch. It is about bloody time.

On New Year's Eve, gangs of some 1,000 men—of mainly foreign descent—amassed around Cologne's main train station and sexually assaulted women with impunity. More than 120 criminal complaints were filed, the vast majority of which had a sexual component.[1] Still, Cologne police described the New Year's celebrations as "peaceful" and officers were instructed to remove the word "rape" from official reports.[2] It took five days for the media to report the incidents. Hans-Peter Friedrich, a former interior minister of Angela Merkel, accused the media of imposing a "news blackout" and operating a "code of silence" over negative news about immigrants. The public broadcaster, ZDF, issued an apology for failing to include the assaults in its main evening news.[3] Following harsh criticism, Cologne Police Chief Wolfgang Albers was forced into early retirement.[4]

Ever since the story became public, Europe has been brooding with indignation. And now, when Sweden has closed its border and the opinion corridor has turned, Swedish media are apparently ready to bring their very own examples to light. Hans contemplates ignoring them, but decides against it and returns the journalist's call. She wonders if he is still willing to talk. Hans swallows his anger and agrees. After all, what matters most is that the truth finally gets out.

Another reporter will call him back, she says. The hours go by and the phone does not ring. Hans contacts the journalist again. She sends a text to let him know that there are several witnesses. In addition, the commanding police officer who had been in charge at We Are Sthlm 2014 a year earlier is willing to make a statement on the record, so there is no need for an anonymous source. "But a warm thanks for your tip. I'm sorry we didn't put it to better use," she writes.

Hans sits back. He feels uneasy. Several witnesses. A police commander willing to talk on the record. What stopped the paper from making these same phone calls back in August? Over the course of the last few months, Hans has lost all confidence in traditional media, and in *Dagens Nyheter* in particular, but now he directs himself to their webpage. The editor-in-chief, Peter Wolodarski, is very critical of how German police and media have handled recent events. "Dangerously silent about the crimes in Cologne," reads the headline of today's editorial. "Media and police tend to be extra careful when it comes to news that risk 'affecting vulnerable groups,'" writes Wolodarski. "But the silence following the assaults in Cologne was a great betrayal of the victims." Hans almost chokes on his coffee. Wolodarski goes on to talk about the unimaginable terror the afflicted women must have experienced that New Year's Eve, when they suddenly found themselves separated from their company and surrounded by men who proceeded to tear off their clothes, steal their valuables, and grope them. "The feeling of horror and powerlessness must be bottomless," he writes. What about our girls? Hans wonders aloud. Wolodarski writes that "both police and traditional media waited unreasonably long with their reports about the events."

According to the editorial, a perpetrator's origins must never become either a mitigating or an aggravating circumstance. "Silence," Wolodarski writes, "is almost never the answer. The news will get out eventually. If traditional media don't do their jobs well, someone else will—much worse." Traditional media, Wolodarski concludes, "must take their responsibility." Two sentences are enlarged and in bold: "If anyone is in an inferior position it is the targeted women. To keep silent or mumble is a great betrayal of the victims." Hans reads and rereads the sentences with growing anger and frustration. He tries to work, to focus on other things, but the words in the editorial, the feelings, and the images from the fall, continue to seep in through the cracks. He goes to bed deeply upset.

The following day, Hans has made up his mind. When he returns home in the evening, he grabs his computer from beside his bed and pulls up his email. His frustration with the mainstream media has led him increasingly to refer to alternate sites for his news. Particularly impressed with the frank and well-researched coverage of *Nyheter Idag*, he brings up their webpage, hits the "Contact Us" section, and reaches out to editor Chang Frick:

January 8, 22:12:15 CET

Hi Chang,

I'm turning to you as I think you might be interested in information that could become a story.

In August I witnessed events in Kungsträdgården, reminiscent of what happened in Cologne, Kalmar, etc at New Year.

I spent a few hours there with two young relatives, both teenagers, when Zara Larsson played on stage.

The police and security guards apprehended/detained about 90 boys/men for sexual assaults in the crowd by the stage where they systematically surrounded girls and touched them everywhere.

No girls wanted to participate in filing complaints and in the chaos of the crowd (Kungsan was packed) it was difficult for police to find plaintiffs.

Hans describes his attempt to reach out to media, and how the events in Cologne finally led the *Dagens Nyheter* journalist to phone him back. He ends with the event that pushed him over the edge:

Wolodarski's editorial the other day was about the importance of established media daring to cover sensitive events—what hypocrisy!!!

Let me know if this sounds interesting, or I'll try to turn to some other possible writer.

Best regards.

SATURDAY 9 JANUARY 2016

It is almost one o'clock in the morning when Chang opens the message. He is tired but doesn't like to go to bed with unread emails in his inbox. One never knows what one could miss. Mechanically he deletes them, one after the other. He receives endless junk mail from all sorts of nut-jobs. People with supposed insights, fueled by conspiracy theories about the real, secret rulers of the world. Ninety-nine times out of a hundred, they are a waste of time. And there is nothing to suggest that this one is any different. "Idea for an important story," the subject reads.

With his mouse hovering over the delete icon, Chang quickly scans the message. He hesitates. The spelling and grammar is flawless, which is more than can be said for most of the psychos who typically reach out to him. He double-clicks to bring up the message in its own window and reads it again, carefully this time: some ninety boys and men have supposedly been detained or evicted for sexually assaulting young girls at a youth festival ... in August. That seems bizarre. He reads on. Established media knew, but chose not to cover it. Chang feels a pang of excitement, combined with disbelief. What if this were true? It would be an unparalleled scandal in the history of Swedish media. All hell would break loose.

Chang replies: "This is super interesting. I'll be in touch tomorrow. Do you have emails, recorded conversations, or anything else to support this?" At 1:08 a.m., he hits send.

* * *

It's a Saturday morning, but as usual Hans wakes up earlier than he would like. He brews his coffee and returns to bed with his laptop. He is pleased to note that Chang has already replied. He writes back to let him know that he has kept the email exchange with the *DN* journalist. It proves she knew about the incident on 17 August. He also has the voice message she left him on 7 January. Hans has made plans to see a friend, but he is eager to have this resolved. "Let's talk after 1 p.m. today, Saturday. I'll be on my cell phone," he writes to Chang. At 9:11 a.m., he hits send.

As Hans prepares his breakfast, he realizes that he forgot to mention that he has also kept the text exchanges with the journalist. At 9:42, he sends Chang another email with that information. "I hope you're able to write something impactful based on these fragments." Hans turns to the news. He starts with *Dagens Nyheter*'s website to see if they've decided to publish anything. They have.

"Is this an attack on Western equality?" wonders journalist Lasse Wierup, in a column talking about a potential link between the attacks in Cologne, and the similar, albeit smaller-scale attacks on the same night in Helsinki and the Swedish city of Kalmar. "Could it really be a coincidence that the phenomenon has suddenly occurred in multiple countries at the same time?" he ponders.

"The first Swedish news reports from Cologne took five days, and in the case of Kalmar even longer. Both police spokespeople and media hesitated, as though not quite trusting the women's stories." Wierup adds that this is similar to what happened in Stockholm last August.[1]

This is where most readers must have lost the thread. What is he talking about? What happened in Stockholm last August? As though in passing, a mere addition to his list of examples, Wierup then describes a scandal hitherto unknown to the Swedish public: at the youth festival We Are Sthlm, large groups of men sexually assaulted young girls, night after night. Struggling to cope, police and guards focused on evicting the perpetrators from the concert. During a single night, some ninety young men were forcefully removed. Meanwhile, detaining perpetrators or filing incident reports was largely neglected, and so far, nobody has been convicted. "One of the police officers who participated, and who had to spend a great deal of time comforting the victimized girls, says that the matter was considered sensitive. The young men who were sent away were judged to be mainly unaccompanied [refugee minors]," Wierup writes. He claims he doesn't know why the extensive sexual harassments ended up in a media blackout. "But the mere suspicion that the abuse was deemed difficult to describe is a betrayal of the victims."[2]

Hans stares at the screen. He can't believe what he has just read. Is *DN* really going to completely dodge its own responsibility like that? He immediately pens another email to Chang. 9:47 a.m.: "I'm sorry to be bombarding you with emails but I just read the story in *DN*..."

* * *

"I can come over. Are you located downtown?" Hans is eager to hand over his email and phone records. After months of frustration, he finally feels this is going somewhere.

Chang replies: "No, I'm in the suburbs. In Hallunda. Havrevägen 11."

"Okay, I'll be there soon."

Hans cuts through the Hallunda commercial center on his way from the subway stop. He walks past several jewelers, pawnshops, and a place called Small World Money Transfers on his left. On his right, Tony's Fashion displays extravagant dresses with much glitter and lace. Most of these establishments certainly don't cater to Swedes, he reflects. It feels like a foreign land.

It is early afternoon when Hans locates the address. He expected some sort of an office, but instead he is standing at the foot of a faintly yellow, eight-story building, typical of the Million Program era. There is an entry code, so Hans phones and Chang comes down to open the door for him. Chang looks unkempt and tired, wearing a worn tracksuit. Hans follows him up the stairs to the fifth floor. An Arabic-sounding name is written on the door. Hans stops to read it. Chang explains that it's a black-market rental from a local Syrian family. "If anyone asks, I'm his brother," he smiles. With his thick black hair and dark stubble, Chang could easily pass for Syrian, Hans figures.

They take off their shoes, then proceed from the narrow hallway into the kitchen.

"Coffee?" offers Chang. He moves toys and papers aside to make room for Hans at the small wooden kitchen table. It's painted in a color known colloquially as "snot-green." Hans can't recall having seen it used on anything since he was a kid in the '80s. There are only two chairs. Hans sits down on one of them and looks around. Chang is standing by the sink. His girlfriend, two young kids, and mother-in-law move around in the background, making the run-down, two-bedroom apartment feel even smaller. "There's no milk," Chang adds as he pours himself some coffee. "Grab a cup." He motions towards the kitchen cabinets. They are made of brown particle boards, with the type of steel handles that were popular in the '60s.

Hans stands up and opens a cupboard at random. Inside there is a mismatch of odd plates and cups of different sizes and patterns. Chang is ready with the coffee pot and empties what remains in Hans' outstretched cup. He puts the pot back down and proceeds past Hans into the other room. "Let's go into the office," he calls. Hans follows him into the small space, where a large Mac screen sits on a white desk. Hard drives, cameras, cords, and boxes fill the area. Chang pulls up a wooden chair for Hans, then takes a seat in his worn, fake-leather office chair.

* * *

"She was very interested and listened, until I told her that the apprehended boys and men were young asylum seekers[3] from Afghanistan and Syria," says Hans. "I noticed a change of tone. But she did say that she would contact the police."

Chang writes the story with Hans right there beside him in his office. He has told him to bring all supporting documents. Hans pulls out his laptop and smartphone, presenting one piece of evidence after another. Chang photographs the texts, makes copies of the voice recordings, and scrutinizes all the material. He creates a new folder where he stores it all. He smiles as he names it "DNgate."

Hans tells Chang how the journalist reached out again after the events in Cologne: "She said she had a lump in her stomach. She was fidgeting when I asked her why she never contacted the police and never wrote an article."

Chang calls Lars, the police source who spent the evening at the festival with Hans, to hear his version. The officer comes across as a quiet, correct, and cautious man. Like Hans, he stresses that he wishes to remain anonymous. He fears his children will pay the price if word gets out that he was the source of the leak. Lars testifies to systematic and extensive assaults, and explains how he and his colleagues had to apprehend a large number of young men who sexually assaulted girls, in large part unaccompanied minors from Afghanistan. When Chang asks about his contact with the *DN* journalist, Lars says her interest faded. "We spoke briefly and she said she would call me back, but she never did. So I tried to reach out again, but she never returned my calls. I called several times, not sure exactly how many, during the course of three or four days," he tells Chang.

They hang up and Chang prepares to confront the journalist. He wonders what she'll say. Will she pick up? He dials her cellphone and she responds almost immediately. "Hi, my name is Chang Frick and I'm calling from *Nyheter Idag.*"

"Okay. Hi." Chang explains that he has spoken to the psychologist who reached out to her in August regarding the events in Kungsträdgården.

"Yes."

"He told you the story, but it didn't result in an article?"

The journalist is quiet. Then says: "I can't talk to you about what my sources have said to me. I can't confirm or deny anything."

Chang explains that he has seen the email conversations and text messages between her and the psychologist. He also explains that the psychologist has contacted him because he feels that *Dagens Nyheter* has covered up the events that took place in Kungsträdgården. "That's why I'd like to ask you a few questions," he adds.

"I'm not going to answer that. No, no, no."

"Was there an editor that prevented you from covering the story?"

"No, no, no, no. I don't want to talk to you. Thanks and goodbye," she says and hangs up.

Shortly thereafter, Hans' phone rings. He turns to Chang. "It's her. What should I say?"

"Don't answer. Let it ring. Don't pick up."

At 4:18 p.m., the journalist leaves a voicemail: "I've just been contacted by a journalist and I feel like I need to talk to you as there may be some misunderstanding. I also feel quite betrayed by that fact that you have shared our conversations. But please call me as soon as you hear this. Bye."

Chang prepares his recorder and instructs Hans to call the journalist back.

"I don't think you fully understand the amount of shit this will stir up," he tells Hans. To openly challenge the Swedish media incumbent like this will not go over well. They will hate him for it and do their best to tear apart his case. Everything must be correct and verifiable. He knows that if there is a single fact that is disputable, that will dominate the discussion and discredit his entire case.

Chang nods to Hans to go ahead and dial the journalist's number. "Welcome to *Dagens Nyheter*. Our hours are..." an automatic response starts to play.

"This must be the landline." Hans checks his notes. "Yup. Then I understand why she's not responding." He dials her cellphone instead. They wait in silence as the ring tones echo. "My pulse is racing," Hans comments. Chang can see that he is agitated. He hopes he'll stay calm. "Why won't she pick up?" says Hans. "She'll record me too, don't you think?" Chang keeps quiet. If she does pick up and hears his voice in the background, she won't say a thing. He makes a face at Hans, attempting to convey that he shouldn't speak to him while it is ringing.

Finally, she answers. Hans introduces himself. "I got your message just now," he adds.

"Yes. Hi! Wait a sec," she says. The line goes quiet. Chang figures she has paused to turn on her recorder. A few seconds later, she is back: "Yes. Well I was very surprised at being contacted..."

"Wait a second," Hans interrupts. "You say in your message that you feel betrayed. Who is betraying who? Haven't you betrayed these girls?" Hans' voice picks up pace and his brow furrows as he reproaches the journalist for her handling of events. "It's a tremendous scandal. How the hell could you do this?" Chang motions for Hans to calm down. Why won't he just let her talk?

The journalist explains that as a columnist she mainly writes editorials. "Are you trying to save your own butt?" Hans asks.

"I'm not at all concerned about my butt. I've had a lot of contact with you. I've handed this over to the Stockholm City Desk where it belongs. Then the Stockholm City Desk decided not to pursue the story. I thought it was a shame."

"How can the Stockholm City Desk decide not to..."

"I don't know," she interrupts.

"But hold on a minute. You told me that the editor of the Stockholm City Desk considered the story to be non-credible and SD [Sweden Democrat] fabrications. How can you not verify this information? All it takes is a phone call."

"No, it's like this..."

"Isn't that what you said the other day?"

"No, I didn't. I said that the editor of the Stockholm City Desk was not excited by this lead. And I left two leads the same day and the other one she was excited about. I don't even remember what it was."

"She wasn't excited about the fact that girls were systematically abused, and that ninety guys were apprehended, and this went on every night throughout the entire festival. That had no news value? Do you expect me to believe that? Listen to yourself! Listen to what you're saying!" Hans says agitatedly.

"You're not even listening to what I am saying. She probably made a judgment call regarding the credibility of this..."

"But it's so easy to check! All you have to do is call the police and get their incident reports. With a phone call you could've verified whether I was telling the truth or not!"

The journalist remains quiet.

"Please answer me," says Hans.

"It's really strange that you don't want to go public with your name."

"No. And you're just confirming why, because the media covers up these things and you know very well what the climate is like on these issues."

* * *

Hours later, Chang is still sitting by his desk, putting the finishing touches to the story. He crafts his article carefully. He double-checks everything. The psychologist is long gone and Chang is alone with the burden of responsibility. He is excited, but there's something else sitting in his gut that he can't quite name. Perhaps his intuition is trying to tell him something. He has another cup of coffee. Then triple-checks the facts. He looks around his tiny office. It's the size of a closet, and if it weren't for his high-end computer one could easily mistake it for a make-believe newsroom, constructed messily by a child pretending to be a reporter in his father's office. Chang never played journalist as a boy. For him it was always all about mechanics. But there's something here that reminds him of his childhood. It takes a minute before he realizes it's the lump in his stomach. The Fear is back. Not like it was back then, just strong enough for him to recognize it. It has been a long time since he last felt it, but he figures it's probably a good sign. After all, he is about to take on Goliath.

He decides to go outside for air. He puts on his shoes but leaves his jacket behind. He wants to feel the cold. He doesn't have a thermometer but knows it's unusually chilly. Just the other day, on 7 January, northern Sweden experienced its coldest day in fifteen years: -42.9 degrees Celsius in Naimakka. Stockholm is not that bad, but brisk enough to make his face tingle. He stares up into the impenetrable January darkness. He has always prided himself on his bravery, but this one requires a few deep breaths even for him.

"Publish and be damned," he mumbles to himself. "Please let there be no mistakes," he repeats as he climbs the stairs back up to his apartment. At 11.41 p.m. he hits publish.

SUNDAY 10 JANUARY 2016

"The Police Covered Up the Assaults at the Festival," reads the *Dagens Nyheter* headline. Two summers in a row, according to the article, systematic sexual assaults of young girls have occurred at the Swedish youth festival We Are Sthlm, Europe's largest festival for teenagers. Yet, instead of informing the public, Swedish police chose to silence internal emergency reports.[1]

Chang reads the story in his office. He hasn't slept much. After publishing his own story, he remained in front of his computer, on guard. At first nothing happened. The minutes dragged by as Chang struggled to suppress a growing feeling of surrealism. Then, at seventeen minutes past midnight, the story was first shared on Flashback, Sweden's largest online forum. At 00:38, Chang posted his fruitless phone conversation with the *DN* journalist on YouTube. Before long, the recording had been shared more than 20,000 times. It is beyond anything Chang could have imagined. *DN* will not be able to ignore it. With a mixture of dread and excitement, he has spent the day awaiting their countermove. It is now evening and he is impressed by the paper's damage control. This is not what he was expecting. With several police sources, countless witnesses and victims, and the massive spread of the story on social media, *DN* must have concluded that trying to deny a cover-up would at this point be pointless. To turn around and blame the police for it is a brilliant move.

Chang reads on: internal memos raised the issues of sexual assaults early, but when Press Officer Hesam Akbari of the Stockholm police summarized the festival on their official site, he reported that there had been "relatively few crimes and few arrests considering the number of visitors." It was noted that the police tents had received "record numbers," but not that these visitors were girls who'd been the victims of crime.

Chang is amazed. They are making it sound like journalists rely on press releases for their news. If they had bothered to lift a phone to verify the information that both Lars and Hans had been trying desperately to make public, this story could have been published long ago. Confirming it now, more than four months later, and even gaining access to internal memos from last summer, has obviously not been a problem. He continues reading. "The youngest girls were only about 11 or 12. I would never have let my own daughter attend the festival if I knew what was going on," a police officer who was on duty tells *DN*. Yet, the assaults were neither a new nor an unexpected phenomenon. Many assaults had also been reported in 2014, including a young girl who had fingers inserted into her vagina. According to *Dagens Nyheter*, the perpetrators were often young, foreign men who had arrived in Sweden without their parents.

Roger Ticoalu, director of events at Stockholm City Council, tells *DN* that sexual assaults have always occurred at festivals, but that from 2014 there has been a major difference in the type of crimes committed: "These cases are very particular. These are groups of young men who intentionally seek out, surround and assault girls. At first, we were completely shocked by their approach. When we received the first indications of what was going on, we simply could not believe it was true," he says. According to internal reports, the number of sexual assaults increased in 2015. After a few days, the police at We Are Sthlm had identified a group of about fifty suspected perpetrators. "They are so-called refugee youths, primarily from Afghanistan. Several from the gang were arrested for sexual harassment. The gang was also responsible for a number of fights during the evening," *DN* quotes from internal police reports. "But there were very few reports in relation to the number of suspected crimes," a police officer explains. "It was crowded, it happened fast and the girls had trouble pointing out who did what."

So instead of taking legal action, police focused on evicting perpetrators from the event. More than 200 young men were forcefully removed through the course of the festival, and police placed great effort on trying to comfort victimized girls and driving them home to their parents. "As soon as we entered the audience, they started grabbing. They would circle you," a young girl recalls. "One of my friends fell and they just threw themselves on top of her. They didn't care that we said no or that we had boyfriends." She says that when she and her friend told the festival's security guards, the perpetrators were simply thrown out. "But they could come back in."

The situation escalated to the point where police considered dividing up the whole audience according to gender. "But, we decided that it would be too invasive. Shouldn't the girls be able to stand with their boyfriends?" Officer Christian Frödén tells *DN*. Instead of cancelling the event, Stockholm City Council's personnel were assigned the task of approaching girls at the festival and warning them. But nothing of this was mentioned in the information provided to the general public and the mass media. Several of the police officers interviewed claim that there is a deliberate effort within the police authority not to report incidents tied to suspected perpetrators with foreign backgrounds.[2]

In 2014 and 2015, thirty-six cases of sexual assault were reported to police at the We Are Sthlm festival, but the actual number of assaults is estimated to be much greater. The vast majority of victims were girls under the age of fifteen.[3] In the end there was only one conviction.[4]

MONDAY 11 JANUARY 2016

The allegations against the police appear in the print version of *Dagens Nyheter*. Without mentioning Chang's name or his site, the paper has also published a rebuttal of the allegations being spread "in a text"—Chang's article—"over social media": "Information that *DN* has participated in a cover-up is a lie: something as important as young women being subjected to systematic abuse is clearly news *DN* would report," writes *Dagens Nyheter's* Managing Editor Caspar Opitz, who claims that the newspaper refrained from publishing in August because they were unable to verify the tip.[1]

The paper's Q&As regarding how events were handled are referenced by other Swedish media, but they do not outline what efforts *Dagens Nyheter* made to verify the tip. *Journalisten*, the journalists' union magazine, conducts its own interview with Opitz, but makes its message to the masses clear in framing its questions: "How should newsrooms handle these types of media frenzies set in motion by rightwing extremist/alternative sites?" Opitz replies: "Generally speaking, we can't devote time to responding to false claims from alternative sites. But sometimes one must make exceptions. Over all I think that we have to show more openness regarding how serious journalism is conducted, how much work is behind our articles, how we verify our sources, etc."[2]

Nobody presses *Dagens Nyheter* on what efforts were actually made to verify the information. Under the headline "*DN* responds to accusations of cover-up—with a scoop," *Resumé* magazine—owned by Bonnier, just like *DN*—also quotes Caspar Opitz answering his own questions, in his own Q&A.[3] Chang phones *Resumé* in an attempt to give his version of the story and offer them access to his evidence and sources, but it quickly becomes apparent that they are not interested in hearing him out.

Meanwhile, the story about Swedish police covering up sexual assaults by young migrants spreads internationally. The same day, *The New York Times*, *L'Express*, and *The Independent* all have extensive reporting on the topic. So do the *Financial Times*, Reuters,[4] and the BBC.[5] *The Guardian* runs a longer piece. The paper includes the allegations directed at *Dagens Nyheter*, but misspells the name of *Nyheter Idag* and discredits Chang's claim by linking him to the far right. The online version of the article doesn't link to Chang's, even though he has translated it into English, but does link to *Dagens Nyheter's* rebuttal:

> an anti-immigrant website linked to the far right Sweden Democrats, *Nyeter Idag* [sic], claimed that *Dagens Nyheter* itself received reports about the assaults very soon after the festival but did not publicize them because they might benefit the far-right party, who campaign to stop immigration. *Dagens Nyheter* vehemently denied the claim, producing a full rebuttal on their website [hyperlinked].[6]

Chang wonders if the misspelling is intentional to make it harder for anyone interested in finding his side of the story.

TUESDAY 12 JANUARY 2016

The next day, *Dagens Nyheter*'s main competitor, *Svenska Dagbladet*, reveals that police officers have been explicitly instructed not to communicate information about ethnicity or nationality when informing the public of criminal cases. In September 2015, a few weeks after the We Are Sthlm festival, police officers were presented with an internal directive from their press department. It stated: "The police is sometimes criticized for reporting on people's skin color. It is perceived as racist. Since the police is not racist and shouldn't be perceived as such, below are the instructions that are henceforth in place." The memo makes clear that "descriptions regarding height, skin color, ethnic origin, or nationality, etc," should not be used in the police's communication with the public.[1]

"We don't want to point the finger at certain ethnic groups as criminals. So we have realized that physical descriptions should not routinely be included in our reports," Varg Gyllander, head of press relations at the Stockholm police, explains to *Svenska Dagbladet*. "Are there any advantages to using physical descriptions?" the reporter asks. "Absolutely, there often are. But we have made a certain consideration regarding when to use this information and when not to. In order not to be suspected of racism, one should not routinely describe appearance or ethnicity," says Gyllander.

When the reporter asks if physical descriptions aren't helpful when trying to catch a suspect, Gyllander replies: "When it comes to everyday crime, our experience is that physical descriptions have no effect whatsoever on incoming leads." The reporter then points out that the internal memo is dated 15 September, just a few weeks after We Are Sthlm; Gyllander insists that there is no connection whatsoever:

> I was not at all involved in those events. This is a general discussion taking place in our organization and in society at large, that we must be careful when it comes to naming ethnicity. Journalists and others have previously criticized us for doing so. This is our attempt at handling this quite difficult issue.[2]

* * *

Meanwhile, *Dagens Nyheter* publishes a number of stories that make it clear that it wasn't just the police who knew of the assaults. As the organizers of the annual festival, the City of Stockholm has known about the assaults for over a decade.

Advertised by the City as an event for children and young people, We Are Sthlm has been marketed as a drug-free place where the young can enjoy themselves in the safe presence of adults. Meanwhile, protocols from City meetings show that the problem with systematic sexual assaults at the festival was present and well known right from its creation in the year 2000.

Ahead of the 2015 festival, members of the organizing committee at Stockholm City wrote in an internal document: "Unfortunately, in the last few years, the number of crying and violated girls who have been subjected to sexual violence has increased." The document also stated that it had become harder for the festival's security personnel to have a dialogue about it, as "the norms have been pushed to the point where they are no longer healthy."[3] In emails to the municipal authorities, teenage girls testified to systematic abuse by men who had surrounded them and forced themselves on them in the cover of the crowd. One girl described how "the hands of strangers" grabbed hold of her breasts, buttocks, and genitals, even though she repeatedly pushed them away and screamed: "Don't touch me!"[4]

During an evaluation meeting in September 2015, head of security Karin Johanessen said that the festival had worked on "getting more young girls to understand how to set boundaries." This did not appear to have helped. She concluded: "As a percentage, the number of crimes has not decreased; if anything they have increased, which is probably because more girls have filed police reports, which was one of the goals. It is still the same boys, but their numbers have grown and they have become smarter and more aggressive." While some city politicians deny having known about the assaults, Social Democrat Roger Mogert has admitted to *Dagens Nyheter* that he knew, and he claims to have passed the information on.[5]

It slowly dawns on the Swedish public that even the would-be victims knew about the risks. As journalists from both *Dagens Nyheter* and *Svenska Dagbladet* set out to interview young people at different schools in Stockholm, the overwhelming response is one of surprise at the sudden interest. "This is really not news. It is so common. Ask any girl," high school student Hamdi Abdiweli tells *DN* reporter Lina Lund. Hamdi and her friends don't believe filing a police complaint would make a difference. "Being a young girl doesn't come with much authority. If one reports that one has been molested, there is no reaction," says Klara Benyamine.[6]

Svenska Dagbladet reporter Karin Thurfjell receives similar responses: "I think that if you ask every girl at this school, they will all have been subjected to something," says 16-year old Kimia Nikbakhsh. "When something uncomfortable happens you tell your friends. But it's so common that one doesn't even think to file a complaint," she adds.[7]

* * *

Vera and her friend Angela, who were assaulted in Kungsträd-gården, both opted neither to file a complaint nor to tell any adult on site. They simply left the festival on shaky legs, walked to the subway and went home. Later that night, Vera wrote a widely shared post on Instagram where she addressed her unknown perpetrators, finishing her entry with "Fuck you." She also told her parents. But not until her dad read about it in the newspapers the following year did they encourage her to go public with her story.[8]

Over the next few weeks and months, as the spotlight stays on sexual violence, it will become clear that these occurrences have by no means been limited to festivals. Young girls and women have been sexually assaulted in public swimming pools, parks, subways, and schools, and on buses. For many young people, this has been a part of everyday life, something one just has to learn to live with. In the 2016 Swedish Crime Survey, 14 per cent of 16- to 24-year-olds reported that they had been subjected to a sex offence that same year. In 2007, there were 12,563 reported sex offences, including 4,749 rapes. By 2016, that number has grown to 20,284 reported sex offences, including 6,715 rapes. Almost half of these rapes (3,010) were perpetrated against children of 0 to 17 years of age. The majority (68 per cent) of all sex offences took place in a public space, in the workplace, or at school. In 65 per cent of cases, the perpetrator was someone the victim had never met before, contrary to the common findings that most rapes are perpetrated by someone known to the victim.[9]

Such high numbers in a country with a mere 10 million inhabitants have ranked Sweden amongst the worst countries in the world when it comes to sexual violence per capita. Differences in how rape is defined and recorded make international compari-sons difficult and unreliable. However, the data leaves no doubt that sexual offences constitute a growing problem in the country. And many anti-immigration advocates believe this is at least partly due to the great influx of immigrants from countries where views of women's rights and of sex differ substantially from those of Sweden.

In 2005, the National Council for Crime Prevention, an agency within the Ministry of Justice, published a study on crime prevalence among immigrants. It concluded that the "relative risk" of people born abroad becoming involved in crime was 2.5 times that of those born in Sweden to two Swedish-born parents. The level of overrepresentation was greatest among immigrants from Africa (four times that of Swedes) and Western Asia (three times that of Swedes), while immigrants from Western Europe or North America displayed negligible differences (1.1 and 0.9 times).[10] The relative risk was also higher for some offences than for others. For example, it was five times as likely for foreign-born individuals to be suspected of rape.[11] Given the intense levels of immigration to Sweden over the past few decades, the Sweden Democrats have long called for a new, updated investigation. However, the government has refused to commission any such report, arguing that it would not "add knowledge with the potential to improve Swedish society."[12] Consequently, in a country that closely monitors virtually everything than can be measured, no official statistics have been produced on crime prevalence among immigrants since 2005.

Since all court verdicts are public records, anyone can gain access to them using the principle of public access. In the absence of further research by the state, this has prompted a number of citizens to put together their own "studies". Published on blogs or alternative sites, these are most frequently focused on asserting a significant overrepresentation of immigrants as perpetrators of sexual violence. The lack of comment or statistics from official agencies means that these arguments cannot be debated with authority.

WEDNESDAY 13 JANUARY 2016

"How do you think the media has handled the story?" The host of *Good Morning Sweden*, a public service television show, turns to his studio guests. It is early in the morning and a panel has been invited to discuss *Dagens Nyheter*'s alleged cover-up of the sexual assaults at We Are Sthlm. Against the backdrop of a large screen featuring the sea of teenagers attending the festival, Kristina Lindquist is sitting on a red sofa. Head of culture at the local newspaper *Uppsala Nya Tidning* and a future *Dagens Nyheter* staff member, she begins by expressing her deep concern: "Under the banner of media criticism, an enormous populist storm has developed aiming to cast doubt on journalists and traditional media. We're seeing established debaters sharing links to racist hate sites who are whipping up a storm, against *DN* in this case."

In addition to Lindquist, the panel consists of Daniel Sandström, literary director of Bonnier—which owns *Dagens Nyheter*—and Kerstin Brunnberg, director of the Swedish Centre for Architecture and Design and former head of Swedish Radio, as well as a board member of the anti-racist Expo Foundation. Chang Frick has not been invited. Neither his name nor his site, *Nyheter Idag*, is mentioned. Instead, the show host explains that "from one direction," *Dagens Nyheter* has been accused of having known about the attacks, but having refrained from publishing because the girls' assailants were allegedly young immigrants, mainly from Afghanistan. "So you don't believe in the cover-up theory?" the host asks Lindquist.

"Cover-up, that is conspiracy theories. When did normal, reasonable people start sharing conspiracy theories?" Lindquist replies.

"Exactly," Kerstin Brunnberg agrees. "I have to say, the media outlets who dedicate themselves to real journalism don't pursue this because they know that the mere thought would be a morass."

"Some of the criticism that should be aimed at the police is being aimed at *Dagens Nyheter*," says Daniel Sandström.

> It is not unusual for the messenger to end up in the line of fire. It was, after all, *Dagens Nyheter* who exposed the story. This has made the international news and is something they should be commended for. But the second thing is, how does one defend against conspiracy theories? Something that isn't there one has to prove doesn't exist. There has been an impossible and completely populist over-interpretation of the debate itself. The new aspect in all of this is that now all stories are equally good whether they are true or not, a complete manipulation of the truth criteria, which places enormous demands on us and puts our democracy under very strong pressure.

The others nod eagerly. "Yes, because it creates distrust in credible information and creates uncertainty in society. And it takes focus from a super important question, which is women's right to their own bodies," Brunnberg adds.

"For some, women's right to their own body is only of interest if it can be used as a bat against The Other," says Lindquist. "As a publicist, it has become impossible to maintain a reasonable position. As soon as one doesn't buy into a racist explanation, one is accused of covering things up." The panelists discuss the media's code of conduct and agree that journalists shouldn't mention ethnicity when it isn't relevant. They end by concluding that professional media are under strong pressure from conspiracy theories and financial challenges, combining to create "a perfect storm."

* * *

"Conspiracy theories" from a "hate site." Chang closes the browser window. Nothing surprises him anymore. Even though the Swedish Press Council has never once found him guilty of violating a single one of their guidelines of good practice.[1]

His stringer, Mattias Albinsson, calls the publisher Ulf Johansson to ask whether he doesn't think it would be fitting to give Chang a chance to present his side of the story, to counter the accusations of being a "hate site" devoted to "conspiracy theories," and to point out that there is evidence, recorded interviews with police sources, and so on. While Johansson does not hang up, he insists that the state-financed television broadcaster has done nothing wrong: "I feel that this was a correct way of handling this on *Good Morning Sweden*, yes."[2]

To have his side of the story heard, Chang is left with only one option—publishing it himself, in an interview on his own site:

> [CF:] It says a great deal that neither Swedish Television, *Journalisten*, or any other Swedish news outlet allow us to express our side of the story or respond to the allegations against us, but instead chooses to publish only one side of the story. I think people are afraid of what I might stir up in the studio. Everything in the story can be verified. Every claim we've published, every allegation. Feel free to contact us and scrutinize our material and our sources.
>
> *So why has no newspaper done so?*
>
> [CF:] They are afraid to.[3]

* * *

In the end, a Norwegian journalist is the only one to take Chang up on his offer of access to material and sources. Helge Øgrim, editor of the Norwegian journalists' association magazine (also called *Journalisten*), scrutinizes Chang's material and tracks down Hans and Lars to conduct his own interviews. Øgrim writes that he considers them credible sources and publishes a story in which he concludes that there is no reason to dismiss Chang's version of events.

Lars tells Øgrim that he called the *Dagens Nyheter* journalist at least five times without being able to speak to her, and that he was not surprised that the media refrained from reporting on the assaults. "No experienced police officer is surprised that this does not receive attention."

"Why?"

"There is an unwillingness to describe reality as it is. It is uncomfortable and does not align with what one has decided it should be. It is propaganda being disseminated." Lars says that he stopped reading *Dagens Nyheter* after the riots in Swedish suburbs such as Rinkeby, Tensta and Husby in 2013. "I was out in the field and worked a lot those weeks. What I read about it in the media simply wasn't accurate."

Øgrim notes that the newspaper has said that it couldn't get the information confirmed, but has not described what efforts were actually made to do so. "How difficult would it be to confirm the information about what took place in Kungsträdgården?" Øgrim asks Lars.

"It would have been easy, incredibly easy. Journalists call the detention centers and the stations' duty officer every day and ask: what is the situation like? How many have been detained or brought into custody? What is the situation like here or there?"

"Do they receive truthful answers?"

"It will never happen that the police officer who responds doesn't tell them how many have been detained or brought into custody. And it wasn't just police officers there. There were organizers, security guards, mothers and fathers, social services, the Church. There were many representatives from society. And what happened took place in spite of the great presence of [civil] society."

Øgrim also conducts a long interview with Hans, but when he contacts *Dagens Nyheter* for answers, Caspar Opitz replies that he is extremely busy and doesn't have time to talk to him. When Øgrim reaches out once more, saying that it's a shame the paper won't comment, Opitz replies: "Hello again Helge, it is up to you if you want to quote accusations from a rightwing populist hate site or not."[4]

* * *

The Norwegian *Journalisten* story is met with silence among traditional Swedish media. But Chang feels vindicated, and he is convinced that established media know it. The article has obviously made an impression on them because it doesn't take long before they open up a new line of attack. Later the same day, Chang reads an editorial in *Svenska Dagbladet* entitled "Russian PR Methods Spread in Sweden." Isobel Hadley-Kamptz writes: "There are parallels between the ongoing rightwing populist campaign against established media in Sweden and Russian methods for destabilizing society." She expresses her surprise that "normal" thinkers and politicians have suddenly begun to refer to "one of the rightwing-populist circle's big propaganda sites" in order to spread the opinion that *Dagens Nyheter* has actively covered up sexual assaults on the grounds that the alleged perpetrators were immigrants. Meanwhile, "the truth," she asserts, "was that the police silenced the abuse." "Carelessly, severe accusations against the media in general, and *DN* in particular, were passed on, and the source was one that decent people had so far not wanted to be associated with."

"Decent people." Chang smiles at the notion. On 11 January alone, he had over 250,000 visitors to his site. Yesterday it was 176,000. Over 1 million in the last month—in a country of 10 million. If he is indecent, so is a significant portion of the population. He reads on:

> Today, we know how Russia ventures to destabilize the rest of the world through the spreading of rumors online. We are aware of their paid armies of trolls, spreading direct Putin propaganda as well as more subtle smoke curtains. The purpose is to decrease the sense of communion and trust in society, and undermine the psychological defense, that is, the will to defend and the power to resist pressure and disinformation.

Chang stares at the screen for a long time, then shouts: "Polina! Tell your mom to bring a Putin t-shirt next time she comes to visit. And a calendar. I want a picture of a bare-chested Putin riding a Siberian tiger to hang in my office."

SAMVEL AND THE COLLECTIVE GUILT

With his cell phone, Samvel films his feet as they make their way over the gray concrete tiles leading through the pedestrian tunnel. As always, he exits the Stockholm subway at Enskede gård. The walls inside the tunnel are clad with new, white tile and colorful Cubist mosaics, but looking down it is all gray. When people fix up public spaces they tend to neglect the ground, Samvel muses. He can attest to that; the ground has been consuming much of his attention lately.

On 13 January, the evening daily *Expressen* published a list of the sexual assault cases from We Are Sthlm 2015 that have resulted in formal complaints. The suspected perpetrators were not all Afghans, *Expressen* concluded. Many were unknown and the newspaper noted that police used descriptions such as "some kind of African descent," "Asian appearance," "African origin," "dark-skinned," "in need of Persian interpreter," or "all men were of foreign descent."

Samvel read about the different cases: a 15-year-old boy of Somalian descent sexually assaulted a 14-year-old girl and punched her friend in the face when she tried to interfere. Some fifty men targeted a 15-year old girl in the cover of the crowd. Some of them pulled up her skirt and stuck their hands in her underwear. Other members of the crowd interfered and helped her out before things could go further. The perpetrators were all of foreign descent. A 14-year old girl was surrounded by some ten men who touched her breasts and buttocks. When they tried to pull down her pants, she elbowed one of them in the stomach. The perpetrators then kicked her and took off with her cell phone. Her friend reports having witnessed another girl being raped in the crowd. A group of men had surrounded her, pulled down her pants and proceeded to rape her. The girl looked too scared to resist, according to the witness. The men were dark-skinned and in their twenties. A 13-year-old girl was molested by a man born in 1981 in Tunisia. A young woman was raped when peeing in the bushes; suspected perpetrator: a 42-year old citizen of Iraq.

The list went on.

"Suspected perpetrator: man from the Middle East wearing a white knitted sweater, blue ripped jeans, cropped hair, stubble, approximately 20–23 years-old."

"Suspected perpetrator: boy born in 2000. In need of interpreter from Persian which is mainly spoken in Iran."

"Suspected perpetrator: unknown. 20–25 years old, 170–175 centimeters tall, dark skin color, short black hair."

"Suspected perpetrator: man born in 1999. In need of interpreter from Dari, a language that is mainly spoken in parts of Afghanistan."

"Suspected perpetrator: born in Pakistan in 1998. Citizen of Afghanistan."

"Suspected perpetrator: man born in 2000. In need of interpreter from Dari, a language that is mainly spoken in parts of Afghanistan."

"Suspected perpetrator: a 15-year-old boy, born in Sweden to parents who immigrated from Somalia."

Only once did it state "Suspected perpetrator: boy born in 2001 in Sweden, citizen of Sweden." Samvel is certain that if one were to read the whole complaint, one would find that he too was of foreign descent. Only one case has resulted in a conviction.

Swedish media never used to report ethnicity, but suddenly, it seems to Samvel that all news stories are about immigrants perpetrating crimes. As the news reports and debates heat up, Samvel feels like both an insider and an outsider at the same time. If immigrants are a source of trouble, that applies to him too. He has to make sure he doesn't do anything wrong; keep his head down, follow every rule to the letter.

Samvel wonders whether he would be capable of committing any of the many atrocities he is reading about. He too is an immigrant. What if there is some hidden evil in him of which he is not aware? A homeless person is physically assaulted outside the Co-op near where he lives. Samvel reads about it in the paper and wonders if it could have been him. He has walked past that same supermarket himself and often sees beggars sitting there. Does he really remember everything he did that day? Perhaps he attacked the beggar? He could have had a blackout.

Before long, Samvel is no longer wondering; he is convinced: there is evil in him. Odds are he is already committing crimes unbeknownst to himself. Whenever he reads of a crime where the perpetrator is unknown, he wonders if it could have been him. A woman has been murdered in Stockholm. There is no indication that the murderer is an immigrant, but Samvel still can't shake the thought that he has done it. When people find out, they'll be even more appalled, because they'll learn that he is doubly evil: both a murderer and an immigrant.

One day, he is walking home from the subway. A man with a long, black coat is walking at a slow pace in front of him. Samvel passes the stranger and continues home. He enters his apartment. But as soon as he closes the door behind him, the doubts set in. Did something happen? Did he attack the anonymous man and forget about it? He doesn't believe so, but how can he be sure? In his nightmares, Samvel perpetrates horrible crimes. Some days he simply can't bring himself to leave the house for fear of what he might do or what he might convince himself he has done.

Samvel decides he has to do a better job of monitoring his own actions. On his phone is a health app that can help him track his steps. He starts using it to monitor what distance he has covered every day, to make sure he hasn't taken any detours he might have forgotten about. But distance alone doesn't prove anything. Using his phone, Samvel starts taking photos to document his own whereabouts at different times of the day. A picture when he leaves the house. A picture when he boards the subway. Another when he exits, and another when he arrives at his destination. But every strategy seems inadequate. There are still gaps in his day, almost as though he wants to give his own brain something to chew on. Before long, Samvel starts to film his feet as he walks home from the subway station every day. That way, when the doubt and angst set in, he can review his digital alibis and put himself at ease.

* * *

Dead leaves and tufts of dry grass peak through the snow as Samvel crosses the green space by the subway exit, making his way over to Odelbergsvägen. There are tire marks in the frost; someone has been driving on the pedestrian path again. The first in a set of three-story apartment buildings appears on his left. It's in great shape, whereas its neighbors could benefit from a fresh coat of paint. His feet continue on autopilot, carrying him all the way to the wooden door to his yellow building, beneath the small, white-box balconies. It has taken 3 minutes to get to this point. He enters and climbs the stairs. They are a glossy gray: polished granite, but gray nonetheless. He likes that his walk both opens and ends in gray. He closes his door behind him and stops his recording.

THURSDAY 14 JANUARY 2016

For the first time since he published his story five days earlier, a Swedish journalist phones Chang. His name is Kolbjörn Guwallius and he works for Bonnier-owned news website *KIT*. But he is not calling to take Chang up on the offer to access his material and verify his sources. In fact, he is not at all interested in talking about the events in Kungsträdgården, or whether Chang can prove his allegations against *DN*. Instead, he has a series of questions about Chang's personal finances. The interview results in an article entitled "The site *Nyheter Idag* is behind the media frenzy against *DN*. But who is behind *Nyheter Idag?*" "Whose errands is the site running?" wonders Guwallius. "Chang Frick declared no income for 2013 and 2014. The previous year he declared an income of 141,000 SEK [roughly $16,800] before tax."[1]

Guwallius devotes more than 1,200 words to interrogating Chang. How does he pay his rent? How does he live? The reporter has also scrutinized Polina's declared income and questions how her annual 52,000 SEK ($6,200) is enough to live on. "Income is one thing," Chang replies. "She has her savings and her mother helps us. I don't understand what these questions have to do with *Nyheter Idag*. We have low expenses. She has some savings and has helped us with rent." Chang explains that he hasn't made enough money from his site to be able to draw a salary, only to cover his work-related expenses. The reporter concludes that Chang and his family live off income that has never been declared.

Chang counters by publishing a blog entry entitled "Bonnier's site *KIT* called—Now I'm accused of being poor." Chang invites Guwallius and his colleagues to come to his apartment in the suburbs and scrutinize his belongings and living conditions, since they still don't seem to want to scrutinize his sources or journalistic methods. "Naturally, *KIT* and Guwallius are welcome to come to my home and inspect my wardrobe and everything I own and possess. It might also do them some good to come out to the suburbs for a change."[2] The post ends with an account number where supporters can deposit donations.

WEDNESDAY 20 JANUARY 2016

A week later, *Dagens Nyheter* reveals that the police have been using a special code to cover up data pertaining to crime and immigrants: "Police refuse to disclose the amount of resources needed to deal with the wave of refugees and the increasingly tense situation at many temporary homes for asylum seekers. Investigations regarding violence, threats and other crime are given the code '291' and kept secret from the media." The paper cites an internal police memo. "Nothing must get out," it reads. The article also quotes an employee from the police communication department: "The situation is becoming dangerous. Anything that touches immigration is to be kept secret and my only conclusion is that there are political reasons for not daring to show reality as it is."[1]

* * *

"The *DN* storm is an attack against us all," writes Helena Giertta, editor-in-chief of Swedish *Journalisten*. She is writing to mark the 250th anniversary of freedom of the press in Sweden. "It's remarkable; yes, a world record. Unfortunately, the atmosphere is not such that one wishes to celebrate," she notes. "The rights we have can too easily be taken away from us." Giertta gives the example of Poland, where "the strike of a pen from the nationalistic winner of the election was enough to make the independence of public service disappear." Both the Polish and Hungarian government have "with all desirable clarity shown what a nationalistic, xenophobic government wants with the media. They want them to be the companions of the state, their henchmen." Then Giertta draws her parallel to Sweden: "The nationalistic, rightwing-extreme, immigrant-hostile forces appear to want the same thing for the media and journalism here. They don't want independent media, who tell it like it is." What they want, she argues, is control over what is being said. "The storm against *Dagens Nyheter* was a typical example of how [these far-right forces] operate."[2]

Chang sits in his fake-leather chair reading the editorial. He is amazed at the discrepancy of worldview between himself and Giertta. Independent media who tell it like it is, that's exactly what he wants. It's what he aspires to be. It's the incumbents who want to maintain control and who refuse to allow alternative voices into the public arena that they monopolize. The only reason the criticism against *Dagens Nyheter* is perceived as criticism against the whole establishment is precisely because they are not independent, but act as one voice, refusing to scrutinize or even question one of their own. He continues to read: "By raising suspicion that the newspaper covered something up, one can then proceed to attack all journalists. The fact that it later turned out to be the police who had covered it up didn't stop the conspiracies."

Chang pulls out his round, white *snus* container and flips open the lid. The last five little linen pouches of LD Vit snuff lie strewn like small pillows across the floor of the container. He's never been a fan of the police. National Police Commissioner Dan Eliasson is a former punk rocker with a 1979 hit called "Fuck in Bangkok." But that anti-establishment infection has long been cured by the system. Now he's the chief defender of the nation's values. This is a guy who, before becoming commissioner, tweeted his aversion to Jimmie Åkesson—that seeing him on television made him "vomit." Eliasson sold out long ago, thinks Chang. He is nothing more than a party loyalist, a drone for the Social Democratic government.

Chang stirs the little white pillows with his finger. He grabs the most comfortable looking of the bunch, stuffs it up under the left side of his front lip, and leans back against the back of his worn chair. There's some truth to these accusations. As the recent leaks of internal documents clearly show, the police have certainly contributed to the distortion of reality. But why so much effort to obfuscate the role that media incumbents themselves have played in this "blackout?" It was the media who set and enforced the norm that one does not talk about crimes related to immigration. Before the tide turned, when police officers would use ethnicity to describe a suspect, the media had been the first to crack down on the practice, criticizing the police and accusing them of racism until the force fell quiet. And now that same quiet has outraged them.

Chang swivels slowly in his chair, taking in the rest of his unkempt office. His article has obviously sped up a shift of the opinion corridor; one that the establishment hadn't quite finished preparing for internally. The sudden change in attitudes among journalists had caused confusion among police officers. The consensus has changed, and apparently no one in the force got the memo. What was okay yesterday is suddenly not—and now everyone has to pretend as though it never was. It reminds Chang of pictures he has seen from 3 September 1967, when, at precisely 5 a.m., Sweden changed from driving on the left to driving on the right. While no one died, there were cars twisted into gridlock strewn diagonally across the roads, surrounded by people looking entirely confused as to how to untangle the mess. Gradual change was not for Sweden. Adjust or hit the wall.

One of those pictures would have made the perfect illustration for an article he read in *Dagens Nyheter* a few days ago. A reporter had asked Ulf Johansson, chief of police for the Stockholm region, when he found out about the assaults against young women at We Are Sthlm. Johansson, obviously puzzled by the question, replied: "Well, as former head of the city police department, I've had a general knowledge of the phenomenon for ten years." Then he added, "We have problems in many areas of society; we hear many young women tell us about their reality and that doesn't just apply to festivals."[3]

Ten goddamn years, Chang reflects. A decade of silence. This whole thing is just so bizarre. He stands up and walks towards the kitchen. He's thirsty. Or hungry. Craving something. He returns with a cup of cold coffee. With his tongue he adjusts his *snus* pouch under his lip, pushing it firmly into the *snusgrop*—the little eroded pit in the gums that develops after years of use. He skims through the rest of Giertta's text: "While discussion and self-criticism are good things, we must also defend what we stand for and not rise to meet these dark forces."

"Dark force"—another epithet to add to his CV.

* * *

Chang doesn't agree with her assessment of the root cause, but Giertta is right to be concerned about the state of the free press. On 26 June 2014, the Swedish government appointed a Media Constitution Committee to review the constitutionally enshrined Freedom of the Press (1766) and the Freedom of Expression Act (1991).[4] The move had been prompted by the creation of a controversial website and database known as Lexbase, enabling users to perform searches on people and companies who had been the subject of criminal trials during the last five years. Since its launch in January 2014, Lexbase had been widely criticized for exposing criminals and publishing sensitive information, including a map function where convicts' addresses were revealed. But Lexbase was based on public records and proved hard to stop.

In December 2017, the government would submit its proposal to Parliament, based on the Commission's recommendations: limit freedom of speech and freedom of expression to allow for a prohibition against publishing certain personal data in compiled and searchable form. Such data included ethnic origin, skin color, religious convictions, or criminal records, and was deemed too sensitive to be accessible to the public, as it could violate the personal integrity of those exposed. Instead, access to such information should be limited to professionals like lawyers, journalists, and researchers. In its proposal, the government stressed that it was "of the greatest importance that serious, investigative journalism is in no way obstructed by the regulation."[5]

But who should decide what constitutes "serious, investigative journalism?" The threat to small media players like Chang was obvious. His site would run the risk of being shut out, while the established players would have a monopoly on access to the records needed for investigative journalism. They could continue to scrutinize the public, while the public would be robbed of that same possibility. Violating the principle of free access to public records, the proposal could further deepen the divide between established actors and the newcomers challenging them.

Changing the constitution requires two parliamentary approvals, with a general election in between. If approved, the change would come into effect in January 2019.

MISSION ACCOMPLISHED

It is 1 September 2016; Samvel's first day at his new job. By now he has spent eight years in Sweden. He has earned his Master's in European Affairs and learnt fluent Swedish. Most strangers he meets ask him what part of Skåne he is from. When he answers that he isn't Swedish, few believe him. "Do your duty, demand your right," the motto goes. Well, today he is finally able to start giving back to society, in a full-time job that is relevant to his political science degree. Östgruppen for Democracy and Human Rights is an NGO working to support activists in Eastern Europe. Fluent in Russian, Armenian, Swedish, and English, Samvel is a great addition to the team.

Walking home from work, Samvel's spirits are unusually light. He takes the tube to Enskede gård. When he crosses the old familiar grass patch to reach Odelbergsvägen, his head is lifted proud. No more staring at the ground. No more filming his feet. He takes his time to stop and listen to the birds. Fall is his favorite Swedish season. The compact darkness of winter is still holding off; the weather is cool, but not excruciatingly cold. Stockholm is once again vibrant, as most holidaymakers have returned to the capital from their summer retreats.

He reaches his apartment building and hears the heavy front door close behind him. He skips up the first flight of stairs.

"It's your fault! People like you fucked up this country!" Samvel shrinks back. It's his neighbor again; a scrawny rocker in his fifties with a long, blond ponytail. He is a Sweden Democrat supporter and constantly looking to engage Samvel in conversation. He must stand peeking out through his windows waiting for Samvel to arrive home. "It's you! You fucking liberals! And the fucking communists too for that matter. How are you going to solve this mess?" He's been drinking, as is usually the case whenever the neighbor comes by to talk sense into Samvel. At first Samvel thought the neighbor was upset at him for being an immigrant, but he soon learned that being a liberal is apparently even worse.

On all other counts, the neighbor likes him. "You are different," he often says. Samvel hears that argument a lot and it makes him uncomfortable. Different from what? From other immigrants? From someone with darker skin? Someone who doesn't speak Swedish? It bothers Samvel that his acceptance hinges on being a "different" type of immigrant. What if one day he were to stop caring about what the homogenous Swedish society wants, stop trying to adapt—would he then be kicked out? Sure, he takes an interest in the Swedish culture and history, but that is a personal preference. It shouldn't be a requirement. Language, on the other hand, should be a requirement. If someone wants to become a Swedish citizen they should learn to speak Swedish. After all, it constitutes the main instrument for being able to function in society. Citizenship is not a human right; if you want to have the ability to influence things, you have to be able to keep yourself informed. Samvel believes that. Democracy depends on it. Samvel agrees that there is some homework he has to do; that any immigrant should do, for their own sake. But he doesn't like being used as an alibi to defend the argument of a Sweden Democrat.

Then again, the formerly communist Left Party is equally suspect in Samvel's book. They used to laud Stalin and his anti-democratic ideology. They subscribed to the dictatorship of the worker's movement, but now they are suddenly considered a normal party just because they removed the word "communist" from their official party name in 1990. Now they are supposedly the great humanists who love immigrants; who love everyone. That happened quite fast. Samvel doesn't buy it. He is bothered by any political ideology that puts the group ahead of the individual.

Ignoring his neighbor, Samvel quickly closes the door behind him. On the doormat a letter lies waiting. It's from the Migration Authorities. Samvel takes off his shoes and puts them away neatly before picking up the letter. He hangs up his coat. Then he remains standing on the doormat, letter in hand, savoring the moment a while longer. No matter the content, once he learns it, his life will never again be the same. He walks over and takes a seat on the sofa. He carefully inches the envelope open and takes out its contents. He unfolds the letter and reads:

Applicant: Atabekyan, Samvel, born 19860226, man, citizen of Armenia

Decision: The Migration Authorities decide to

– Reject your application for permanent residency
– Deport you from the country in accordance with chap. 8, 6 §
  Aliens Act (2005:716).

Samvel isn't sure how much time has passed when he becomes aware of his surroundings again. How is it possible? What will he do now? What is he supposed to tell work? Has he been irresponsible to accept their offer without knowing what the outcome of his application would be? The letter says he is summoned to a meeting with the Migration Authorities on 15 September. He calls his friend Henrik, who promises to help.

If he does nothing, he'll be kicked out within three weeks. But he has a job now. On 8 September, Samvel applies for a working visa. He and Henrik call the Migration Authorities several times a day, but each time the person on the other end has a different answer. No matter what they try, they can't get a clear response. Then, on 12 September, another letter arrives from the Authorities: the rejection process has been paused and his case is under investigation. Once again, Samvel phones the Authorities. Does he still have to show up for the meeting on 15 September? Yes, that would probably be best, he is advised.

REJECTED AT THE GATES

It is 15 September 2016. "Hello. Who's the customer?" The middle-aged, blonde bureaucrat enters the room and gets straight to the point, in brisk Swedish with a thick Stockholm accent. She doesn't introduce herself or extend her hand to greet Samvel or his friend Henrik, who has joined him at the interview with the Migration Authorities. She simply takes a seat across the desk from them and fires up the computer.

"I am," Samvel replies.

"Well, your application has been rejected." She flips through the papers in the folder that she brought with her. Without looking up, she continues, "And I can see you've applied for a work permit as well. This has also been rejected."

Samvel looks around the barren room. There are no personal touches, no private belongings; it is obvious no one sits here permanently. It must just be an office where people come to get their notice. And now here he is, informed of his verdict. It's surreal. Just three days earlier, he received the letter stating that his case was being investigated.

"You didn't know?" the lady asks. "Well, that's how it is. The purpose of this meeting is to talk about your return home." Samvel feels like he has just been diagnosed with a terminal disease, and there she is, hardly stopping to breathe.

"I can see in my file that you have a job. That means you'll have to buy your own ticket."

"Of course, I was never planning on taking any money from you or your department."

"Now I have to ask what your attitude is on this matter?"

"Attitude? What do you mean?"

"I mean do you intend to abide by the rules or not? I can explain the consequences to you if you don't return voluntarily." Samvel stares at her dumbfounded. "So, do you intend to follow the rules?" she asks again.

"Yes, I've never had any intention of not following the rules."

"Okay. Good. Let's move on then." Shifting her gaze to the computer, she continues: "We have to book a meeting when you are to return and show us your ticket. Then we'll give you your passport back. What day shall it be, 20 September?"

"Well, today is the 15th, that feels very stressful."

"Okay, so what day then?"

"At the end of the month?"

"Okay, I'm making an appointment for 29 September. You are to come here and show us your ticket." Her fingers march determinedly over the bulky, black keyboard as she enters the information.

"I guess you don't get any empathy courses here," Henrik intervenes.

"I'm sorry you feel that way. I think we do a pretty good job. Most people who come here think that everything is always positive. They don't consider that the outcome can also be negative."

"You have to understand. I've started a new job. I have a life here. It's not easy," Samvel intersects.

"Did you not know that you don't meet the demands?"

"No, I filed an application and then it's up to the Migration Authorities to determine whether I meet the demands or not."

"You were just looking to buy time."

The meeting takes about 15 minutes to bring eight years to an end. The Migration Authorities conclude Samvel has certain ties to Sweden, but not strong enough to be allowed to stay. After all, he arrived in Sweden as an adult. And he still has a mother and a brother living in Armenia. Samvel also listed health reasons in his application. Lacking pigmentation made it impossible for him to lead a normal life in Armenia. But since returning there would not pose an immediate threat to his life, his health reasons have also been rejected.

How long does one have to stay in a country to develop a strong connection, Samvel wonders as he walks home. He has spent the better part of his adulthood here. Sweden—becoming Swedish—has been his life's achievement. He has learned the language, embraced the culture, and knows much more about Swedish history and literature than most Swedes. But more importantly, he felt Swedish before he even set foot in Sweden. Arriving only confirmed what he has always known; this is where he belongs.

Sweden brags about its equal and mutually independent citizens, but for immigrants, the laws still revolve around family. Blood ties trump all others. As an individual, he doesn't count. He feels like the decision goes against the Swedish ethos of the individual's right to freedom and pursuit of happiness. If he had family here—if he had married someone, or had a child with someone—he would be allowed to stay. Then it wouldn't have mattered even if he had no connection to the country and didn't speak a word of Swedish.

But ironically, he is now too Swedish to try to pull a stunt like that.

THE CULPRIT

"As soon as someone spoke of volumes, we began to question their mental health and what they really believed. I was a part of this myself. It resulted in chaos and a 180-degree turnaround where we pulled the emergency brake. We owe the Swedish people an apology. I owe the Swedish people an apology." On a balmy July afternoon in 2016, Hanif Bali, a Moderate Party MP, addressed the public from a small stage in Almedalen, Visby. He apologized for having failed to take the migration crises seriously.

Visby, the medieval capital of the Swedish island of Gotland, is a stunning old fortress city, still surrounded by its ancient wall. In summer, it is one of the surest places to encounter the few rays of sunshine that Sweden is allotted in a given year. A popular holiday destination, it is also a stage for political intrigue. Each July, the political elite, the lobbyists, and the media descend on the small island to forge alliances, make pacts, and party. This started in 1968, when Olof Palme climbed onto the back of a lorry and gave an impromptu speech to people who had gathered in Almedalen Park. Since then, the combination of political speeches, debates, and cocktail receptions has been an annual tradition.

Across the rest of Sweden, the season for summer festivals was underway. In an attempt to tackle the widespread, and now much discussed, problem of groping and sexual assaults, National

Police Commissioner Dan Eliasson had initiated a campaign providing young people with armbands that read "Police cordon, don't grope," as though the issue were that the girls aren't being clear enough with their boundaries. At the Almedalen week in Gotland, the Sweden Democrats responded by handing out armbands with the message "Resign Dan Eliasson."

Whether the police intentionally covered up the assaults at We Are Sthlm or not, there is no doubt that they, like everyone else, were affected by the prevailing Swedish norm that said one didn't talk about immigrant-related crimes. The fact that all investigations regarding violence, threats, and other crimes that involved refugees had been given the secret code "291" proved it. But this secrecy didn't just apply to the police department. The government, which usually loves statistics, had refused to publish any stats related to crime prevalence among immigrants, leaving citizens to draw their own conclusions based on public records.

And then there was the media. On 12 August 2015, the state broadcaster Radio Sweden had aired its short story about the fact that We Are Sthlm had for years struggled with problems of sexual assaults.[1] The story caused no reaction in Swedish society. Radio Sweden is an important medium, so it seems unlikely that no journalist had heard the broadcast or read the accompanying article. Yet, neither Radio Sweden nor other media outlets chose to follow up with the organizers at the end of the festival to find out how many girls had been assaulted. It wasn't just *Dagens Nyheter* that refrained from covering the assaults; all media did. Perhaps this explains why no newsroom wants to point fingers at the paper now. They are all equally guilty of having looked the other way.

But if the police knew, the media knew, the city knew, local politicians knew, and even the young people attending the festival knew that systematic, sexual assaults were taking place, then who is to blame? And, more interestingly, what caused the sudden change in attitude? Why were the assaults quietly tolerated for more than a decade, only to be strongly condemned now in 2016? The perception of common sense had no doubt shifted. In the collective subconscious, the Unimind, the whispers grew louder; the list of inconvenient facts and unpunished trespasses against its unspoken norms grew longer. It was like adding tension to an electrical circuit: initially nothing happens, but eventually there comes a point when the increasing current overloads the system. To prevent damage to the circuit, a fuse blows and—in an instant—everything changes.

Afterwards, most people seemed to think that the previous way of looking at the world had been naïve, or even wrong, yet no one stood up to be held to account for it. Everyone simply acted in accordance with the prevailing norms; the prevailing understanding of reality. No explicit instructions were necessary; people instinctively knew what was expected of them.

When the culprit is systemic, everyone is complicit, and no one is accountable.

THE DISSIDENT IN THE HEART OF DARKNESS

Almedalen week in Gotland is a microcosm of Sweden. However sunny and pleasant the atmosphere, the usual rules of engagement still apply. There can be no real debate on sensitive topics. Instead, panelists who agree with each other are invited to add to each other's points and nod approvingly at each other's comments.

Chang has arrived to listen to one of these "debates" about his and other so-called "alternative" news sites. As usual, he has not been invited to participate. In a session entitled "Do the Media Lie? Migration, Distrust and Cover-Ups," a panel of established media representatives debate the issue. None of the sites discussed have been invited to participate. However, media and communications expert Kristoffer Holt presents his research about "immigration-critical alternative sites." Chang's *Nyheter Idag* is one of the sites scrutinized. Holt summarizes his study by stating that there are important differences between the various sites and their positions. However, they are joined by a common raison d'être, which is their belief that established media intentionally withhold facts from the public in an effort to control people's opinions, and that they try to bar people with divergent opinions from sharing them.

Then follows a discussion with representatives of the established media, including Anna Gullberg, editor-in-chief of Gävle's local paper *Gefle Dagblad*, and Rouzbeh Djalaie from Radio Sweden. Gullberg acknowledges that the media do "cover things up" in the sense that they are "constantly making different kinds of ethical considerations." This, she adds, can of course be interpreted as covering things up, but it can also be interpreted as being responsible.

The room is so packed that people are sitting on the stairs or standing. It is obvious that this is still a hot topic among the public. Chang has arrived early to get a seat near the front. Even though he is not allowed to participate, he wants the panelists to see him when they are speaking about him. When the seminar is over, it is time for mingling. But before the wine and canapés are brought out, the organizers make it clear that all members of the public who have not specifically been invited must clear out. This, of course, includes Chang.

It is just after 6 p.m. when he steps out into the balmy Swedish summer evening.

He watches Stockholm's elites stream past. A few who obviously recognize him cast a quick glare his way, but most are too caught up in their own airs. He is still shunned. The Tattare. The immigrant. The racist. The hatemonger. He feels the sun's faint warmth on his face and smiles. He wouldn't touch their wine if they begged him. He doesn't have to; he's won. Uncomfortable truths have been exposed, and society is having to face them. The opinion corridor has shifted.

Chang watches as the last of the audience members exit the building onto the bright green grass. They meander towards Gunpowder Tower and the 800-year-old walls of medieval Visby, well at home on the thin, paved path between history and the imposing, blue-black Baltic Sea. For a brief moment, he is overwhelmed by the sense of being stuck in time—that these same people have walked, every day, amongst the false security of their stone walls, huddled within the fortress of their collective thoughts. He pops a *snus* pouch behind his lip and watches the crowd disappear along the shore. The corridor has indeed shifted. And with the herd heading in a new direction, perhaps the time has come for him to expand his spotlight.

He turns and begins instinctively to walk the other way.

* * *

In September 2016, Chang publishes an article about misconduct among Sweden Democrat parliamentarians, exposing MP Kent Ekeroth's secret trip to a refugee camp in Greece to film and produce a propaganda video for the anti-immigration site *Avpixlat*.[1] Later, he exposes another MP's gross misbehavior on a trip to Russia.[2]

In December 2016, Chang goes after anti-immigrant "fake news." A Kristianstad newspaper reports that a local church is forced to hire guards because "a new clientele" of visitors is misbehaving. They are defecating on the church floor, openly masturbating, and stealing the church silver, in addition to a long list of other offenses.[3] Several national media outlets pick up the story, and on social media the rumor spreads that this "new clientele" are EU migrants. Using his contacts in Kristianstad, Chang is quickly able to ascertain that the culprits are in fact Swedes, and is thus able to stop the further spread of misinformation.[4]

About two months later, *Dagens Nyheter* publishes a story about fake news, using the misreporting on the Kristianstad church incidents as one of its examples. The article refrains from mentioning that it was Chang who broke the story.[5]

CHESS ON THE BEACH

WAITING FOR DEATH

It is a gray, cold, and windy day in early October 2016 when Samvel arrives on Gotland by boat. He has come in search of Ingmar Bergman's house on the tiny island of Fårö. He knows it is situated in a secret location, hidden away in the forest; near the water, but not visible from the shoreline. He also knows asking locals for help won't work. While alive, Bergman made a pact with the few residents of Fårö not to reveal his address. Even after his death, they still honor that promise. Not that it would have made a difference. Samvel doesn't run into anyone. On this autumn day, the island seems completely deserted.

Samvel has done his research. Using different satellite and map applications, he has figured out roughly where to look. It takes some searching, but Fårö isn't big. Eventually Samvel stands beneath the security fence and surveillance cameras that signal he has arrived. He walks around, tracing the fence, but finds neither an opening nor a place where he can catch a glimpse. He knew he wouldn't be able to enter, but at least to see the building where his idol had lived—that was all he'd hoped for. He's come all this way. But all he can see is thick forest. He cannot get past the fence.

Disappointed, he makes his way to the towering *raukar* of Fårö's shores. The wind slaps at his cheeks. He picks up a couple of gray rocks and sticks them in his pocket as a memento. On these rocky beaches the films of his youth were shot; films such as *Persona*, *Through a Glass Darkly*, *Hour of the Wolf*, *Shame*, and *Scenes from a Marriage*. Films that suited his temperament; films that sparked his dream of Sweden. Samvel takes a seat and stares out at the gray ocean one last time. He half expects Bergman's Grim Reaper to arrive so that he can challenge him to a game of chess; bargain for more time. But in his heart he knows: his time is already up.

On 10 October 2016, Samvel returns to Armenia.

THE UNIMIND STRIKES AGAIN

On 9 January 2017, Katerina Janouch, a Swedish author born in the Czech Republic, is interviewed by Czech television. Janouch is well known for her popular children's books, as well as a wide range of books on adult topics, but on this occasion the host, Martin Veselovský, wants to ask her about the situation in Sweden and how the country is coping with the high levels of immigration. Janouch conveys her opinion. She talks about no-go zones, asylum seekers who lie about their age to pass for minors, about how increasing numbers of Swedes feel unsafe and how, as a result, she and others are learning to handle guns for self-defense. She talks about pensioners who can't afford to eat and about patients dying because of long queues in an over-whelmed healthcare system. All in all, she paints a pretty dark picture of her homeland.[1]

Although, internally, national media have increasingly begun to acknowledge Sweden's challenges, it is still taboo to make comments that can hurt the nation's brand abroad. Problems are to be kept in the family. Consequently, the reactions to Janouch's statements are merciless. In *Dagens Nyheter*, she is accused of spreading "rumors and prejudice."[2]

A few days later, the newspaper also contacts Piratförlaget, Janouch's publishers, to find out how their author's comments will affect their relationship with her. Piratförlaget opt to "strongly distance themselves from her comments."[3] In Uppsala, a bookstore announces that it has removed all of Janouch's children's books from its shelves. "My decision has nothing to do with the contents of Katerina Janouch's children's books. It's about her name being associated with comments and opinions that I wish to distance myself from," Elja Lietoff Schüssler, head of the bookstore, tells local newspaper *Uppsala Nya Tidning*.[4]

Even Prime Minister Stefan Löfven comments on Janouch's decision to speak ill of Sweden abroad. "This is a person who, in my opinion, makes a very strange statement," he tells Swedish media, all the way from the World Economic Forum in Davos. "There is great respect for the Swedish and Nordic model; that we combine productivity with equality and good working conditions for employees with productive and effective companies and a welfare state that contributes. There is great faith in that," he says.[5]

On Facebook, Janouch replies: "Just like in the days of the good dictatorship, the 'image' of the country is more important than what is actually going on in the country. Now Löfven is condemning my comments! Exactly like Brezhnev, Husak, and Ceauşescu did with many cultural workers. Sweden 2017."[6]

Shortly thereafter Janouch receives a phone call. "Katerina! This is Chang Frick..."

In the spring of 2017 she begins to write for *Nyheter Idag*.

AFTERWORD

"Hi, my name is Kajsa Norman..." Click. The line goes dead. Katerina Janouch just hung up on me. Or were we disconnected? I dial her number again. This time there is no response. I write a long SMS explaining that I'd like to ask her about the reactions to her interview on Czech television. I had emailed her on this topic weeks ago, but received no response.

She texts back: "I can't talk right now."

"Ok, when might be a better time?" I ask. The days go by and there is no reply.

Finally, I reach out to Chang. "I guess she really doesn't want to talk to me," I write. "Any idea why?"

"Let me call her and ask," he replies. The next day, he messages: "Try reaching out to her again."

This time Katerina picks up. As I listen to her story, it's easy to understand her hesitation to take my call. If she has googled me, she'll know that I'm published by established media houses, and it is established media that have vilified her. She has no reason to believe that this interview should be any different.

Her story is a book in itself; one that she has, in fact, just finished writing.

The Image of Sweden is the story of her fall; a year of persecution, sleep deprivation, *ångest*, depression, and alienation. She lost friends, her community, her publisher of fifteen years, and her place in the Swedish establishment.

Her story and Chang's are very different in that respect. He was always the outcast; Katerina Janouch, on the other hand, is one of Sweden's most well-known and popular authors. In addition to her many children's books, she has published dozens of fiction and non-fiction titles for adults, on topics ranging from co-dependency to sex and pregnancy.

But that was then. Before she criticized Sweden in her interview on Czech TV. Now, she's forced to self-publish. She sends me the book. I read it with a knot in my stomach: "I have committed the mortal sin of saying something unfavorable, albeit true, about the state of the country," she writes, before including the quote by former Prime Minister Göran Persson—the same quote that many people have used to caution me: "I, as well as the government to which I belong, will, in every context, forcefully *brännmärka* those who speak ill of Sweden abroad."

The associations the verb *brännmärka* spurs in me become more unpleasant each time I read it. In my head I hear the sizzling sound of glowing hot metal searing into flesh. I see the burnt edges of the indelible mark on skin. I can almost smell burnt meat. But, unlike Katerina, I haven't felt it. Not yet.

Whether one physically marks a heretic or merely expels them from the community, the outcome is roughly the same; the shunned person will inevitably go in search of new community. And when this person stumbles across someone else with a blistered "B" burnt into their forehead, the two will invariably experience kinship—even if there is nothing but the "B" that binds them. As the stories of the black Nazis illustrate, Swedish contemporary history provides many examples of unlikely alliances, in which the shared stigma of exclusion is the only common denominator.

It is this powerful sense of permanent shame that many fear most about being branded. So, when Swedes begin to wear the

mark with pride—as a source of strength—something founda-
tional is changing in our collective society. Chang felt the sting
of the brand his whole life. The *svartskalle*. The *tattare*. The
dissident. Eventually, however, those brands became badges of
honor, his reminders of the perceived injustice against which he
was fighting. In many ways, he's reminiscent of a Scandinavian
Noir protagonist: deeply flawed and troubled, both a victim and
an opponent of the system he is fighting—the system that created him. Driven by a personal sense of justice, wearing his brand
with pride, he becomes a rallying point for other outcasts in
search of belonging.

* * *

When Noir pioneer and avid socialist Henning Mankell offered
to critique my writing, I was ecstatic. He didn't do it because he
found me particularly talented, nor because he saw any similari-
ties between his voice and mine; quite the opposite. He did it
because we were different. "Her eye isn't mine," he noted in the
preface to *Bridge Over Blood River*. Henning could disagree vehe-
mently with my interpretation of reality, but still yearn to read
it, fight for it to be published (which he did), and devote countless hours to helping me craft my message. The reward for all his
efforts, he said, was "fresh perspectives on what the world is
really like." Among Swedes, that is a rare position.

In writing this book, I became overwhelmed with sadness and
shame by the very Swedish ways in which we punish difference.
From the early days of race biology and forced sterilizations, one
could argue that Sweden has come a long way, embracing—or at
least claiming to embrace—ethnic diversity. However, despite its
progressive legislation, when it comes to differences of opinion,
Swedish society is far from a pluralistic utopia. On the contrary,
as we've seen in this book, the methodical way in which we keep
down, stigmatize, and deny alternative perspectives—even when

they are true—is frightening. It is a commonly held belief that the right to free speech is the cornerstone, the foundation, of a healthy democratic society. For me, writing this book came with the realization that, without the personal commitment to open-mindedness; the desire to listen; the endeavor to understand those who think differently from ourselves; free speech is nothing more than an impotent platitude.

If I have a hope, it is that we, as a collective, will replace our righteousness with the confidence we need as a nation, as a people, to hear criticism; to consider it, and to accommodate it where it makes sense to do so. But that would require each of us, as individuals, first to lay down our branding irons and begin to listen.

In spite of the efforts to mark them as such, people like Chang and Katerina are not Nazis, racists, or dangerous wrongdoers. They are dissidents, cast out simply for shining a light on the dark side of our self-proclaimed utopia.

NOTES

PREFACE

1. The Swedish Institute, "Sweden beyond the Millennium and Stieg Larsson," 2012, p. 8, https://issuu.com/swedish_institute/docs/sweden_beyond_the_millennium [accessed 18 June 2018].
2. Ibid., p. 34.

WEDNESDAY 12 AUGUST 2015

1. Hannu, Filip, 'Problem med sexuella trakasserier på festival för unga', *Radio Sweden*, 12 August 2015, http://sverigesradio.se/sida/artikel.aspx?programid=1 646&artikel=6230084 [accessed 31 January 2018].

SUNDAY 16 AUGUST 2015

1. Örstadius, Kristoffer, "Förenings-Sverige tynar bort," *Dagens Nyheter*, 16 August 2015, https://www.dn.se/nyheter/sverige/forenings-sverige-tynar-bort/ [accessed 13 June 2018].

IN THE BEGINNING THERE WAS DARKNESS

1. Hagerman, Maja, *Det rena landet—om konsten att uppfinna sina förfäder*, Stockholm: Prisma, 2006, p. 22.
2. Berggren, Henrik and Lars Trägårdh, *Är svensken människa?—Gemenskap och oberoende i det moderna Sverige*, Stockholm: Norstedts Förlag, Second Edition, 2015, pp. 392–3.
3. Ibid., pp. 399–406.
4. Thurfjell, David, *Det gudlösa folket: de postkristna svenskarna och religionen*, Stockholm: Molin Sorgenfrei Förlag, 2015, pp. 18–19.
5. Lindqvist, Herman, *Våra kolonier—de vi hade och de som aldrig blev av*, Stockholm: Albert Bonniers förlag, 2016, p. 12.

NOTES

GO BACK TO POLAND, CHANG!

1. Author's translation. *För vad Sorg och Smärta* (Stockholm: Albert Bonniers Förlag, 2016) is about the experiences of the Traveler people in Sweden. Quote from p. 87.

THE FALL OF THE SWEDISH EMPIRE

1. Englund, Peter "Karl XII:s död—Fallet är avslutat," Peter Englund blog, 3 September 2015, https://peterenglundsnyawebb.wordpress.com/2015/09/03/karl-xiis-dod-fallet-ar-avslutat/ [accessed 13 June 2018].

SWEDISH COLONIALISM

1. Lindqvist, p. 274.
2. Ibid., p. 183.
3. Ibid., pp. 182–7.
4. Kent, Neil, *The Soul of the North: A Social, Architectural, and Cultural History of the Nordic Countries, 1700–1940*, London: Reaktion, 2000, p. 362; Lindqvist, pp. 222–3.
5. Lindqvist, p. 187.
6. Ibid., p. 201.
7. Ibid., pp. 222–3.
8. Ibid., pp. 194–5.
9. Ibid., p. 201.
10. Ibid., p. 205.
11. Kent, p. 362.
12. Lindqvist, pp. 236–7, 222–3.
13. Ibid., pp. 237–42.

VIKING REVIVAL

1. Translated in *The Northern Review*, vol. 3, no. 10 (January 1918), p. 22 (uncredited).
2. Hagerman, p. 137.
3. Berggren and Trägårdh, p. 101.
4. Ibid., pp. 98–101.
5. Hagerman, pp. 139–40.
6. Nilsson, Torbjörn, "Unionsupplösningen 1905: Krisen chockade kungen," *Populär Historia*, vol. 2 (2005), https://popularhistoria.se/artiklar/unionsupplosningen-1905-krisen-chockade-kungen [accessed 24 May 2018].

THE CRADLE OF COLLECTIVE MENTALITY

1. Huntford, Roland, *The New Totalitarians*, London: Allen Lane, 1975 (paperback edition), pp. 42–4.
2. Ibid., p. 88.
3. Ibid., pp. 87–8.
4. Hagerman, pp. 248–249.
5. Huntford, pp. 89–90.

SHAPING THE *VOLKSGEIST*

1. Hagerman, pp. 254–5.
2. Berggren and Trägårdh, pp. 188–91.
3. Sundbärg, Gustav, *Det svenska folklynnet*, Stockholm: Norstedt & Söners Förlag, 1921 (15th edn), p. 8.
4. Berggren & Trägårdh, pp. 188–91.
5. Ibid., p. 146.
6. Ibid., p. 149.
7. Ibid., p. 159.
8. Hagerman, pp. 243–251.
9. Ibid., pp. 254–5.
10. Ibid.
11. Ibid., pp. 256–7.
12. Author's translation (originally "Fosterländsk läsning för barn och ungdom"). Hagerman, pp. 252–7.
13. A literary, linguistic and cultural movement aiming to promote the Nordic spirit and shared cultural history of Scandinavia. For some, it also had a political dimension—aspirations for a unified Scandinavian state.
14. Hagerman, pp. 258–259.
15. Ibid., pp. 261–2.

CHANG'S SILENT VICTORY

1. Sandemose, Aksel, *A Fugitive Crosses His Tracks* (trans. Eugene Gay-Tifft), New York: Alfred A. Knopf, 1936.
2. Berggren and Trägårdh, p. 53.

THE BIRTH OF THE PEOPLE'S HOME

1. Huntford, pp. 90–2.
2. Berggren and Trägårdh, pp. 222–5.
3. Ibid.
4. Ibid., pp. 216–19.
5. Etzemüller, Thomas, *Alva and Gunnar Myrdal: Social Engineering in the Modern World*, London: Lexington Books, 2014, Kindle version, location 2247.

6. Berggren and Trägårdh, pp. 222–5.
7. Hansson, Per-Albin, *Folkhemstalet* (People's Home Speech), Swedish Parliament, 18 January 1928. Author's translation.
8. Berggren and Trägårdh, pp. 222–5.
9. Ibid., p. 206.
10. Ibid., pp. 211–19.

SAMVEL DISCOVERS BERGMAN

1. *Raukar* or "sea stacks" are geological formations in the shape of vertical columns that eroded from reef cliffs during the last ice age.

WEEDING OUT THE DREGS: ENGINEERING BIOLOGICAL HOMOGENEITY

1. Etzemüller, p. 87.
2. Broberg, Gunnar and Mattias Tydén, *Oönskade i folhemmet—rashygien och sterilisering i Sverige*, Stockholm: Dialogos, 2005, pp. 38, 183.
3. Lindqvist, Ursula, "The Cultural Archive of the IKEA store," *Space and Culture*, vol. 12, no. 1, February 2009, pp. 50–1.
4. Broberg and Tydén, pp. 55–6.
5. Etzemüller, pp. 20–1.
6. Ibid., p. 11.
7. Ibid., p. 88.
8. Ibid., p. 117.
9. Runcis, Maija, *Steriliseringar i folkhemmet*, Stockholm: Ordfront, 1998, p. 26.
10. Myrdal, Alva and Gunnar Myrdal, *Kris i befolkningsfrågan*, Stockholm: Albert Bonniers Förlag, 1935, pp. 74–5.
11. Myrdal and Myrdal, p. 217.
12. Runcis, pp. 27–51.
13. Zaremba, Maciej, *De rena och de andra—Om tvångssteriliseringar, rashygien och arvsynd*, Stockholm: Forum, 1999, p. 277.
14. Zaremba, pp. 285–6.
15. Ibid., pp. 289–90.
16. Etzemüller, p. 88.
17. Zaremba, p. 247.
18. Ibid., pp. 247–344.
19. Runcis.
20. Zaremba, p. 338.
21. Ibid., pp. 296–7.
22. Runcis, p. 107.
23. Zaremba, pp. 331–3.

24. Ibid, pp. 327–8.
25. Ibid, pp. 333–5.
26. Ibid., p. 10.
27. Runcis, p. 51.
28. Zaremba, pp. 325–6.
29. Berggren and Trägårdh, p. 231.
30. Zaremba, p. 367.
31. The National Board of Health and Welfare, "Report on 'the *tattare* issue'", 28 June 1937, National Archives, quoted in Zaremba, p. 346.
32. Zaremba, pp. 335–47.
33. Ibid., p. 367.
34. Etzemüller, p. 88.

CHANG VISITS HIS FATHER

1. Equivalent to £855.

ENGINEERING SOCIAL HOMOGENEITY

1. Hermansson, Daniel and Robin Olovsson, "Alva Myrdal," *Historiepodden*, Episode 138, first broadcast 21 January 2017, https://www.radioplay.se/podcast/historiepodden?episode-id=30654 [accessed 31 May 2018].
2. Myrdal and Myrdal, pp. 16–17.
3. Etzemüller, p. 112.
4. Ibid., pp. 186–7.
5. Myrdal, Alva, *Stadsbarn: En bok om deras fostran i storbarnkammare*, Stockholm: Kooperativa Förbundet, 1935, p. 87.
6. Ibid., p. 94.
7. Etzemüller, p. 112.
8. Ibid., p. 120.
9. Etzemüller, Kindle version, location 2156.
10. Björkman, Jenny, "När vi fick lära oss ta av oss skorna", *Forskning & Framsteg*, no. 6 (2007).
11. Swedish Television, "1930-talet," *Historieätarna*, season 2, episode 6, first broadcast 17 December 2014.
12. Björkman.
13. Berggren and Trägårdh, p. 240.
14. Björkman.
15. Myrdal, Gunnar, "Bostadsfrågan såsom socialt planläggningsproblem" [lecture in Copenhagen], quoted in Etzemüller, p. 174.
16. Myrdal, Gunnar, "Kosta sociala reformer pengar?", *Arkitektur och samhälle*, Stockholm: Spektrum, 1932, p. 43.
17. Myrdal and Myrdal, p. 226.

18. Myrdal and Myrdal, p. 203.
19. Hirdman, Yvonne, *Att lägga livet till rätta—studier i svensk folkhemspolitik*, Stockholm: Carlsson Bokförlag, 2010, p. 142.
20. Hedenmo, Martin and Fredrik von Platen, "Bostadspolitiken: Svensk politik för boende, planering och byggande under 130 år," National Board of Housing, Building and Planning (Boverket) report, 2007, p. 54, https://www.boverket.se/globalassets/publikationer/dokument/2007/bostadspolitiken.pdf [accessed 13 June 2018].
21. Etzemüller, p. 173.
22. Huntford, p. 85.
23. Björkman.
24. Ibid.
25. Ibid.
26. Swedish Television, "Nationalromantiken," *Historieätarna*, season 2, episode 3, first broadcast 27 November 2014.
27. Björkman.
28. Ibid.
29. Hirdman, pp. 223–30.

CONSTRUCTING UTOPIA: THE SWEDISH MODEL

1. Etzemüller, Kindle version, location 4076.
2. Lundin, Sara, *P3 Dokumentär: Skotten i Ådalen-31*, Radio Sweden, first broadcast 30 October 2011, http://sverigesradio.se/sida/avsnitt/54030?programid=2519 [accessed 11 July 2017].
3. Elmbrant, Björn, *Så föll den svenska modellen*, Stockholm: Fischer & Co, 1993, p. 14.
4. Elmbrant, p. 16.
5. Mats Svegfors, former editor-in-chief of the Swedish daily *Svenska Dagbladet*, in Tove Lifvendal's book *Från sagoland till framtidsland: Om svensk identitet, utveckling och emigration*, Stockholm: Hjalmarson & Högberg Bokförlag, 2012, p. 181.
6. Elmbrant, p. 16.
7. Huntford, p. 57.
8. Ibid., pp. 60, 69–70.
9. Etzemüller, p. 81.
10. Kristoffersson, Sara, *IKEA—en kulturhistoria*, Stockholm: Atlantis, 2015, p. 126.

GARBO FEVER

1. The Ingmar Bergman Foundation, "Bergman and Sweden," 18 October 2011, http://www.ingmarbergman.se/en/universe/bergman-and-sweden [accessed 31 May 2018].

2. Ibid.
3. Lifvendal, Tove, *Från sagoland till framtidsland: Om svensk identitet, utveckling och emigration*, Stockholm: Hjalmarson & Högberg Bokförlag, 2012, pp. 187–8.
4. Huntford, p. 326.
5. Ibid., p. 326–7.

SWEDISH NEUTRALITY

1. Boëthius, Maria-Pia, *Heder och samvete*, Stockholm: Ordfront, 1999, p. 20.
2. Leitz, Christian, *Nazi Germany and Neutral Europe During the Second World War*, Manchester: Manchester University Press, 2000, p. 56.
3. Boëthius, p. 32.
4. Leitz, pp. 56–8.
5. Boëthius, pp. 105–7.
6. Leitz, pp. 56–8.
7. Boëthius, p. 48.
8. Leitz, p. 63.
9. Leitz, pp. 65–71.
10. Boëthius, pp. 65–71, 110.
11. Boëthius, pp. 110–12.
12. Leitz, p. 72.
13. Ibid., p. 74.
14. Ibid., p. 66.
15. Statens Offentliga Utredningar (SOU 2005:56), "Det blågula glashuset—strukturell diskriminering i Sverige," state-appointed commission report, 2005, pp. 106–8.
16. Ibid.
17. Leitz, p. 77.
18. Ibid., pp. 72–4.
19. Boëthius, pp. 57–9.
20. Berggren, Henrik, *Underbara dagar framför oss—En biografi över Olof Palme*, Stockholm: Norstedts, 2010, p. 190.
21. Hawkins, Derek, "Nazi past followed Ikea founder Ingvar Kamprad to his death," *The Washington Post*, 29 January 2018, https://www.washingtonpost.com/news/morning-mix/wp/2018/01/29/nazi-past-followed-ikea-founder-ingvar-kamprad-to-his-death/?utm_term=.da2eada30b7a [accessed 19 June 2018].
22. Kristoffersson, p. 128.
23. Ibid., p. 129.
24. Person from the southern Swedish province of Småland, famous for their frugality. *Smålänning* can also be used condescendingly to label someone cheap.
25. Kristoffersson, pp. 45–46.

THE RISE OF THE MORAL SUPERPOWER

1. Berggren, pp. 190–214.
2. Statens offentliga utredningar (SOU 2005:56), "Det blågula glashuset—strukturell diskriminering i Sverige," 2005, p. 109.
3. Johansson Heinö, Andreas, *Farväl till Folkhemmet*, Stockholm: Timbro, 2015, pp. 25–6.
4. Ibid., p. 29.
5. Ibid., pp. 31, 34–5, 40.
6. Ibid., p. 40.
7. Ibid., pp. 8, 31.
8. Mattsson, Pontus, *Tvärvändningen—om svängningen i flyktingpolitiken*, Swedish Television, first broadcast 29 October 2017.
9. Johansson Heinö, p. 34.
10. Ibid., p. 41.
11. Ibid., p. 42.
12. Ibid., p. 44.

THE SWEDISH MODEL II: THE CONTRACT

1. Berggren, pp. 282–4.
2. Ibid., pp. 345–91.
3. Ibid., p. 225.
4. Ibid., pp. 415–17.
5. Ibid., pp. 111–41.
6. Ibid., pp. 460–1.
7. Elmbrant, pp. 29–31.
8. Almqvist, Carl Jonas Love, *Det går an*, Stockholm: Modernista, 2017 (first published in 1838).
9. Berggren and Trägårdh, pp. 253–5.
10. Ibid., pp. 254, 265.
11. Ibid., pp. 273–4.
12. Ibid., pp. 276–7.
13. Ibid., pp. 242–5.
14. Ibid., pp. 253–5.
15. Ibid., pp. 242–5.
16. Hall, Bengt, "Dags för Palmes penndrag," *Kristianstadsbladet*, 29 April 2017, http://www.kristianstadsbladet.se/debatt/dags-for-palmes-penndrag/ [accessed 12 June 2018].
17. Berggren and Trägårdh, pp. 282–3.
18. Ibid., p. 288.
19. Ibid., pp. 290–5.
20. Berggren, pp. 460–1.

21. Berggren and Trägårdh, pp. 310–11.
22. Berggren, pp. 460–1.
23. Berggren and Trägårdh, p. 306.
24. Ibid., pp. 266–304.
25. Hinde, Dominic, *A Utopia Like Any Other: Inside the Swedish Model*, Edinburgh: Luath Press Limited, 2016, Kindle version, location 209.

AGENTS OF THE UNIMIND

1. Björk, Gunnela, *Olof Palme och medierna*, Stockholm: Boréa Bokförlag, 2006.
2. Lifvendal, p. 153.
3. Ibid., p. 232.
4. Huntford, p. 287.
5. Ibid.
6. Lind, Kalle, *Snedtänkt: Om SVT:s sjuttiotal*, Radio Sweden, first broadcast 10 December 2015.
7. Hammar, Filip and Fredrik Wikingsson, *Två nötcreme och en Moviebox— Hisnande generaliseringar om vår uppväxt i DDR-Sverige*, Stockholm: Bonnier Fakta, 2003, p. 137.
8. Bildt, Carl et al (Moderate Party), "En fri radio och TV," Proposal to Parliament, 1989/90:K401.
9. Huntford, pp. 292–3.
10. Swedish Government, "The Swedish Press Act: 250 years of freedom of the press," http://www.government.se/articles/2016/06/the-swedish-press-act-250-years-of-freedom-of-the-press/ [accessed 4 June 2018].
11. Swedish Institute, "20 milestones of Swedish press freedom," 18 January 2018, https://sweden.se/society/20-milestones-of-swedish-press-freedom/ [accessed 4 June 2018].
12. Huntford, p. 293.
13. Ibid., pp. 300, 296–9.
14. Ibid., pp. 295–6.

THE MURDER OF THE PROPHET

1. Hermansson, Daniel and Robin Olovsson, "Palmemordet," *Historiepodden*, Episode 93, first broadcast 27 February 2016.
2. Ellung, Göran, *Palme—sista timmarna*, TV4, broadcast 24 February 2016. This documentary was made for the thirtieth anniversary of the assassination.
3. Ibid.
4. Billger, Ola, "The Millennium author's theories concerning the murder of Olof Palme," *Svenska Dagbladet*, 24 February 2014, https://www.svd.se/the-millennium-authors-theories-concerning-the-murder-of-olof-palme [accessed 5 June 2018].

5. Ellung.
6. Ibid.
7. Ibid.
8. Ibid.
9. Ibid.
10. Borgäs, Lars, *SVT Dokument Inifrån—Mannen, Mordet, Mysteriet*, Swedish Television, 1999.
11. Brown, Andrew, *Fishing in Utopia: Sweden and the Future that Disappeared*, London: Granta Books, 2008, Kindle edition, location 1654.
12. Hermansson and Olovsson, "Palmemordet."
13. Ibid.
14. Ibid.
15. Radio Sweden, "Time Limits on Murder Cases Removed," 3 February 2010, https://sverigesradio.se/sida/artikel.aspx?programid=254&artikel=3417924 [accessed 12 June 2018].
16. Berggren, p. 648.
17. Ibid., pp. 655–6.
18. Hermansson and Olovsson, "Palmemordet."
19. Fichtelius, Erik, Kjell Tunegård and Paolo Rodriguez, *Ordförande Persson*, Swedish Television, first broadcast in March 2007.
20. Edman, Gustav, "90-talskrisen," *P3 Dokumentär*, Radio Sweden, 12 October 2008, http://sverigesradio.se/sida/avsnitt/87426?programid=2519 [accessed 5 June 2018].
21. Ibid.
22. Ibid.

SAMVEL AND SWEDISH ANGST

1. Author's translation.

SWEDISH GLASNOST

1. Berggren and Trägårdh, pp. 354-356.
2. Häger, Björn, "Problempartiet—Mediernas villrådighet kring SD valet 2010," Stockholm: Stiftelsen Institutet för mediestudier, 2012, p. 35.
3. Elmbrant, p. 256.
4. Häger, p. 36.
5. Ibid., pp. 36–7.
6. Elmbrant, p. 256.

UNINTENDED VICTIMS OF THE UNIMIND

1. Tamas, Gellert, *Lasermannen—en berättelse om Sverige*, Stockholm: Ordfront, 2016 (first edition 2002), p. 59.

2. Ibid., p. 80.
3. Ibid., p. 143.
4. Ibid., p. 145.
5. Tamas, Gellert and Malcolm Dixelius, *Lasermannen—Dokumentären*, Swedish Television, Channel 2, 11 December 2005.
6. Tamas, pp. 200–5, 229–30.
7. Ibid., p. 232.
8. Tamas and Dixelius.
9. Tamas, p. 276.
10. Tamas and Dixelius.

MEDIA HANGOVER

1. Tamas, Gellert, *Lasermannen—en berättelse om Sverige*, p. 295.
2. Tamas, Gellert, and Malcolm Dixelius, *Lasermannen—Dokumentären*.
3. Häger, p. 44
4. Ibid.
5. Ibid.

THE BLACK NAZIS: BASTARDS OF THE PEOPLE'S HOME

1. A type of emergency tractor made from a car or truck, EPA tractors were originally made to keep farming going during the Second World War, when there was a shortage of spare parts. They were named after EPA discount stores, as a way to signal that they were basic and cheap.
2. Interview with Lars Johnsson, 26 October 2016, Stockholm.
3. Tamas, pp. 240, 242.
4. Ibid., p. 242.
5. Interview with Benjamin Teitelbaum, Boulder, Colorado, 2 November 2017.
6. Sandelin, Magnus, *Den svarte nazisten—en dokumentär om Jackie Arklöf*, Stockholm: Bokförlaget Forum, Månpocket, 2010, pp. 24–5, 29, 33.
7. Ibid., p. 35.
8. Ibid., pp. 37–40.
9. Ibid., pp. 41–5.
10. Ibid., pp. 45–83.
11. Ibid., pp. 98–104.
12. Ibid., pp. 98–112.
13. Ibid., p. 110.
14. Ibid., pp. 123–4.
15. Ibid., pp. 132–5.
16. Ibid., p. 135.
17. Ibid., pp. 132–62.

18. Ibid., pp. 164–71
19. Ibid., pp. 171–7, 201.
20. Ibid., p. 190.
21. Karim, Osmond, *De ensamma—en film om adoption*, Swedish Television, 20 April 2017, https://www.svtplay.se/video/13246808/de-ensamma-en-film-om-adoption/de-ensamma-en-film-om-adoption-avsnitt-1?start=auto&tab=senaste [acessed 25 August 2017].
22. Öberg, Martin, "Jag blev ert monster," *SVT Opinion*, Swedish Television, 5 July 2014, https://www.svt.se/opinion/article2167728.svt [accessed 25 August 2017].
23. Hübinette, Tobias, "Psykisk hälsa bland utlandsadopterade i Sverige" [Mental health among international adoptees in Sweden], *Psykisk Hälsa* vol. 44, no. 1 (2003), pp. 17–30.
24. Karim.

CHANG MAKES A FRIEND

1. Teitelbaum, Benjamin R., *Lions of the North—Sounds of the New Nordic Radical Nationalism*, New York, NY: Oxford University Press, 2017, p. 34.
2. Larsson, Stieg, "The New Popular Movement," *Expo/Svartvitt*, no. 3/4, 1999.
3. Teitelbaum, pp. 21–34.
4. Odmalm, Pontus and Eve Hepburn (eds), *The European Mainstream and the Populist Radical Right*, London: Routledge, 2017; Widfeldt, Anders, 'The Radical Right in the Nordic Countries', in Rydgren, Jens (ed.), *The Oxford Handbook of the Radical Right*, New York: Oxford University Press, 2018.
5. Baas, David, *Bevara Sverige Svenskt—ett reportage om Sverigedemokraterna*, Stockholm: Bonniers, 2014, Månpocket, 2015, pp. 31–3.
6. Ibid., pp. 31–3, 35, 38–9.

CHANG AT HOME AT THE SCRAPYARD

1. Johansson Heinö, Andreas, *Farväl till Folkhemmet*, Stockholm: Timbro, 2015, p. 70.
2. Mattsson, Pontus, *Tvärvändningen—om svängningen i flyktingpolitiken*, Swedish Television, first broadcast 29 October 2017.
3. Cetin, Evin, "Sabuni kravlar fram i populistisk lervällning," *Aftonbladet*, 17 August 2010, https://www.aftonbladet.se/debatt/article12430379.ab [accessed 1 November 2017].
4. Kamali, Masoud, "Med de nya statsråden ökar rasismen i Sverige," *Dagens Nyheter*, 13 October 2006, https://www.dn.se/arkiv/debatt/med-de-nya-statsraden-okar-rasismen-i-sverige/ [accessed 5 June 2018].
5. Skogkär, Mats, "Ministern som stör," *Sydsvenskan*, 17 October 2006, https://www.sydsvenskan.se/2006-10-16/ministern-som-stor [accessed 12 June 2018].

6. Mattsson.
7. Ibid.
8. Johansson Heinö, p. 74.

SWEDISH IMMERSION

1. Lifvendal, p. 227.

THE UNIMIND ENFORCES ITS BOUNDARIES

1. Baas, p. 288.

MOTHER'S FROWN

1. Johansson Heinö, p. 85.
2. Ibid., pp. 73–4, 85.
3. Baas, p. 187.
4. Swedish International Liberal Centre, "Rapport från valövervakning av de svenska valen till riksdag, kommun och landsting: Rekommendationer och iakttagelser," 14 September 2014, http://silc.se/wp-content/uploads/2016/07/Val%C3%B6vervakning-av-de-svenska-riksdagsvalen-2014.pdf [accessed 20 June 2018].
5. Orrenius, Niklas, "Martyrrollen stärks Motvinden är SD:s medvind," *Sydsvenskan*, 1 October 2009; Sverigedemokraterna, "Omfattande valsabotage redan efter 2 dagars förtidsröstning," press release, 3 September 2010, http://www.mynewsdesk.com/se/sverigedemokraterna/pressreleases/omfattande-valsabotage-redan-efter-2-dagars-foertidsroestning-463781 [accessed 20 June 2018].
6. Orrenius, Niklas, "Sd serveras martyrskapet gratis," *Sydsvenskan*, 2 November 2007.

THE FIGHT FOR CONTROL OF THE UNIMIND BEGINS

1. De Benoist, Alain, "The New Right: Forty Years After" (Preface), in Sunić, Tomislav, *Against Democracy and Equality: The European New Right* (3rd edition), London: Arktos Media, 2011, p. 22.
2. Lindgren, Petter, "Poesiprotest i arktisk kyla," *Aftonbladet*, 25 November 2010, https://www.aftonbladet.se/kultur/article12677782.ab [accessed 7 November 2017].
3. Ibid.
4. Frick, Chang, "Plötsligt en förening," *Chang Frick Blogspot*, 29 November 2010, http://changfrick.blogspot.com/2010/11/plotsligt-en-forening.html [accessed 7 November 2017].
5. Teitelbaum, pp. 42–3.
6. Ibid., p. 53.

SAMVEL STARES INTO THE VOID

1. Thurfjell, David, *Det gudlösa folket: de postkristna svenskarna och religionen*, Stockholm: Molin Sorgenfrei Förlag, 2015, pp. 23–9.
2. Ibid, pp. 72, 111–12.

THE CONSEQUENCES OF DISOBEDIENCE

1. Tagesson, Eric, Anders Johansson, and Kerstin Danielson, "Han lämnar SD efter överfallet," *Aftonbladet*, 24 September 2010, http://www.aftonbladet.se/nyheter/valet2010/article12528820.ab [accessed 7 June 2018].
2. Sulaiman, Haore, "Issa fick 18 knivhugg—för att han är med i SD," *Dagen*, 12 January 2011, http://www.dagen.se/issa-fick-18-knivhugg-for-att-han-ar-med-i-sd-1.121478 [accessed 7 June 2018].
3. Ibid.
4. Ibid.
5. Poolh, Daniel, "Misshandlades för att han var Sverigedemokrat," *Expo*, 28 September 2010, http://expo.se/2010/misshandlades-for-att-han-var-sverigedemokrat_3398.html [accessed 7 June 2018].
6. Baas, p. 290.
7. Ibid., pp. 288–9.
8. Ibid., pp. 290–1.
9. Thurfjell, Karin, "Läkare: Ristade själv in hakkors," *Svenska Dagbladet* (TT), 18 September 2010, https://www.svd.se/lakare-ristade-sjalv-in-hakkors; Klint, Lars, Anna Skarin and Fredrik Sjöshult, "Polisen: SD-kandidaten ristade sig själv i pannan," *Expressen*, 19 September 2010, http://www.expressen.se/nyheter/val-2010/polisen-sd-kandidaten-ristade-sig-sjalv-i-pannan/; Rosén, Eric, 'Utredningen om hakkors i pannan på sd-politikern nedlagd', *Nyheter24*, 11 November 2010, https://nyheter24.se/nyheter/inrikes/486055-utredningen-om-hakkors-i-pannan-pa-sd-politikern-nedlagd [all accessed 7 June 2018].

HUSBY RIOTS

1. Wallroth, Emmelie, and Sofia Roström Andersson, "Våldsamma upplopp i Husby i natt," *Aftonbladet*, 19 May 2013, https://www.aftonbladet.se/nyheter/article16804681.ab [accessed 7 June 2018].
2. Orange, Richard, "Swedish riots spark surprise and anger," *The Guardian*, 25 May 2013, https://www.theguardian.com/world/2013/may/25/sweden-europe-news [accessed 7 June 2018].
3. 'Sweden riots spread beyond Stockholm despite extra police', BBC News, 25 May 2013, http://www.bbc.com/news/world-europe-22656657 [accessed 7 June 2018].

THE LONELY HOLOGRAM

1. Berggren, Henrik and Lars Trägårdh, *Är svensken människa?—Gemenskap och oberoende i det moderna Sverige*, Stockholm: Norstedts Förlag, Second Edition, 2015, p. 441.

2. Gandini, Erik, *The Swedish Theory of Love*, Fasad Cine AB, 2015.

3. Berggren and Trägårdh, pp. 21–3.

4. Ibid., p. 55.

5. Augustine Lawler, Peter, "The Problem of Democratic Individualism," *The University Bookman*, vol. 28, no. 3 (Spring 1988), http://www.kirkcenter.org/index.php/bookman/article/the-problem-of-democratic-individualism/ [accessed 10 September 2017].

BLINDSPOTS OF THE UNIMIND

1. The Swedish Police Authority, The National Operations Department (Nationella operativa avdelningen Underrättelseenheten), "Rapport: 'Utsatta områden—sociala risker, kollektiv förmåga och oönskade händelser' av Polismyndigheten/Noa," December 2015, https://polisen.se/siteassets/dokument/ovriga_rapporter/utsatta-omraden-sociala-risker-kollektiv-formaga-och-oonskade-handelser.pdf [accessed 18 June 2018].

2. Höjer, Henrik, 'Därför ökar de kriminella gängens makt', *Forskning & Framsteg*, 11 May 2015, http://fof.se/tidning/2015/5/artikel/darfor-okar-de-kriminella-gangens-makt [accessed 6 October 2017].

3. The Swedish Police Authority.

4. Ibid., p. 8.

5. Björkman, Jenny, "När vi fick lära oss ta av oss skorna," *Forskning & Framsteg*, no. 6 (2007).

6. Nordström, Ludvig, *Lort-Sverige*, Sundsvall: Tidsspegeln, 1984 [1st edn 1938], p. 11.

7. Björkman.

8. Hedenmo, Martin and Fredrik von Platen, "Bostadspolitiken: Svensk politik för boende, planering och byggande under 130 år," National Board of Housing, Building and Planning (Boverket) report, 2007, https://www.boverket.se/globalassets/publikationer/dokument/2007/bostadspolitiken.pdf [accessed 8 June 2018], p. 55.

9. Huntford, Roland, *The New Totalitarians*, London: Allen Lane, 1971, p. 283.

10. Hall, Thomas, *Stockholm: The Making of a Metropolis*, London and New York: Routledge, 2009, p. 112.

11. Huntford, pp. 262–3.

12. Rudberg, Eva, *Sven Markelius, arkitekt*, Stockholm: Arkitektur Förlag, 1989, p. 156.

13. Huntford, pp. 272–3.
14. Government prop. 1967:100, quoted in Hedenmo and von Platen, p. 56.
15. Hinde, Dominic, *A Utopia Like Any Other: Inside the Swedish Model*, Edinburgh: Luath Press Limited, 2016, Kindle version, location 1759.
16. Huntford, pp. 250–1.
17. Ibid., p. 254.
18. Brown, Andrew, *Fishing in Utopia: Sweden and the Future that Disappeared*, London: Granta Books, 2008, Kindle edition, location 253.
19. The Swedish Police Authority.
20. Ibid., p. 8.
21. Ibid., p. 18.
22. Ibid., p. 19.
23. Ibid., pp. 15–17.
24. Larsson, Jens, "Polischef i Rinkeby: 'De kriminella skrattar åt oss,'" *SVT Nyheter*, Swedish Television, 7 March 2017, https://www.svt.se/nyheter/lokalt/stockholm/polischef-i-rinkeby-de-kriminella-skrattar-at-oss [accessed 19 September 2017].
25. In 2017, there were forty-three deadly shootings in Sweden, the vast majority of which took place in "vulnerable areas." This compares to the early 1990s, when there was an average of four deaths a year that could be attributed to gang-related shootings. Sundberg, Marit, "Polisen: 43 personer sköts till döds 2017," 19 January 2018, https://www.svt.se/nyheter/inrikes/polisen-43-personer-skots-till-dods-2017 [accessed 8 June 2018]; Björklund, Andreas, "Rekordmånga ouppklarade mord i Sverige," *SVT Nyheter*, Swedish Television, 9 October 2016, https://www.svt.se/nyheter/inrikes/rekordmanga-ouppklarade-mord-i-sverige [accessed 8 June 2018].
26. Persson, Daniel, *Forskare: Fler skottdraman i Sverige*, Radio Sweden, 5 September 2017, http://sverigesradio.se/sida/artikel.aspx?programid=96&artikel=6770039&utm_source=dlvr.it&utm_medium=twitter [accessed 4 October 2017].
27. Ejneberg, Rasmus, "Våldet i Sverige omfattande—jämförs nu med Mexiko," *Expressen*, 5 September 2017, https://www.expressen.se/nyheter/brottscentralen/valdet-i-sverige-omfattande-jamfors-nu-med-mexiko/ [accessed 12 June 2018].
28. The Swedish Police Authority.
29. Ibid., p. 20.
30. Svensson, Anna H., "Säpo-chefen om radikaliseringen i Sverige: Enorm ökning," *SVT Nyheter*, Swedish Television, 17 September 2017, https://www.svt.se/nyheter/inrikes/sapo-chefen-om-radikaliseringen-i-sverige-enorm-okning [accessed 15 February 2018].
31. Klinghoffer, Sanna, "Terrorforskaren: 'Utvecklingen är oroande,'" *SVT Nyheter*,

Swedish Television, 15 September 2017, https://www.svt.se/nyheter/inrikes/utvecklingen-ar-oroande, [accessed 15 February 2018].

32. Capatides, Christina, "Which European countries have produced the most ISIS fighters?," CBS News, 25 January 2016, https://www.cbsnews.com/news/isis-terror-recruiting-europe-belgium-france-denmark-sweden-germany/ [accessed 15 February 2018].

33. The Swedish Police Authority, p. 20.

34. Ibid., pp. 18–19.

35. Sanandaji, Tino, *Massutmaning—ekonomisk politik mot utanförskap & antisocialt beteende*, Stockholm: Kuhzad Media, 2017, pp. 5–6, and pp. 94–109.

36. Johansson, Anders and Linda Hjertén, "Polisens hemliga rapport: Här är Stockholms läns farligaste områden," *Aftonbladet*, 4 February 2016, http://www.aftonbladet.se/nyheter/krim/article22190105.ab [accessed 5 March 2017].

37. Moreno, Federico, "Ett parallellt samhälle växer fram," *Expressen*, 30 June 2016, https://www.expressen.se/nyheter/longread/utanforskapet-inifran/ett-parallellt-samhalle-vaxer-fram/ [accessed 27 June 2018].

38. Sanandaji, pp. 138–41.

39. Speech broadcast on Mattsson, Pontus, *Tvärvändningen—om svängningen i flyktingpolitiken*, Swedish Television, 29 October 2017.

40. Johansson Heinö, pp. 85–6.

41. Mattsson, Pontus, *104 dagar—en nyhetsdokumentär om den politiska turbulensen efter 2014 års val*, Swedish Television, Channel 2, broadcast 23 December 2015. In 1957, the Social Democrats formed a coalition with the Centre party. It collapsed and a new election had to be announced.

42. Sanandaji, pp. 58–61.

43. Ibid., pp. 39–41.

44. The survey defines a person with foreign background as someone whose parents were both born outside of Sweden. A person with one parent born in Sweden is regarded as Swedish regardless of whether they themselves were born in Sweden or abroad. Wernersson, Annie, "SD ökar kraftigt bland väljare med utländsk bakgrund," *SVT Nyheter*, Swedish Television, 7 June 2017, https://www.svt.se/nyheter/inrikes/sd-okar-kraftigt-bland-utrikes-fodda [accessed 8 June 2018].

45. Baas, p. 319.

46. Ibid., pp. 324–5.

47. Johansson Heinö, Andreas, *Gillar vi olika? Hur den svenska likhetsnormen hindrar integrationen*, Stockholm: Timbro, 2012, p. 109.

48. Ibid.

49. Ibid., pp. 110, 123.

50. Thurfjell, p. 27.

51. Berggren and Trägårdh, pp. 84–5.

52. Statistics Sweden, "Antal personer efter utländsk/svensk bakgrund och år, 2016," http://www.statistikdatabasen.scb.se/pxweb/sv/ssd/START__BE__ BE0101__BE0101Q/UtlSvBakgFin/table/tableViewLayout1/?rxid=63a8bae6– 3541–4a94-bb7d-6a00c1e2ea52 [accessed 8 June 2018]; UK Office for National Statistics, 'Statistical bulletin: Population of the UK by country of birth and nationality: 2017', 24 May 2018, https://www.ons.gov.uk/peoplepopulation-andcommunity/populationandmigration/internationalmigration/bulletins/ ukpopulationbycountryofbirthandnationality/2017 [accessed 8 June 2018].

53. Johansson Heinö, *Farväl till Folkhemmet*, p. 88.

54. Statistics Sweden, "Utrikesfödda efter födelseland och invandringsår," 31 December 2017, available at www.scb.se [accessed 17 May 2018].

55. Johansson Heinö, *Farväl till Folkhemmet*, p. 88.

56. Sanandaji, p. 42.

57. Statistics Sweden, "Var fjärde i Sverige är högutbildad, Befolkningens utbild-ning 2016," https://www.scb.se/hitta-statistik/sverige-i-siffror/utbildning-jobb-och-pengar/befolkningens-utbildning/ [accessed 16 May 2018].

58. Sanandaji, p. 41.

59. Jelmini, Maria, "SvD prisas för Gula Båtarna-kampanj och affärsmodell," *Svenska Dagbladet*, 24 May 2016, https://www.svd.se/svd-vann-pris-for-gula-batarna-kampanj [accessed 8 June 2018].

60. Sanandaji, p. 49.

61. Carp, Ossi, "'Tjänar över en halv miljard på invandringen,'" *Dagens Nyheter*, 31 May 2014, https://www.dn.se/nyheter/sverige/tjanar-over-en-halv-miljard-pa-invandringen/ [accessed 8 June 2018].

62. The numbers and many errors of the report are explained in detail by Tino Sanandaji, economics researcher at the Stockholm School of Economics: "Invandring lönsam i Sandvikens kommun! (finstilt: 'om statens och landstin-gens kostnader exkluderas'...)," Tino Sanandaji blog, 1 June 2014, http://tino. us/2014/06/rapport-om-sandviken-invandring-lonsam-finstila-om-stat-och-landstingens-kostnader-exkluderats/ [accessed 8 June 2018].

63. Hägg, Joanna, Magnus Höijer, and Samir Sandberg, "Rådgivningsrapport: Socioekonomisk analys Invandring Sandvikens kommun," Pricewaterhouse-coopers, March 2014.

64. Truedson, Lars et al., "Misstron mot medier," Stockholm: Institutet för medi-estudier, 2017, p. 10.

65. Frick, Chang, "Man skjuten i Stockholm—Här jagar tungt beväpnad polis gärningsmännen," *Nyheter Idag*, 5 September 2016, https://nyheteridag.se/ man-skjuten-i-stockholm-har-jagar-tungt-bevapnad-polis-garningsmannen/ [accessed 8 June 2018].

66. Magnusson, Erik, "Så blev flyktingkrisen en svensk beredskapskatastrof," *Sydsvenskan*, 26 December 2015, https://www.sydsvenskan.se/2015-12-26/sa-blev-flyktingkrisen-en-svensk-beredskapskatastrof [accessed 17 October 2017].
67. Mattsson, *Tvärvändningen*.

THE PEOPLE'S CONTAINER

1. Kristoffersson, Sara, *IKEA—en kulturhistoria*, Stockholm: Atlantis, 2015, p. 25.
2. Interview with Thomas Melin, SEM-System Fritidshus AB (owner of the property at the time of the vandalism), June 2017.

THE FUSE BLOWS: THE UNIMIND CHANGES ITS MIND

1. Radio Sweden, "Tidslinje över flyktingkrisen," November 11, 2015, http://sverigesradio.se/sida/artikel.aspx?programid=83&artikel=6299595 [accessed October 17, 2017].
2. Magnusson.
3. Tidningarnas Telegrambyrå, "Tusen ensamkommande flyktingbarn har försvunnit," *Göteborgsposten*, 14 October 2015, http://www.gp.se/nyheter/sverige/tusen-ensamkommande-flyktingbarn-har-f%C3%B6rsvunnit-1.151349 [accessed 17 October 2017].
4. Magnusson.
5. Gudmunson, Per, "SD näst störst—M ner på 20 procent," *Svenska Dagbladet*, 23 October 2015, https://www.svd.se/sd-nast-storst-m-ner-pa-20-procent [accessed 11 June 2018].
6. Wallroth, Emmelie, "Yougov: Nu är SD Sveriges största parti," *Metro*, 20 August 2015, https://www.metro.se/artikel/yougov-nu-%C3%A4r-sd-sveriges-st%C3%B6rsta-parti-xr [accessed 11 June 2018].
7. Frick, Chang, "Efter flyktingkrisen: SD största parti med högsta noteringen någonsin," *Nyheter Idag*, 10 September 2015, https://nyheteridag.se/efter-flyktingkrisen-sd-storsta-parti-med-hogsta-noteringen-nagonsin/ [accessed 11 June 2018].
8. Albinsson, Mattias, "All time high för SD—26,8 procent i Nyheter Idag/Sentios opinionsmätning", *Nyheter Idag*, 12 November 2015, https://nyheteridag.se/all-time-high-for-sd-268-procent-i-nyheter-idagsentios-opinionsmatning/ [accessed 11 June 2018].
9. Magnusson.
10. Radio Sweden, "Tidslinje över flyktingkrisen."
11. Swedish Migration Agency (Migrationsverket), "Nästan 163 000 människor sökte asyl i Sverige 2015," 1 January 2016, http://www.mynewsdesk.com/se/migrationsverket/news/naestan-163-000-maenniskor-soekte-asyl-i-sverige-2015-153237 [accessed 11 June 2018].
12. Sanandaji, *Massutmaning*, pp. 70–1.

NOTES

THE OPINION CORRIDOR

1. Hakelius, Johan, 'När det som var suspekt plötsligt blir sunt förnuft', *Aftonbladet*, 26 October 2015, https://www.aftonbladet.se/nyheter/kolumnister/johanhakelius/article21647404.ab [accessed 4 November 2017].

THURSDAY 7 JANUARY 2016

1. Huggler, Justin, "'Cover-up' over Cologne sex assaults blamed on migration sensitivities," *The Telegraph*, 6 January 2016, https://www.telegraph.co.uk/news/worldnews/europe/germany/12085182/Cover-up-over-Cologne-sex-assaults-blamed-on-migration-sensitivities.html [accessed 12 June 2018].
2. Withnall, Adam, "Cologne police ordered to remove word 'rape' from reports into New Year's Eve sexual assaults amid cover-up claims," *The Independent*, 7 April 2016, http://www.independent.co.uk/news/world/europe/cologne-police-ordered-to-remove-word-rape-from-reports-into-new-year-s-eve-sexual-assaults-a6972471.html [accessed 10 March 2017].
3. Huggler.
4. Withnall.

SATURDAY 9 JANUARY 2016

1. Wierup, Lasse, "Kvinnors rätt att festa säkert kan inte offras," *Dagens Nyheter*, 9 January 2016, http://www.dn.se/nyheter/varlden/kvinnors-ratt-att-festa-sakert-kan-inte-offras/?forceScript=1&variantType=large [accessed 11 March 2017].
2. Ibid.
3. In Swedish the term is *ensamkommande*, literally "unaccompanied", meaning an asylum seeker who has arrived without parents and who is, or claims to be, a minor.

SUNDAY 10 JANUARY 2016

1. Bouvin, Emma, "Polisen mörkade övergreppen på festivalen," *Dagens Nyheter*, 10 January 2016, http://www.dn.se/nyheter/sverige/polisen-morkade-overgreppen-pa-festivalen/?forceScript=1&variantType=large [accessed 9 March 2017].
2. Ibid.
3. Pirttisalo Sallinen, Jani, "38 flickor utsattes för sexbrott på festivalen," *Svenska Dagbladet*, 11 January 2016, https://www.svd.se/38-flickor-utsattes-for-ofredande-pa-festivalen [accessed 12 June 2018].
4. Salihu, Diamant, Åsa Asplid, and Michael Syrén, "Här är anmälningarna från 'We are Sthlm'," *Expressen*, 13 January 2016, https://www.expressen.se/nyheter/har-ar-anmalningarna-fran-we-are-sthlm/ [accessed 12 June 2018].

MONDAY 11 JANUARY 2016

1. *Dagens Nyheter*, "Questions and answers on DN's handling of events in the Kungsträdgården," 11 January 2016, http://www.dn.se/nyheter/sverige/questions-and-answers-on-dns-handling-of-events-in-the-kungstradgarden/ [accessed 10 March 2017].

2. Lundquist, Hanna, "Opitz: 'Behövs mer öppenhet om våra arbetssätt,'" *Journalisten*, 11 January 2016, https://www.journalisten.se/nyheter/opitz-behovs-mer-oppenhet-om-vara-arbetssatt [accessed 12 June 2018].

3. Rågsjö Thorell, Andreas, "DN svarar på anklagelserna om mörkläggning—med avslöjande," *Resumé*, 11 January 2016, https://www.resume.se/nyheter/artiklar/2016/01/11/dn-svarar-pa-anklagelserna-om-morklaggning—med-avslojande/ [accessed 12 June 2018].

4. Nordenstam, Sven, "Swedish police to investigate sexual assault cover-up allegations," Reuters, 11 January 2016, https://uk.reuters.com/article/uk-sweden-assaults/swedish-police-to-investigate-sexual-assault-cover-up-allegations-idUK-KCN0UP1PQ20160112 [accessed 12 June 2018].

5. BBC News, "Swedish police probe 'cover-up of migrant sex assaults,'" 11 January 2016, http://www.bbc.com/news/world-europe-35285086 [accessed 12 June 2018].

6. Crouch, David, "Swedish police accused of covering up sex attacks by refugees at music festival," *The Guardian*, 11 January 2016, https://www.theguardian.com/world/2016/jan/11/swedish-police-accused-cover-up-sex-attacks-refugees-festival [accessed 12 June 2018].

TUESDAY 12 JANUARY 2016

1. Pirttisalo Sallinen, Jani, "Polisen får nya direktiv om signalement vid vardagsbrott," *Svenska Dagbladet*, 12 January 2016, https://www.svd.se/internt-polisbrev-stoppar-signalement [accessed 12 June 2018].

2. Ibid.

3. Carlsson, Mattias, and Mikael Delin, "Stockholms stad kände till övergreppen i flera år," *Dagens Nyheter*, 12 January 2016, https://www.dn.se/nyheter/sverige/stockholms-stad-kande-till-overgreppen-i-flera-ar/ [accessed 12 June 2018].

4. Ibid.

5. Ibid.

6. Lund, Lina, "Sexuella ofredanden—en del av ungas vardag," *Dagens Nyheter*, 11 January 2016, https://www.dn.se/sthlm/sexuella-ofredanden-en-del-av-ungas-vardag/ [accessed 12 June 2018].

7. Thurfjell, Karin, "'Det är så vanligt—man tänker inte på att anmäla,'" *Svenska Dagbladet*, 12 January 2016, https://www.svd.se/sa-vanligt—man-tanker-inte-pa-att-anmala [accessed 12 June 2018].

8. Interview with Vera Söderström, 4 April 2018.

9. The National Council for Crime Prevention (Brå), "Rape and sexual offences," 2016, https://www.bra.se/bra-in-english/home/crime-and-statistics/rape-and-sex-offences.html [accessed 12 June 2018].

10. National Council for Crime Prevention (Brå), "Brottslighet bland personer födda i Sverige och i utlandet," report no. 17, 2005, p. 37.

11. Ibid., p. 43.

12. Barr, Björn, Arne Lapidus, and Karin Sörbring, "Sprickan om invandrare och brottsligheten," *Expressen*, 25 February 2017, https://www.expressen.se/nyheter/sprickan-om-invandrare-och-brottsligheten/ [accessed 2 March 2018].

WEDNESDAY 13 JANUARY 2016

1. A few months later, on 31 May 2016, *Nyheter Idag* was found to be in violation of good journalistic practice for the first time—for using the headline "love mingle" when publishing photos of a nightclub encounter between rightwing nationalist Daniel Friberg and author/human rights activist Alexandra Pascalidou. To date (16 May 2018), this remains the site's only violation. Swedish Press Council PO-PON (Allmänhetens Pressombudsman-Pressens Opinionsnämnd), "Mötet var inget 'kärleksmingel,'" Exp. nr: 59/2016, dnr: 37/2016, 19 October 2016, https://po.se/fallningar/moetet-var-inget-kaerleksmingel/ [accessed 12 June 2018]; Frick, Chang, "BILDEXTRA: Se hela kärleksminglet mellan Daniel Friberg och Alexandra Pascalidou," *Nyheter Idag*, 1 February 2016, https://nyheteridag.se/bildextra-se-hela-karleksminglet-mellan-daniel-friberg-och-alexandra-pascalidou/ [accessed 12 June 2018].

2. Albinsson, Mattias, "SVT:s attack på Nyheter Idag efter DN-avslöjandet: 'Konspirationsteori,'" *Nyheter Idag*, 13 January 2016, https://nyheteridag.se/svts-attack-pa-nyheter-idag-efter-dn-avslojandet-konspirationsteori/ [accessed 12 June 2018].

3. Ibid.

4. Øgrim, Helge, "Overgrep mot unge jenter—halvt års taushet i svenske medier," *Journalisten*, 13 January 2016, http://journalisten.no/2016/01/overgrep-mot-unge-jenter-taust-i-dagens-nyheter [accessed 11 March 2017].

THURSDAY 14 JANUARY 2016

1. Guwallius, Kolbjörn, "Sajten Nyheter Idag står bakom drevet mot DN. Men vem står bakom Nyheter Idag?," *KIT*, 14 January 2016, https://kit.se/2016/01/14/30489/sajten-nyheter-idag-star-bakom-drevet-mot-dn-men-vem-star-bakom-nyheter-idag/ [accessed 12 June 2018].

2. Frick, Chang, "Bonniers sajt KIT ringde—Nu anklagas jag för att vara fattig," *Nyheter Idag*, 14 January 2016, https://nyheteridag.se/bonniers-sajt-kit-ringde-nu-anklagas-jag-for-att-vara-fattig/ [accessed 12 June 2018].

WEDNESDAY 20 JANUARY 2016

1. Wierup, Lasse, "Polisen hemlighåller fakta om sitt flyktingarbete," *Dagens Nyheter*, 20 January 2016, http://www.dn.se/nyheter/sverige/polisen-hemlighaller-fakta-om-sitt-flyktingarbete/ [accessed 9 March 2017].
2. Giertta, Helena, "DN-drevet är en attack mot oss alla," *Journalisten*, 20 January 2016, https://www.journalisten.se/ledare/dn-drevet-ar-en-attack-mot-oss-alla [accessed 12 June 2018].
3. Wierup, Lasse, "Kameror kan sättas in vid festivalen We are Sthlm," *Dagens Nyheter*, 15 January 2016, https://www.dn.se/nyheter/sverige/kameror-kan-sattas-in-vid-festivalen-we-are-sthlm/ [accessed 18 June 2018].
4. Statens Offentliga Utredningar (SOU 2016:58), "Ändrade mediegrundlagar," 2016.
5. Swedish Government Proposal (Regeringens proposition) 2017/18:49, "Ändrade mediegrundlagar," p. 153.

THE CULPRIT

1. Hannu, Filip, "Problem med sexuella trakasserier på festival för unga," *Radio Sweden*, 12 August 2015, http://sverigesradio.se/sida/artikel.aspx?programid=1 646&artikel=6230084 [accessed 31 January 2018].

THE DISSIDENT IN THE HEART OF DARKNESS

1. Frick, Chang, and Mathias Wåg, "Ekeroth och Putilov hemliga medarbetare på Avpixlat," *Nyheter Idag*, 12 September 2016, https://nyheteridag.se/ekeroth-och-putilov-hemliga-medarbetare-pa-avpixlat/ [accessed 12 June 2018].
2. Frick, Chang, "Den svenska diplomaten," *Nyheter Idag*, 8 November 2017, https://nyheteridag.se/den-svenska-diplomaten/ [accessed 12 June 2018].
3. Stenrosen, Matti, "Tvingas ha vakter vid dop," *Kristianstadsbladet*, 7 December 2016, http://www.kristianstadsbladet.se/kristianstad/tvingas-ha-vakter-vid-dop/ [accessed 12 June 2018].
4. Frick, Chang, "De bajsar, onanerar och tar barn från prästen i kyrkan," *Nyheter Idag*, 7 December 2016, https://nyheteridag.se/de-bajsar-onanerar-och-tar-barn-fran-prasten-i-kyrkan/ [accessed 12 June 2018].
5. Mosesson, Måns, "Fejknyheter sprids från 'trollfabrik' i Makedonien," *Dagens Nyheter*, 16 February 2017, https://www.dn.se/nyheter/sverige/fejknyheter-sprids-fran-trollfabrik-i-makedonien/ [accessed 12 June 2018].

THE UNIMIND STRIKES AGAIN

1. Aktualne.cz, "Švédsko přestává zvládat migraci, narůstá kriminalita i strach místních lidí, říká Janouchová," 9 January 2017, https://video.aktualne.cz/dvtv/sved-

sko-prestava-zvladat-migraci-narusta-kriminalita-i-strac/r-0ab6755ad5de11e68
1020025900fea04/ [accessed 12 June 2018].

2. Pallas, Hynek, "Hynek Pallas: Tv-intervjun med Katerina Janouch sprider rykten och fördomar," *Dagens Nyheter*, 10 January 2017, https://www.dn.se/kul-
tur-noje/kulturdebatt/hynek-pallas-tv-intervjun-med-katerina-janouch-sprider-
rykten-och-fordomar/ [accessed 12 June 2018].

3. Jones, Evelyn, "Janouchs förlag tar avstånd från uttalanden," *Dagens Nyheter*,
12 January 2017, https://www.dn.se/arkiv/kultur/janouchs-forlag-tar-avstand-
fran-uttalanden/ [accessed 12 June 2018].

4. Sterner, Göran, "Därför tar hon bort Katerina Janouchs böcker," *Uppsala Nya
Tidning*, 13 January 2017, http://unt.se/kultur-noje/darfor-tar-hon-bort-kat-
erina-janouchs-bocker-4501817.aspx [accessed 12 June 2018].

5. Holmqvist, Anette, "Bildt: 'Det har spridits bekymmersamma bilder av Sverige,'"
Aftonbladet, 17 January 2017, https://www.aftonbladet.se/nyheter/samhalle/a/
7zRpK/bildt-det-har-spridits-bekymmersamma-bilder-av-sverige [accessed 12
June 2018].

6. Svensson, Niklas, "Stefan Löfvens svar till Katerina Janouch," *Expressen*, 18
January 2017, https://www.expressen.se/nyheter/stefan-lofvens-svar-till-kat-
erina-janouch/ [accessed 12 June 2018].

BIBLIOGRAPHY

Books

Almqvist, Carl Jonas Love, *Det går an*, Stockholm: Modernista, 2017 (first published in 1838).

Arklöf, Jackie, *Marionettmänniskan*, Stockholm: Vulkan, 2011.

Baas, David, *Bevara Sverige Svenskt—ett reportage om Sverigedemokraterna*, Stockholm: Månpocket, 2015 (paperback edition).

Berggren, Henrik, *Underbara dagar framför oss—En biografi över Olof Palme*, Stockholm: Norstedts Förlag, 2010.

—— and Lars Trägårdh, *Är svensken människa?—Gemenskap och oberoende i det moderna Sverige*, Stockholm: Norstedts Förlag, 2015 (second edition).

Boëthius, Maria-Pia, *Heder och samvete*, Stockholm: Ordfront, 1999.

Björk, Gunnela, *Olof Palme och medierna*, Stockholm: Boréa Bokförlag, 2006.

Brown, Andrew, *Fishing in Utopia: Sweden and the Future that Disappeared*, London: Granta Books, 2008 (Kindle edition).

Broberg, Gunnar and Mattias Tydén, *Oönskade i folkhemmet—rashygien och sterilisering i Sverige*, Stockholm: Dialogos, 2005.

De Benoist, Alain, "The New Right: Forty Years After" (Preface), in Sunić, Tomislav, *Against Democracy and Equality: The European New Right* (3rd edition), London: Arktos Media, 2011.

Elmbrant, Björn, *Så föll den svenska modellen*, Stockholm: Fischer & Co, 1993.

Etzemüller, Thomas, *Alva and Gunnar Myrdal: Social Engineering in the Modern World*, London: Lexington Books, 2014.

Häger, Björn, *Problempartiet—Mediernas villrådighet kring SD valet 2010*, Stockholm: Stiftelsen Institutet för mediestudier, 2012.

Hagerman, Maja, *Det rena landet—om konsten att uppfinna sina förfäder*, Stockholm: Prisma, 2006.

BIBLIOGRAPHY

Hall, Thomas, *Stockholm: The Making of a Metropolis*, London and New York: Routledge, 2009.

Hammar, Filip and Fredrik Wikingsson, *Två nötcreme och en Moviebox—Hisnande generaliseringar om vår uppväxt i DDR-Sverige*, Stockholm: Bonnier Fakta, 2003.

Hinde, Dominic, *A Utopia Like Any Other: Inside the Swedish Model*, Edinburgh: Luath Press Limited, 2016 (Kindle edition).

Hirdman, Yvonne, *Att lägga livet till rätta—studier i svensk folkhemspolitik*, Stockholm: Carlsson Bokförlag, 2010 (first published 1989).

Huntford, Roland, *The New Totalitarians*, London: Allen Lane, 1975 (paperback edition).

Johansson Heinö, Andreas, *Gillar vi olika? Hur den svenska likhetsnormen hindrar integrationen*, Stockholm: Timbro, 2012.

Kent, Neil, *The Soul of the North: A Social, Architectural, and Cultural History of the Nordic Countries, 1700–1940*, London: Reaktion, 2000.

———, *Farväl till Folkhemmet*, Stockholm: Timbro, 2015.

Kristoffersson, Sara, *IKEA—en kulturhistoria*, Stockholm: Atlantis, 2015.

Leitz, Christian, *Nazi Germany and Neutral Europe During the Second World War*, Manchester: Manchester University Press, 2000.

Lifvendal, Tove, *Från sagoland till framtidsland: Om svensk identitet, utveckling och emigration*, Stockholm: Hjalmarson & Högberg Bokförlag, 2012.

Lindqvist, Herman, *Våra kolonier—de vi hade och de som aldrig blev av*, Stockholm: Albert Bonniers Förlag, 2016.

Lundberg, Thom, *För vad Sorg och Smärta*, Stockholm: Albert Bonniers Förlag, 2016.

Myrdal, Alva, *Stadsbarn: En bok om deras fostran i storbarnkammare*, Stockholm: Kooperativa Förbundet, 1935.

——— and Gunnar Myrdal, *Kris i befolkningsfrågan*, Stockholm: Albert Bonniers Förlag, 1935.

Nordström, Ludvig, *Lort-Sverige*, Sundsvall: Tidsspegeln, 1984 (first published 1938).

Rudberg, Eva, *Sven Markelius, arkitekt*, Stockholm: Arkitektur Förlag, 1989.

Runcis, Maija, *Steriliseringar i folkhemmet*, Stockholm: Ordfront, 1998.

Sanandaji, Tino, *Massutmaning—ekonomisk politik mot utanförskap & antisocialt beteende*, Stockholm: Kuhzad Media, 2017.

Sandelin, Magnus, *Den svarte nazisten—en dokumentär om Jackie Arklöf*, Stockholm: Bokförlaget Forum, Månpocket, 2010.

Sandemose, Aksel, *A Fugitive Crosses His Tracks* (trans. Eugene Gay-Tifft), New York: Alfred A. Knopf, 1936.

Sundbärg, Gustav, *Det svenska folklynnet*, Stockholm: Norstedt & Söners Förlag, 1921 (15th edn).

BIBLIOGRAPHY

Tamas, Gellert, *Lasermannen—en berättelse om Sverige*, Stockholm: Ordfront, 2016 (first published 2002).

Teitelbaum, Benjamin R., *Lions of the North: Sounds of the New Nordic Radical Nationalism*, New York, NY: Oxford University Press, 2017.

Thurfjell, David, *Det gudlösa folket: de postkristna svenskarna och religionen*, Stockholm: Molin Sorgenfrei Förlag, 2015.

Truedson, Lars et al., *Misstron mot medier*, Stockholm: Institutet för mediestudier, 2017.

Zaremba, Maciej, *De rena och de andra—Om tvångssteriliseringar, rashygien och arvsynd*, Stockholm: Forum, 1999.

Key articles

Albinsson, Mattias, "All time high för SD—26,8 procent i Nyheter Idag/Sentios opinionsmätning', *Nyheter Idag*, 12 November 2015, https://nyheteridag.se/all-time-high-for-sd-268-procent-i-nyheter-idagsentios-opinionsmatning/ [accessed 11 June 2018].

———, "SVT:s attack på Nyheter Idag efter DN-avslöjandet: 'Konspirationsteori,'" *Nyheter Idag*, 13 January 2016, https://nyheteridag.se/svts-attack-pa-nyheter-idag-efter-dn-avslojandet-konspirationsteori/ [accessed 12 June 2018].

Augustine Lawler, Peter, "The Problem of Democratic Individualism," *The University Bookman*, vol. 28, no. 3 (Spring 1988), http://www.kirkcenter.org/index.php/bookman/article/the-problem-of-democratic-individualism/ [accessed 10 September 2017].

Barr, Björn, Arne Lapidus, and Karin Sörbring, "Sprickan om invandrare och brottsligheten," *Expressen*, 25 February 2017, https://www.expressen.se/nyheter/sprickan-om-invandrare-och-brottsligheten/ [accessed 2 March 2018].

BBC News, "Sweden riots spread beyond Stockholm despite extra police," 25 May 2013, http://www.bbc.com/news/world-europe-22656657 [accessed 7 June 2018].

———, "Swedish police probe 'cover-up of migrant sex assaults,'" 11 January 2016, http://www.bbc.com/news/world-europe-35285086 [accessed 12 June 2018].

Billger, Ola, "The Millennium author's theories concerning the murder of Olof Palme," *Svenska Dagbladet*, 24 February 2014, https://www.svd.se/the-millennium-authors-theories-concerning-the-murder-of-olof-palme [accessed 5 June 2018].

Björkman, Jenny, "När vi fick lära oss ta av oss skorna," *Forskning & Framsteg*, no. 6 (2007).

Bouvin, Emma, "Polisen mörkade övergreppen på festivalen," *Dagens Nyheter*, 10 January 2016, http://www.dn.se/nyheter/sverige/polisen-morkade-overgreppen-pa-festivalen/?forceScript=1&variantType=large [accessed 9 March 2017].

BIBLIOGRAPHY

Capatides, Christina, "Which European countries have produced the most ISIS fighters?," CBS News, 25 January 2016, https://ww.cbsnews.com/news/isis-terror-recruiting-europe-belgium-france-denmark-sweden-germany/ [accessed 15 February 2018].

Carlsson, Mattias, and Mikael Delin, "Stockholms stad kände till övergreppen i flera år," *Dagens Nyheter*, 12 January 2016, https://www.dn.se/nyheter/sverige/stockholms-stad-kande-till-overgreppen-i-flera-ar/ [accessed 12 June 2018].

Carp, Ossi, "'Tjänar över en halv miljard på invandringen,'" *Dagens Nyheter*, 31 May 2014, https://www.dn.se/nyheter/sverige/tjanar-over-en-halv-miljard-pa-invandringen/ [accessed 8 June 2018].

Cetin, Evin, "Sabuni kravlar fram i populistisk lervällning," *Aftonbladet*, 17 August 2010, https://www.aftonbladet.se/debatt/article12430379.ab [accessed 1 November 2017].

Crouch, David, "Swedish police accused of covering up sex attacks by refugees at music festival," *The Guardian*, 11 January 2016, https://www.theguardian.com/world/2016/jan/11/swedish-police-accused-cover-up-sex-attacks-refugees-festival [accessed 12 June 2018].

Dagens Nyheter, "Questions and answers on DN's handling of events in the Kungsträdgården," 11 January 2016, http://www.dn.se/nyheter/sverige/questions-and-answers-on-dns-handling-of-events-in-the-kungstradgarden/ [accessed 10 March 2017].

Ejneberg, Rasmus, "Våldet i Sverige omfattande—jämförs nu med Mexiko," *Expressen*, 5 September 2017, https://www.expressen.se/nyheter/brottscentralen/valdet-i-sverige-omfattande-jamfors-nu-med-mexiko/ [accessed 12 June 2018].

Englund, Peter, "Karl XII:s död—Fallet är avslutat," Peter Englund blog, 3 September 2015, https://peterenglundsnyawebb.wordpress.com/2015/09/03/karl-xiis-dod-fallet-ar-avslutat/ [accessed 13 June 2018].

Frick, Chang, "Plötsligt en förening," *Chang Frick Blogspot*, 29 November 2010, http://changfrick.blogspot.com/2010/11/plotsligt-en-forening.html [accessed 7 November 2017].

———, "Efter flyktingkrisen: SD största parti med högsta noteringen någonsin," *Nyheter Idag*, 10 September 2015, https://nyheteridag.se/efter-flyktingkrisen-sd-storsta-parti-med-hogsta-noteringen-nagonsin/ [accessed 11 June 2018].

———, "Bonniers sajt KIT ringde—Nu anklagas jag för att vara fattig," *Nyheter Idag*, 14 January 2016, https://nyheteridag.se/bonniers-sajt-kit-ringde-nu-anklagas-jag-for-att-vara-fattig/ [accessed 12 June 2018].

———, "Man skjuten i Stockholm—Här jagar tungt beväpnad polis gärningsmännen," *Nyheter Idag*, 5 September 2016, https://nyheteridag.se/man-skjuten-i-stockholm-har-jagar-tungt-bevapnad-polis-garningsmannen/ [accessed 8 June 2018].

BIBLIOGRAPHY

———, "De bajsar, onanerar och tar barn från prästen i kyrkan," *Nyheter Idag*, 7 December 2016, https://nyheteridag.se/de-bajsar-onanerar-och-tar-barn-fran-prasten-i-kyrkan/ [accessed 12 June 2018].

———, "Den svenska diplomaten," *Nyheter Idag*, 8 November 2017, https://nyheteridag.se/den-svenska-diplomaten/ [accessed 12 June 2018].

——— and Mathias Wåg, "Ekeroth och Putilov hemliga medarbetare på Avpixlat," *Nyheter Idag*, 12 September 2016, https://nyheteridag.se/ekeroth-och-putilov-hemliga-medarbetare-pa-avpixlat/ [accessed 12 June 2018].

Giertta, Helena, "DN-drevet är en attack mot oss alla," *Journalisten*, 20 January 2016, https://www.journalisten.se/ledare/dn-drevet-ar-en-attack-mot-oss-alla [accessed 12 June 2018].

Gudmunson, Per, "SD näst störst—M ner på 20 procent," *Svenska Dagbladet*, 23 October 2015, https://www.svd.se/sd-nast-storst-m-ner-pa-20-procent [accessed 11 June 2018].

Guwallius, Kolbjörn, "Sajten Nyheter Idag står bakom drevet mot DN. Men vem står bakom Nyheter Idag?," *KIT*, 14 January 2016, https://kit.se/2016/01/14/30489/sajten-nyheter-idag-star-bakom-drevet-mot-dn-men-vem-star-bakom-nyheter-idag/ [accessed 12 June 2018].

Hakelius, Johan, 'När det som var suspekt plötsligt blir sunt förnuft', *Aftonbladet*, 26 October 2015, https://www.aftonbladet.se/nyheter/kolumnister/johanhakelius/article21647404.ab [accessed 4 November 2017].

Hall, Bengt, "Dags för Palmes penndrag," *Kristianstadsbladet*, 29 April 2017, http://www.kristianstadsbladet.se/debatt/dags-for-palmes-penndrag/ [accessed 12 June 2018].

Hannu, Filip, "Problem med sexuella trakasserier på festival för unga," Radio Sweden, 12 August 2015, http://sverigesradio.sesida/artikel.aspx?programid=1646&artikel=6230084 [accessed 31 January 2018].

Hawkins, Derek, "Nazi past followed Ikea founder Ingvar Kamprad to his death," *The Washington Post*, 29 January 2018, https://www.washingtonpost.com/news/morning-mix/wp/2018/01/29/nazi-past-followed-ikea-founder-ingvar-kamprad-to-his-death/?utm_term=.da2eada30b7a [accessed 19 June 2018].

Höjer, Henrik, 'Därför ökar de kriminella gängens makt', *Forskning & Framsteg*, 11 May 2015, http://fof.se/tidning/2015/5/artikel/darfor-okar-de-kriminella-gangens-makt [accessed 6 October 2017].

Holmqvist, Anette, "Bildt: 'Det har spridits bekymmersamma bilder av Sverige,'" *Aftonbladet*, 17 January 2017, https://www.aftnbladet.se/nyheter/samhalle/a/7zRpK/bildt-det-har-spridits-bekymmersamma-bilder-av-sverige [accessed 12 June 2018].

Hübinette, Tobias, "Psykisk hälsa bland utlandsadopterade i Sverige", *Psykisk Hälsa* vol. 44, no. 1 (2003).

BIBLIOGRAPHY

Huggler, Justin, "'Cover-up' over Cologne sex assaults blamed on migration sensitivities," *The Telegraph*, 6 January 2016, https://www.telegraph.co.uk/news/worldnews/europe/germany/12085182/Cover-up-over-Cologne-sex-assaults-blamed-on-migration-sensitivities.html [accessed 12 June 2018].

Jelmini, Maria, "SvD prisas för Gula Båtarna-kampanj och affärsmodell," *Svenska Dagbladet*, 24 May 2016, https://www.svd.se/svd-vann-pris-for-gula-batarna-kampanj [accessed 8 June 2018].

Johansson, Anders and Linda Hjertén, "Polisens hemliga rapport: Här är Stockholms läns farligaste områden," *Aftonbladet*, 4 February 2016, http://www.aftonbladet.se/nyheter/krim/article22190105.ab [accessed 5 March 2017].

Jones, Evelyn, "Janouchs förlag tar avstån från uttalanden," *Dagens Nyheter*, 12 January 2017, https://www.dn.se/arkiv/kultur/janouchs-forlag-tar-avstand-fran-uttalanden/ [accessed 12 June 2018].

Kamali, Masoud, "Med de nya statsråden ökar rasismen i Sverige," *Dagens Nyheter*, 13 October 2006, https://www.dn.se/arkiv/debatt/med-de-nya-statsraden-okar-rasismen-i-sverige/ [accessed 5 June 2018].

Klinghoffer, Sanna, "Terrorforskaren: 'Utvecklingen är oroande,'" *SVT Nyheter*, 15 September 2017, https://www.svt.se/nyheter/inrikes/utvecklingen-ar-oroande, [accessed 15 February 2018].

Klint, Lars, Anna Skarin and Fredrik Sjöshult, "Polisen: SD-kandidaten ristade sig själv i pannan," *Expressen*, 19 September 2010, http://www.expressen.se/nyheter/val-2010/polisen-sd-kandidaten-ristade-sig-sjalv-i-pannan/ [accessed 7 June 2018].

Larsson, Jens, "Polischef i Rinkeby: 'De kriminella skrattar åt oss,'" *SVT Nyheter*, 7 March 2017, https://www.svt.se/nyheter/lokalt/stockholm/polischef-i-rinkeby-de-kriminella-skrattar-at-oss [accessed 19 September 2017].

Larsson, Stieg, "The New Popular Movement," *Expo/Svartvitt*, no. 3/4, 1999.

Lindgren, Petter, "Poesiprotest i arktisk kyla," *Aftonbladet*, 25 November 2010, https://www.aftonbladet.se/kultur/article12677782.ab [accessed 7 November 2017].

Lindqvist, Ursula, "The Cultural Archive of the IKEA store," *Space and Culture*, vol. 12, no. 1, February 2009.

Lund, Lina, "Sexuella ofredanden—en del av ungas vardag," *Dagens Nyheter*, 11 January 2016, https://www.dn.se/sthlm/sexuellaofredanden-en-del-av-ungas-vardag/ [accessed 12 June 2018].

Lundquist, Hanna, "Opitz: 'Behövs mer öppenhet om våra arbetssätt,'" *Journalisten*, 11 January 2016, https://www.journalisten.se/nyheter/opitz-behovs-mer-oppen-het-om-vara-arbetssatt [accessed 12 June 2018].

Magnusson, Erik, "Så blev flyktingkrisen en svensk beredskapskatastrof," *Sydsvenskan*, 26 December 2015, https://www.sydsvenskan.se/2015-12-26/sa-blev-flyktingkrisen-en-svensk-beredskapskatastrof [accessed 17 October 2017].

BIBLIOGRAPHY

Moreno, Federico, "Ett parallellt samhälle växer fram," *Expressen*, 30 June 2016, https://www.expressen.se/nyheter/longread/utanforskapet-inifran/ett-parallellt-samhalle-vaxer-fram/ [accessed 27 June 2018].

Mosesson, Måns, "Fejknyheter sprids från 'trollfabrik' i Makedonien," *Dagens Nyheter*, 16 February 2017, https://www.dn.se/nyheter/sverige/fejknyheter-sprids-fran-trollfabrik-i-makedonien/ [accessed 12 June 2018].

Myrdal, Gunnar, "Kosta sociala reformer pengar?", *Arkitektur och samhälle*, Stockholm: Spektrum, 1932.

Nilsson, Torbjörn, "Unionsupplösningen 1905: Krisen chockade kungen," *Populär Historia*, vol. 2 (2005), https://popularhistoria.se/artiklar/unionsupplosningen-1905-krisen-chockade-kungen [accessed 24 May 2018].

Nordenstam, Sven, "Swedish police to investigate sexual assault cover-up allegations," *Reuters*, 11 January 2016, https://uk.reuters.com/article/uk-sweden-assaults/swedish-police-to-investigate-sexual-assault-cover-up-allegations-idUKKCN0UP1PQ20160112 [accessed 12 June 2018].

Öberg, Martin, "Jag blev ert monster," *SVT Opinion*, Swedish Television, 5 July 2014, https://www.svt.se/opinion/article2167728.svt [accessed 25 August 2017].

Øgrim, Helge, "Overgrep mot unge jenter—halvt års taushet i svenske medier," *Journalisten*, 13 January 2016, http://journalisten.no/2016/01/overgrep-mot-unge-jenter-taust-i-dagens-nyheter [accessed 11 March 2017].

Orange, Richard, "Swedis riots spark surprise and anger," *The Guardian*, 25 May 2013, https://www.theguardian.com/world/2013/may/25/sweden-europe-news [accessed 7 June 2018].

Orrenius, Niklas, "Martyrrollen stärks Motvinden är SD:s medvind," *Sydsvenskan*, 1 October 2009.

Orrenius, Niklas, "Sd serveras martyrskapet gratis," *Sydsvenskan*, 2 November 2007.

Örstadius, Kristoffer, "Förenings-Sverige tynar bort," *Dagens Nyheter*, 16 August 2015, https://www.dn.se/nyheter/sverige/forenings-sverige-tynar-bort/ [accessed 13 June 2018].

Pallas, Hynek, "Hynek Pallas: Tv-intervjun med Katerina Janouch sprider rykten och fördomar," *Dagens Nyheter*, 10 January 2017, https://www.dn.se/kultur-noje/kulturdebatt/hynek-pallas-tv-intervjun-med-katerina-janouch-sprider-rykten-och-fordomar/ [accessed 12 June 2018].

Pirttisalo Sallinen, Jani, "38 flickor utsattes för sexbrott på festivalen," *Svenska Dagbladet*, 11 January 2016, https://www.svd.se/38-flickor-utsattes-for-ofre-dande-pa-festivalen [accessed 12 June 2018].

———, "Polisen får nya direktiv om signalement vid vardagsbrott," *Svenska Dagbladet*, 12 January 2016, https://www.svd.se/internt-polisbrev-stoppar-sig-nalement [accessed 12 June 2018].

Poolh, Daniel, "Misshandlades för att han var Sverigedemokrat," *Expo*, 28

BIBLIOGRAPHY

September 2010, http://expo.se/2010/misshandlades-for-att-han-var-sverigede-mokrat_3398.html [accessed 7 June 2018].

Radio Sweden, "Time Limits on Murder Cases Removed," 3 February 2010, https://sverigesradio.se/sida/artikel.aspx?programid=254&artikel=3417924 [accessed 12 June 2018].

————, "Tidslinje över flyktingkrisen," 11 November 2015, http://sverigesradio.se/sida/artikel.aspx?programid=83&artikel=6299595 [accessed 17 October 2017].

Rågsjö Thorell, Andreas, "DN svarar på anklagelserna om mörkläggning—med avslöjande," *Resumé*, 11 January 2016, https://www.resume.se/nyheter/artik-lar/2016/01/11/dn-svarar-pa-anklagelserna-om-morklaggning—med-avslo-jande/ [accessed 12 June 2018].

Rosén, Eric, 'Utredningen om hakkors i pannan på sd-politikern nedlagd', *Nyheter24*, 11 November 2010, https://nyheter24.se/nyheter/inrikes/486055-utredningen-om-hakkors-i-pannan-pa-sd-politikern-nedlagd [accessed 7 June 2018].

Salihu, Diamant, Åsa Asplid, and Michael Syrén, "Här är anmälningarna från 'We are Sthlm'," *Expressen*, 13 January 2016, https://www.expressen.se/nyheter/har-ar-anmalningarna-fran-we-are-sthlm/ [accessed 12 June 2018].

Skogkär, Mats, "Ministern som stör," *Sydsvenskan*, 17 October 2006, https://www.sydsvenskan.se/2006-10-16/ministern-som-stor [accessed 12 June 2018].

Stenrosen, Matti, "Tvingas ha vakter vid dop," *Kristianstadsbladet*, 7 December 2016, http://www.kristianstadsbladet.se/kristianstad/tvingas-ha-vakter-vid-dop/ [accessed 12 June 2018].

Sterner, Göran, "Därför tar hon bort Katerina Janouchs böcker," *Uppsala Nya Tidning*, 13 January 2017, http://unt.se/kultur-noje/darfor-tar-hon-bort-kat-erina-janouchs-bocker-4501817.aspx [accessed 12 June 2018].

Sulaiman, Haore, "Issa fick 18 knivhugg—för att han år med i SD," *Dagen*, 12 January 2011, http://www.dagen.se/issa-fick-18-knivhugg-for-att-han-ar-med-i-sd-1.121478 [accessed 7 June 2018].

Svensson, Anna H., "Säpo-chefen om radikaliseringen i Sverige: Enorm ökning," *SVT Nyheter*, Swedish Television, 17 September 2017, https://www.svt.se/nyheter/inrikes/sapo-chefen-om-radikaliseringen-i-sverige-enorm-okning [accessed 15 February 2018].

Svensson, Niklas, "Stefan Löfvens svar till Katerina Janouch," *Expressen*, 18 January 2017, https://www.expressen.se/nyheter/stefan-lofvens-svar-till-katerina-janouch/ [accessed 12 June 2018].

Sverigedemokraterna, "Omfattande valsabotage redan efter 2 dagars förtidsröstning," press release, 3 September 2010, http://www.mynewsdesk.com/se/sverigede-mokraterna/pressreleases/omfattande-valsabotage-redan-efter-2-dagars-foertid-sroestning-463781 [accessed 20 June 2018].

BIBLIOGRAPHY

The Swedish Institute, "Sweden beyond the Millennium and Stieg Larsson," 2012, p. 8, https://issuu.com/swedish_institute/docs/sweden_beyond_the_millennium [accessed 18 June 2018].

Tagesson, Eric, Anders Johansson, and Kerstin Danielson, "Han lämnar SD efter överfallet," *Aftonbladet*, 24 September 2010, http://www.aftonbladet.se/nyheter/valet2010/article12528820.ab [accessed 7 June 2018].

The Ingmar Bergman Foundation, "Bergman and Sweden," 18 October 2011, http://www.ingmarbergman.se/en/universe/bergman-and-sweden [accessed 31 May 2018].

Thurfjell, Karin, "Läkare: Ristade själv in hakkors," *Svenska Dagbladet* (TT), 18 September 2010, https://www.svd.se/lakare-ristade-sjalv-in-hakkors [accessed 7 June 2018].

———, "'Det är så vanligt—man tänker inte på att anmäla,'" *Svenska Dagbladet*, 12 January 2016, https://www.svd.se/sa-vanligt—man-tanker-inte-pa-att-anmala [accessed 12 June 2018].

Tidningarnas Telegrambyrå, "Tusen ensamkommande flyktingbarn har försvunnit," *Göteborgsposten*, 14 October 2015, http://www.gp.se/nyheter/sverige/tusen-ensamkommande-flyktingbarn-har-f%C3%B6rsvunnit-1.151349 [accessed 17 October 2017].

Wallroth, Emmelie, "Yougov: Nu är SD Sveriges största parti," *Metro*, 20 August 2015, https://www.metro.se/artikel/yougov-nu-%3%A4r-sd-sveriges-st%C3%B6rsta-parti-xr [accessed 11 June 2018].

——— and Sofia Roström Andersson, "Våldsamma upplopp i Husby i natt," *Aftonbladet*, 19 May 2013, https://www.aftonbladet.se/nyheter/article16804681.ab [accessed 7 June 2018].

Wernersson, Annie, "SD ökar kraftigt bland väljare med utländsk bakgrund," *SVT Nyheter*, Swedish Television, 7 June 2017, https://www.svt.se/nyheter/inrikes/sd-okar-kraftigt-bland-utrikes-fodda [accessed 8 June 2018].

Wierup, Lasse, "Kvinnors rätt att festa säkert kan inte offras," *Dagens Nyheter*, 9 January 2016, http://www.dn.se/nyheter/varlden/kvinnors-ratt-att-festa-sakert-kan-inte-offras/?forceScript=1&variantType=large [accessed 11 March 2017].

———, "Polisen hemlighåller fakta om sitt flyktingarbete," *Dagens Nyheter*, 20 January 2016, http://www.dn.se/nyheter/sverige/polisen-hemlighaller-fakta-om-sitt-flyktingarbete/ [accessed 9 March 2017].

Withnall, Adam, "Cologne police ordered to remove word 'rape' from reports into New Year's Eve sexual assaults amid cover-up claims," *The Independent*, 7 April 2016, http://www.independent.co.uk/news/world/europe/cologne-police-ordered-to-remove-word-rape-from-reports-into-new-year-s-eve-sexual-assaults-a6972471.html [accessed 10 March 2017].

BIBLIOGRAPHY

TV, film, radio, and podcasts

Aktualne.cz, "Švédsko přestává zvládat migraci, narůstá kriminalita i strach místních lidí, říká Janouchová," 9 January 2017, https://video.aktualne.cz/dvtv/svedsko-prestava-zvladat-migraci-narusta-kriminalita-i-strac/r-0ab6755ad5de11e681020025900fea04/ [accessed 12 June 2018].

Bergman, Ingmar, *Wild Strawberries*, AB Svensk Filmindustri, 1957.

Borgäs, Lars, *SVT Dokument Inifrån—Mannen, Mordet, Mysteriet*, Swedish Television, 1999.

Edman, Gustav, "90-talskrisen," *P3 Dokumentär*, Radio Sweden, 12 October 2008, http://sverigesradio.se/sida/avsnitt/87426?programid=2519 [accessed 5 June 2018].

Ellung, Göran, *Palme—sista timmarna*, TV4, broadcast 24 February 2016.

Fichtelius, Erik, Kjell Tunegård and Paolo Rodriguez, *Ordförande Persson*, Swedish Television, first broadcast in March 2007.

Gandini, Erik, *The Swedish Theory of Love*, Fasad Cine AB, 2015.

Hermansson, Daniel and Robin Olovsson, "Alva Myrdal," *Historiepodden*, Episode 138, first broadcast 21 January 2017, https://www.radioplay.se/podcast/historiepodden?episode-id=30654 [accessed 31 May 2018].

———, "Palmemordet," *Historiepodden*, Episode 93, first broadcast 27 February 2016.

Karim, Osmond, *De ensamma—en film om adoption*, Swedish Television, 20 April 2017, https://www.svtplay.se/video/13246808/de-ensamma-en-film-om-adoption/de-ensamma-en-film-om-adoption-avsnitt-1?start=auto&tab=senaste [acessed 25 August 2017].

Lind, Kalle, *Snedtänkt: Om SVT:s sjuttiotal*, Radio Sweden, first broadcast 10 December 2015.

Lundin, Sara, *P3 Dokumentär: Skotten i Ådalen-31*, Radio Sweden, first broadcast 30 October 2011, http://sverigesradio.se/sida/avsnitt/54030?programid=2519 [accessed 11 July 2017].

Mattsson, Pontus, *104 dagar—en nyhetsdokumentär om den politiska turbulensen efter 2014 års val*, Swedish Television, Channel 2, broadcast 23 December 2015.

———, *Tvärvändningen—om svängningen i flyktingpolitiken*, Swedish Television, first broadcast 29 October 2017.

Nycander, Maud and Kristina Lindström, *Palme*, Swedish Film Institute, 2012.

Persson, Daniel, *Forskare: Fler skottdraman i Sverige*, Radio Sweden, 5 September 2017, http://sverigesradio.se/sida/artikel.aspx?programid=96&artikel=6770039&utm_source=dlvr.it&utm_medium=twitter [accessed 4 October 2017].

Swedish Television, "1930-talet," *Historieätarna*, season 2, episode 6, first broadcast 17 December 2014.

———, "Nationalromantiken," *Historieätarna*, season 2, episode 3, first broadcast 27 November 2014.

BIBLIOGRAPHY

Tamas, Gellert and Malcolm Dixelius, *Lasermannen—Dokumentären*, Swedish Television, Channel 2, 11 December 2005.

Official Reports and Parliamentary Bills:

Bildt, Carl et al. (Moderate Party), "En fri radio och TV," Proposal to Parliament, 1989/90:K401.

Hägg, Joanna, Magnus Höijer, and Samir Sandberg, "Rådgivningsrapport: Socioekonomisk analys Invandring Sandvikens kommun," Pricewaterhousecoopers, March 2014.

Hedenmo, Martin and Fredrik von Platen, "Bostadspolitiken: Svensk politik för boende, planering och byggande under 130 år," National Board of Housing, Building and Planning (Boverket) report, 2007, https://www.boverket.se/globalassets/publikationer/dokument/2007/bostadspolitiken.pdf [accessed 13 June 2018].

National Council for Crime Prevention (Brå), "Brottslighet bland personer födda i Sverige och i utlandet," report no. 17, 2005.

———, "Rape and sexual offences," 2016, https://www.bra.se/bra-in-english/home/crime-and-statistics/rape-and-sex-offences.html [accessed 12 June 2018].

Statens Offentliga Utredningar (SOU 2005:56), "Det blågula glashuset—strukturell diskriminering i Sverige," state-appointed commission report, 2005.

——— (SOU 2016:58), "Ändrade mediegrundlagar," state-appointed commission report, 2016.

Swedish Government Proposal (Regeringens proposition) 2017/18:49, "Ändrade mediegrundlagar."

Swedish International Liberal Centre, "Rapport från valövervakning av de svenska valen till riksdag, kommun och landsting: Rekommendationer och iakttagelser," 14 September 2014, http://silc.se/wp-content/uploads/2016/07/Val%C3%B6vervakning-av-de-svenska-riksdagsvalen-2014.pdf [accessed 20 June 2018].

The Swedish Police Authority, The National Operations Department (Nationella operativa avdelningen Underrättelseenheten), "Rapport: 'Utsatta områden—sociala risker, kollektiv förmåga och oönskade händelser' av Polismyndigheten/Noa," December 2015, https://polisen.se/siteassets/dokument/ovriga_rapporter/utsatta-omraden-sociala-risker-kollektiv-formaga-och-oonskade-handelser.pdf [accessed 18 June 2018].

Other

Statistics Sweden, "Antal personer efter utländsk/svensk bakgrund och år, 2016," http://www.statistikdatabasen.scb.se/pxweb/sv/ssd/START__BE__BE0101__BE0101Q/UtlSvBakgFin/table/tableViewLayout1/?rxid=63a8bae6–3541-4a94-bb7d-6a00c1e2ea52 [accessed 8 June 2018].

BIBLIOGRAPHY

———, "Var fjärde i Sverige är högutbildad, Befolkningens utbildning 2016," https://www.scb.se/hitta-statistik/sverige-i-siffror/utbildning-jobb-och-pengar/befolkningens-utbildning/ [accessed 16 May 2018].

———, "Utrikesfödda efter födelseland och invandringsår," 31 December 2017, available at www.scb.se [accessed 17 May 2018].

Swedish Government, "The Swedish Press Act: 250 years of freedom of the press," http://www.government.se/articles/2016/06/the-swedish-press-act-250-years-of-freedom-of-the-press/ [accessed 4 June 2018].

Swedish Institute, "20 milestones of Swedish press freedom," 18 January 2018, https://sweden.se/society/20-milestones-of-swedsh-press-freedom/ [accessed 4 June 2018].

Swedish Migration Agency (Migrationsverket), "Nästan 163 000 människor sökte asyl i Sverige 2015," 1 January 2016, http://www.mynewsdesk.com/se/migrationsverket/news/naestan-163–000-maenniskor-soekte-asyl-i-sverige-2015-153237 [accessed 11 June 2018].

Swedish International Liberal Centre, "Rapport från valövervakning av de svenska valen till riksdag, kommun och landsting: Rekommendationer och iakttagelser," 14 September 2014, http://silc.se/wp-content/uploads/2016/07/Val%C3%B6vervakning-av-de-svenska-riksdagsvalen-2014.pdf [accessed 20 June 2018].